mustsees
Italy

Tempio della Concordia, Agrigento and La Valle dei Templi, Sicily / © Diego Barucco/Dreamstime.com

mustsees **Italy**

Editorial Director	Cynthia Clayton Ochterbeck
Principal Writer	Judy Edelhoff
Production Manager	Natasha George
Updating, Photo Editing,	Buysschaert&Malerba, Milan
and Layout	Francesca del Puglia and Zino Malerba
	(photo editing and layout)
Cartography	Peter Wrenn
Interior Design	Chris Bell, cbdesign, Natasha George
Cover Design	Chris Bell, cbdesign, Natasha George

Contact Us	Michelin Travel and Lifestyle North America
	One Parkway South
	Greenville, SC 29615, USA
	travel.lifestyle@michelin.com
	Michelin Travel Partner
	Hannay House
	39 Clarendon Road
	Watford, Herts WD17 1JA, UK
	www.ViaMichelin.com
	travelpubsales@uk.michelin.com

Special Sales	For information regarding bulk sales, customized editions and premium sales, please contact us at: travel.lifestyle@michelin.com

Michelin Travel Partner

Société par actions simplifiées au capital de 11 288 880 EUR
27 cours de l'Île Seguin - 92100 Boulogne Billancourt (France)
R.C.S. Nanterre 433 677 721

© Michelin Travel Partner
ISBN 978-2-067216-16-7
Printed: January 2017
Printed and bound in Italy

Note to the reader:
While every effort is made to ensure that all information printed in this guide is correct
and up-to-date, Michelin Travel Partner accepts no liability for any direct, indirect or
consequential losses howsoever caused so far as such can be excluded by law. Admission
prices listed for sights in this guide are for a single adult, unless otherwise specified.

Welcome to Italy

Fontana di Trevi, Rome
© S. Greg Panosian/iStockphoto.com

© Dan Breckwoldt/iStockphoto.com

Introduction

Must See

p 144

p 152

p 36

© Luciano Mortula/iStockphoto.com

p.68

©Risphoto2/iStockphoto.com

Must Do

Must Eat

Must Stay

Must Know

TABLE OF CONTENTS

★★★ATTRACTIONS

Unmissable attractions awarded three stars in this guide

Statue of Augustus, Monte Solaro, Capri p 143

Mosaics, Basilica di Sant'Ambrogio, Milan p 46

Basilica di San Marco, Venice p 72

Foro Romano, Rome   p 118

© Alex Timaios/Dreamstime.com

Turin with the Mole Antonelliana   p 62

© J. Elliott/age fotostock

San Gimignano, Tuscany   p 99

© Shargaljut/Dreamstime.com

STAR ATTRACTIONS

Pompeii p 140

Portofino p 59

Courtyard, Pinacoteca di Brera, Milan p 45

ACTIVITIES

Unmissable activities and entertainment

Colosseum, Rome   p 118

© Piotr Rzeszutek/Dreamstime.com

Palio delle Contrade, Siena   p 98

©Mrohana/Dreamstime.com

Carnevale in Venice   p 14

© Ary6/iStockphoto.com

Ski in the Dolomites   p 64

© Norman7/Dreamstime.com

★★★ ATTRACTIONS

Unmissable sights in and around Italy

For more than 100 years people have used Michelin stars to take the guesswork out of travel. Our star-rating system helps you make the best decision on where to go, what to do, and what to see.

★★★	Unmissable	★	Worth a detour
★★	Worth a trip	No star	Recommended

MUST KNOW

★★Two Star

12

ACTIVITIES

Unmissable Italian events, shows, restaurants and more
We recommend every activity in this guide, but our top picks are highlighted with the Michelin Man logo. *Look-out for the Michelin Man throughout the guide for the top activities.*

Events

Carnevale in Venice *p 14*
Venice Film Festival *p 187*
Biennale, Venice *p 16, p 187*
Palio in Siena *p 98, 188*
Calcio Storico Fiorentino *p 16*
Historic regatta Venice *p 16*

For Families

Family fun at the theme park *p 176*
Mummies, Museum of Egyptian Antiquities, Turin *p 63*
Colosseum, Rome *p 118*
Hike up to watch volcanic activity on Vesuvius *p 138*
Ski in the Dolomites *p 64, 177*
Wander the ghost town of Pompeii *p 141*
Cycling in Rome along the Appia Antica or Tiber River *p 124, p 177*
Vaporetto and gondola rides Venice *p 69*

Bars

Caffè Florian Venice *p 193*
Harry's Bar Venice *p 193*
Caffè Greco Rome *p 195*
Caffe Gambrinus Naples *p 196*

Food Wine

Cuisine in Bologna *p 181, 182*
Wine tasting around Verona *p 181*
Taste Tuscan reds in Chianti, Montalcino and Montepulciano *p 15*

On the Water

Boat through the Aeolian Islands *p 175*
Boating on the Venetian lagoon *p 179*

Leisure

Music in - Venice *p 186*, Verona *p 187*, Florence *p 187*
Shopping in - Milan *p 181*, Rome *p 183*
The spas at - Montecatini *p 176*

Active

Hiking Italy's long-distance footpaths *p 177*

STAR ATTRACTIONS

CALENDAR OF EVENTS

January

1st – New Year.

6th – Epiphany holiday- Befana, the Christmas witch, delivers presents to children. Markets.

Aosta – St Orso Fair – Craft fair in the Valle d'Aosta. *www.fieradisantorso.it*

Venezia – Regata della Befana – Epiphany boat race with contestants dressed as witches racing to a giant stocking at Rialto Bridge!

February

🎭 **Carnevale celebrations:**

Ivrea – Battle of the Oranges. *www.storicocarnevaleivrea.it*

Rome – Commedia dell'arte, equestrian shows in piazzas.

Venice – Parties and events in the *calli* and *campi*. *www.carnevale.venezia.it*

Verona – "Venerdì gnocolar" procession.

Viareggio – Procession of allegorical and political floats. **viareggio.ilcarnevale.com**

Agrigento – Almond Blossom Festival.

March

19th – S. Giuseppe (Fathers' Day).

25th – Festa delle Donne (Women's Day), women give and receive mimosa flowers.

Rome – Marathon of Rome. *www.maratonadiroma.it*

Holy Week rites – Pasqua (Easter Sunday holiday) **Pasquetta** (Monday after Easter holiday, traditional for picnics).

Florence – Scoppio del Carro – Explosion of the Cart, Piazza del Duomo, fireworks from a float, parade in Renaissance costume.

Verona-Vinitaly wine fair. *www.vinitaly.com*

February / Carnival participants, Venice

April: Design Week – FuoriSalone, Milan

April

Pasqua/Easter – see March.
Pasquetta – see March.
21st – Rome's birthday, parades.
25th – Liberation Day holiday.
25th – Venice - Festa di San Marco, St Mark Evangelist festival.
1st – San Marino – **Investiture of the regents of the Republic.** Cultural Heritage Week- free/ reduced entry (or in May).
www.visitsanmarino.com
Milano – **Design Week** – *FuoriSalone, held during the weeklong Salone del Mobile.* This unmissable event turns galleries, museums, stores and other institutions into jam-packed meeting places. The press publishes the programme. *www.fuorisalone.it.*

May

1st – Festa del Lavoro- Labour holiday. Parades and fiery speeches honour the nation's labourers. Businesses are closed on this popular holiday.

Naples – **Feast of the Miracle of St Januarius (Gennaro)** cathedral, "blood miracle" of patron saint. *sangennaro.eu*
Cagliari – **Feast of Sant'Efisio.** *www.festadisantefisio.com*
Assisi – **First Thurs after 1 May** Calendimaggio – Ides of May medieval traditions. *www.calendimaggiodiassisi.com*
Chianti – Chianti classico è wine tastings in/around 8 Chianti classico zones.
Florence – Festa del Grillo- Cricket Festival in Cascine Park.
Gubbio – **Ceri ("candle") race** – Uphill foot race in medieval garb to the Basilica of St Ubaldo. *www.ceri.it*
Sassari – **Cavalcata Sarda**.
Gubbio – **Palio della Balestra**.
Venice – **Vogalonga** – Rowing enthusiasts crowd the lagoons with boats. *www.vogalonga.com*
Taormina – **Festival of Sicilian costumes and carts**.

June

Cavalcata Oswald von Wolkenstein – medieval equestrian events Alto Adige Outdoor cinema through summer in Rome and Florence.
www.ovwritt.com

2nd – Festa della Repubblica d´Italia Republic of Italy holiday.
www.festadellarepubblica.it

29th – St. Peter and St Paul Rome holiday.

Venice – 🎭 **Biennale**.
www.labiennale.org

Pisa –16 **Luminara di San Ranieri**, 70,000 candles along the Arno.

Roma – **Estate Romana** (**June– August**) – (Roman Summer, *www.estateromana.comune.roma. it*): Concerts and spectacles held (especially in Caracalla's Baths).

Florence – 🎭 **Calcio Storico Fiorentino** – Historic Football game Piazza S. Croce, parade, both in 16C costumes.

Taormina – Film Festival.
www.taorminafilmfest.net

Verona – **Opera season in the Roman amphitheatre**.
www.arena.it

July

Regata delle Repubbliche Marinare – boat race in historic costume rotates among Pisa Venezia, Genoa and Amalfi.

Palermo – Festa di Santa Rosalia.

Spoleto – **Spoleto Due Mondi Festival** – International theatre, music and dance festival.
www.festivaldispoleto.com

Perugia – **Umbria Jazz Festival**.
www.umbriajazz.com

Siena – 🎭 **Palio** – Historic horse race. Also in Aug. *www.ilpalio.org*

Venice – **Feast of the Redeemer** – Fireworks Sat night; religious services and regatta on Sun.

August

15th – Ferragosto/ Assunzione di Maria in Cielo holiday. The entire nation goes on holiday – often for weeks.

Sassari – **Feast of the candles**.

Nuoro – **Feast of the Redeemer**.
www.festadelredentorenuoro.it

Ferrara – **Buskers Festival** – Street music. *www.ferrarabuskers.com*

Venice – 🎭 **International Film Festival** at the Lido.
www.labiennale.org/it/cinema

September

Late september (and october) – European Heritage Day: Private gardens and palaces open their doors on the fourth Sunday. Freebies, discounts and related events in the most important museums.

3rd – Festa di San Marino, foundation of the Republic 301.

Asti – **Festival delle Sagre and "Douja d'or" wine festival**.
www.doujador.it

Cannara – Onion Festival.
www.festadellacipolla.com

Lucca – **Luminara di S. Croce**.

Venice – 🎭 **Historical Regatta on the Grand Canal** – Gondoliers in period costume compete.
www.regatastoricavenezia.it

Florence – **Feast of the Rificolona** (coloured paper lanterns). Music and folklore.

Loreto – **Feast of the Nativity of the Virgin**. *www.santuarioloreto.it*

Marostica – **Partita a scacchi** – Chess tournament with human chess pieces.
www.marosticascacchi.it

Montefalco – Tasting Sagrantino wine. *www.settimanaenologica.it*

19th – Naples – **Feast of the Miracle of St Januarius (Gennaro)** in the cathedral.

Asti – Palio di Asti – Horse race.
www.palio.asti.it
Festa del Vino – Grape harvest,
wine festivals in Italy.
www.festedelvino.it
www.lagrandefestadelvino.it

October
1st – San Marino – **Investiture of
the Republic's regents**.
Perugia – Eurochocolate –
chocolate fair on town streets.
www.eurochocolate.com
Festa del Vino – Wine festivals.

November
1st – Ognissanti - All Saints holiday.
Costumed children race in the
squares, flinging confetti
and shaving cream. Snack on the
"bones of the dead" (osso di morto)
from a pastry shop.
2nd – Commemorazione dei
defunti - cemetery visits.
4th – Giorno dell'Unità Nazionale
Italia, Unification of Italy.

6th – Vino Novello- "New Wine".
Festa dell'olio- Olive oil festivals.
www.novelloinfesta.it
Asti – Truffle festival.
**Venice – Madonna della
Salute Feast**.
**Bolzano, Bressanone, Merano –
Christmas markets**.
www.mercatini-natale.com

December
8th – Immaculate Conception
– Rome: Pope places wreath on
Mary's statue, Piazza di Spagna.
25th – Christmas holiday.
26th – Santo Stefano holiday.
**Milano – Fiera degli "Oh bej,
oh bej!"** – *7-10 Dec, Castello
Sforzesco.* The name is dialect
for "Beautiful things." Christmas
market with the sale of handcrafts,
secondhand goods and regional
specialities.
Orvieto – Umbria Jazz Festival.
www.umbriajazz.com

September: *Feast of the Rificolona, Florence*

©Thefinalmi/Dreamstime.com

PRACTICAL INFORMATION

WHEN TO GO

Roughly half of Italy's visitors come specifically for tourism related to art and history, for which Italy is an ideal destination year round. Food and wine are great tourism draws, too; except for specific seasonal specialities or the harvest, these delight the visitor year round. April, May, September and October are best for city breaks, with cooler temperatures. Many Italian cities use the seasons to theatrical advantage and are worth visiting off peak – Venice's winter mists (and floods) lend it an air of mystery, while a crisp winter morning in a deserted Florentine piazza is exceptionally pleasant. June and September are best for beach holidays, providing sultry heat without uncomfortable humidity, high prices and peak crowds. However, in the Alps and Apennines short, cool summers between May and September are optimum times for walking and outdoor activity holidays. The Italian ski season is typically from December to late March, with year-round skiing on the higher reaches of Mont Blanc.

KNOW BEFORE YOU GO
Useful Websites

www.italiantouristboard.co.uk – Website of the Italian State Tourist Board. Accommodation, events, museums and holiday experiences. Tour operator search.

www.italiantourism.com – Website of the Italian Tourist Board in North America. Travel tips and holiday planning, plus regional information.

www.USTOA.com – US Tour Operators Association; has a list of agencies that specialise in Italy for package tours, including independent traveller options.

www.beniculturali.it – Website of the Ministry of Culture (in Italian only). Museum details, cultural event programmes, news on restorations and publications.

whc.unesco.org – Italy has more World Heritage properties (51 total, plus 41 pending) than any other country in the world, "having outstanding universal value."

International Visitors
Tourist Organisations

Italian State Tourist Office – For information, brochures, maps and assistance in planning a trip to Italy, apply to the **ENIT** (Ente Nazionale Italiano per il Turismo) in your country or consult www.enit.it.

UK

- 1 Princes Street, London W1B 2AY, *(020) 7408 1254*, www.italiantouristboard.co.uk

USA

- 686 Park Avenue, New York, 3rd Floor, NY 10065 *(212) 245 5618*
- 10850 Wilshire Boulevard, Suite 725, Los Angeles, CA 90024. *(310) 820 1898,*
- 3800 Division Street, Stone Park, Chicago IL 60165. *(312) 644 0996.*

Canada

- 69 Yonge Street, Suite 1404. Toronto Ontario M5E 1K3. *(416) 925 4882.*

Rome viewed from Basilica di San Pietro

Italian Embassies
UK
- 14 Three Kings' Yard, London
  W1K 4EH. *(020) 7312 2200.*
  www.amblondra.esteri.it.

USA
- 3000 Whitehaven Street,
  NW Washington, DC 20008.
  (202) 612 4400.
  www.ambwashingtondc.esteri.it.

Canada
- 274 Slater Street,
  21st Floor, Ottawa, Ontario K1P
  5H9. *(613) 232 2401.*
  www.ambottawa.esteri.it.

Italian Consulates
UK
- Harp House, 83/86 Farringdon
  Street, London, EC4A 4BL.
  (020) 79365900.
  consolato.londra@esteri.it.
  www.conslondra.esteri.it.
- 32 Melville Street, Edinburgh
  EH3 7HA. *(0131) 226 3631.*
  www.consedimburgo.esteri.it.
- Union Street, Bedford
  MK40 1HJ. (01234) 356647.
  www.consbedford.esteri.it.

USA
- 690 Park Avenue, New York,
  NY 10065. *(212) 737 9100.*
  Fax (212) 249 4945.
  www.consnewyork.esteri.it.
- 600 Atlantic Avenue, 17th Floor,
  Boston, MA 02210 -2206.
  617 722 9201.
  www.consboston.esteri.it.
- 500 North Michigan Avenue,
  Suite 1850, Chicago, IL 60611.
  (312) 467 1550.
  www.conschicago.esteri.it.
- 1900 Avenue of the Stars, Suite
  1250, Los Angeles, CA 90067.
  (310) 820 0622.
  www.conslosangeles.esteri.it.

Canada
- 3489 Drummond Street,
  Montreal, Quebec H3G 1X6.
  (514) 849 8351.
  www.consmontreal.esteri.it.
- 136 Beverly Street, Toronto,
  Ontario M5T 1Y5. *(416) 977 1566.*
  www.constoronto.esteri.it.
- Standard Building, 510 West
  Hastings Street, Suite 1100,
  V6B 1L8 Vancouver,
  British Columbia. *604 684 7288.*
  www.consvancouver.esteri.it.

PRACTICAL INFORMATION

Foreign Embassies and Consulates in Italy

Australia
Consulate: 3rd Floor, Via Borgogna 2, Milan. *02 777 04 217.*
Embassy: Via Antonio Bosio 5, Rome. *06 85 27 21.* www.italy.embassy.gov.au.

Canada
Consulate: Piazza Cavour 3, Milan. *02 626 94 238.*
Embassy: Via Zara 30, Rome. *06 85 44 42 911.* www.canada.it

Ireland
For consulate see UK below.
Embassy: Villa Spada, Via Giacomo Medici 1, Rome. *06 58 52 381.* www.embassyofireland.it.

UK
Consulate: Via S. Paolo 7, Milan. *02 723 001.*
British embassy: Via XX Settembre 80a, Rome. *06 42 20 00 01.* www.italiantouristboard.co.uk.

USA
Consulate: Via Principe Amedeo 2/10, Milan. *02 290 351.* italian.milan.usconsulate.gov.
Embassy: Via Vittorio Veneto 121, Roma. *06 46 741.* http://italy.usembassy.gov.

Documents

Passport – Visitors entering Italy must be in possession of a valid national passport. Citizens of European Union countries need only a National Identity Card. Report loss or theft to the embassy or consulate and the local police.

Visa – Entry visas are required by Australian, New Zealand, Canadian and US citizens (if their intended stay exceeds three months). Apply to the Italian Consulate (visa issued same day; delay if submitted by mail). US citizens should obtain the booklet "A Safe Trip Abroad", which provides useful information on visa requirements, customs regulations and medical care for international travellers. Published by the Government Printing Office, it can be ordered or online at: **www.travel.state.gov.**

Driving licence – Nationals of EU countries require a valid national driving licence. Nationals of non-EU countries require an International Driving Permit. This is available in the USA from the American Automobile Association for $20 (an application form can be found at www.aaa.com) and in Canada from the Canadian Automobile Association for $25 (*see www.caa.ca for details*). If you are bringing your own car into the country, you will need the vehicle registration papers.

Car insurance – If you are bringing your own car to Italy, an International Insurance Certificate (Green Card), although no longer a legal requirement, is the most

effective proof of insurance cover and is internationally recognised by the police and other authorities. This is available from your insurer.

Customs Regulations

As of 30 June 1999, those travelling between countries within the European Union can no longer purchase "duty-free" goods. For further information on customs regulations, travellers should contact Her Majesty's Revenue & Customs (HMRC) *0845 010 9000*; **www.hmrc.gov.uk** (and enter "Travel" in the Search option). For the US Customs and Border Protection consult the website **www.cbp.gov**.

Health

British citizens should apply to the Department of Health for a **European Health Insurance Card** (EHIC), which entitles the holder to urgent treatment for accident or unexpected illness in EU countries. It does not provide cover for repatriation in the event of an emergency. The EHIC is free, and can be obtained by calling *0800 67 89 10 11* (from outside the EU *0032 22 99 96 96*) or at **www.dh.gov.uk**. Nationals of non-EU countries should check that their insurance policy covers them specifically for overseas travel, including doctors' visits, medication and hospitalisation in Italy (most take out supplementary insurance). The US State Dept lists some insurance companies at http://travel.state. gov. American Express offers its cardholders a service called Global Assist to help in financial, legal, medical or personal emergencies. For further information, consult: www.americanexpress.com.

Prescription drugs should always be clearly labelled, and it is also recommended that you carry a prescription copy. Chemists' shops (*farmacia* – green cross sign) post a list of colleagues open at night or on Sundays.

First aid service (*pronto soccorso*) is available in hospitals at some airports and railway stations.

Accessibility

For further information, contact **Roma per tutti**. For information and to have an idea about accessible tourist attractions and events in the city for the disabled or people with particular needs, we suggest visiting the website www.turismoroma.it or contact the service-centre for tourism, information and mobility for persons with special needs in Rome: *06 57 17 70 94*.

Information and the assistance-request service for traveling on the Italian State railways are available at the number *199 30 30 60* (Mon–Sun 6.45am–9.30pm) or free number *800 90 60 60* (from landlines only).

You can also consult the site **www.trenitalia.com.** To request assistance (at least two days in advance) on the Trenord railway network, call *800 210 955* (www. trenord.it).

Tourism for All UK (formerly Holiday Care), *0845 124 9971*. www.tourismforall.org.uk.

Disability Rights UK, CAN Mezzanine, 49-51 East Rd, London N1 6AH. *(020) 7250 8181*. www.disabilityrightsuk.org.

Society for Accessible Travel & Hospitality – 347 Fifth Ave, Suite 605, NY 10016-5010. *(212) 447 7284*. www.sath.org.

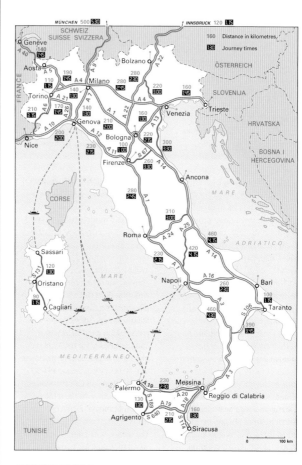

GETTING THERE

Discounts: Before you book, check for discounts for families, groups (sometimes of four or less), youths, and senior citizens, as well as for special offers.

By Plane

Many international carriers operate services to Rome and the country's major provincial airports (Milan, Turin, Verona, Venice, Genoa, Bologna, Florence, Pisa, Naples, Catania and Palermo). Discounts may be available for families, groups (sometimes of four or less), youths, and senior citizens. Numerous no-frills airlines offer low-cost flights from many regional airports in the UK, Ireland and other European cities. These usually connect to more remote urban airports or those in regional capitals like Bergamo, Pescara or Verona. Some discount fares from London have been as low as €19, plus taxes. However, travellers should research the airport's location, transport options and all expenses before booking.

Air Canada www.aircanada.com
Alitalia www.alitalia.com
American
www.americanairlines.com
British Airways
www.britishairways.com
Bmi regional
www.bmiregional.com
Delta www.delta.com

Easyjet
Flights to Bari, Bologna, Brindisi, Cagliari, Catania, Milan, Naples, Olbia, Palermo, Pisa, Rome, Turin, Verona and Venice from London and regional UK airports;
www.easyjet.com

Monarch Airlines
Flights to Naples, Rome, Turin, Verona and Venice.
www.monarch.co.uk

Ryanair
Flights to Alghero (Sardinia; from London Stansted and Luton), Ancona, Bari, Bologna, Bergamo, Brindisi, Cagliari, Genoa, Lamezia Terme, Milan, Palermo, Parma, Perugia, Pescara, Pisa, Rome, Trapani, Treviso (Venice), Trieste and Turin from London Stansted.
www.ryanair.com

US Airways
www.usairways.com

By Ship
Passenger ferries, car-ferries and luxury cruise ships can offer a scenic arrival, from economical to luxury. Italy is reachable by trans-Atlantic crossings (including bargain repositioning cruises), from European ports in Spain, Greece, France, Croatia, Albania, and from further points such as Egypt. Some cruise lines that call on Italian ports: Carnival; Celebrity; Crystal; Cunard; Holland; America; Princess; MSC; Sea Cloud.

Additional cruise and ferry lines may be obtained from travel agents and online by searching port cities by "porto di" and the Italian name: Ancona; Bari; Brindisi; Catania; Civitavecchia; Genoa; La Spezia/Cinque Terre; Napoli; Venezia. Civitavecchia is the busiest Mediterranean passenger port after Barcelona.

By Train
From London, the Channel ports and other European cities there are rail services to many Italian towns, including high-speed passenger trains and motorail services. Tourists residing outside Italy can buy rail passes that offer unlimited travel during a specific period. Parties may purchase discounted group tickets.
Italian State Railway –
www.fsitaliane.it.
Trenitalia – *89 20 21*.
www.trenitalia.it.
Rail Europe – *800-622-8600 toll-free from US). 0844 848 5848 (from UK)*.
www.raileurope.com.
help.uk.voyages-sncf.com..
Eurostar – *03432 186 186 (from UK)*.
www.eurostar.com.uk.

Tickets are also available from the main British and American Rail Travel Centres and travel agencies. The Eurail Pass can be purchased before going abroad, from certain European destinations, or online at www.eurail.com.

Rail is a particularly good way of getting to Milan, Venice, Florence and Rome, as the stations are within easy reach of the cities' centres. Italo, a private company, launched high-speed trains, www.italotreno.it.

By Coach/Bus

Regular coach services operate from London to Rome and to other large provincial Italian towns and cities. Services from Victoria Coach Station in London to Italy are operated by:
Eurolines – *0871 781 81 81.* www.eurolines.co.uk. Alternatively, contact **National Express** – *0871 781 81 81.* www.nationalexpress.com.

By Car

Roads from France into Italy, with the exception of the Menton/ Ventimiglia (Riviera) coast road, are dependent on Alpine passes and tunnels. The main roads go through the Montgenèvre Pass near Briançon, the Fréjus Tunnel and Mont-Cenis Pass near Saint-Jean-de-Maurienne, the Petit-Saint-Bernard Pass near Bourg-Saint-Maurice and the Mont-Blanc Tunnel near Chamonix.
Via Switzerland, three main routes are possible – through the tunnel or pass at Grand-Saint-Bernard, through the Simplon Pass, and through the St Gottard Pass, which goes via Ticino and Lugano to the great lakes of Lombardy. Be sure to budget for the Swiss road tax (*vignette*), which is levied on all motor vehicles and trailers with a maximum weight of 3.5 tons, instead of charging tolls on the motorways.

The *vignette* costs 40 Swiss francs and can be bought at border crossings, post offices, petrol stations, garages and cantonal motor registries, or in advance from the Switzerland Travel Centre, 30 Bedford Street, 1st Floor, London WC2E 9ED; (020) 74 20 49 34; www.stc.co.uk.
The Brenner Pass south of Innsbruck greets drivers from Germany and Austria. Remember that most of these tunnels or passes levy tolls (*see By Car in Getting Around, below*).
Use **Michelin maps 719, 721** and **735** or the **Michelin Atlas Europe** to help plan your route.

GETTING AROUND

Discounts: Before you book, check for discounts for families, groups (sometimes of four or less), youths and senior citizens, as well as for special offers.

By Plane

Frequent domestic flights cover the whole country. Transfer buses serve town bus terminals and railway stations. For further information, contact:

Air Dolomiti
045 28 86 140.
www.airdolomiti.it

Airone
895 898 95 78.
www.fly-go.it/Airone

Alitalia
03335 66 55 44 (from UK), 00353 124 765 46 (from Ireland), 800 223 5730 (toll-free from US) www.alitalia.com

Meridiana

89 29 28 (+44 20 38 68 1778 from UK and *+ 1 718 751 4499* from USA).
www.meridiana.it

By Ship

Sicily and Sardinia

These two islands are linked to the mainland by ferries and hydrofoils, especially popular during the summer months.

Visitors are advised to book early, especially if travelling with a car or if a cabin is required. Deck tickets are available until a few hours before departure at the terminal. Again, it's wise to book ahead, even for less luxurious spots.

The main ferry services to Sicily (Catania, Messina, Palermo, Trapani) and Sardegna (Arbatax, Cagliari, Olbia) depart from Genoa, Livorno, Civitavecchia, Fiumicino, Naples, Salerno and Cagliari. Crossings range from about 7–18 hours, depending on departure and arrival ports. **www.aliscafi.it** connects Naples to southern ports, including along the Amalfi Coast, Salerno, and the Cilento Coast. From Calabria (Ponte San Giovanni or Reggio) crossings can take

15 to 45 minutes, depending on whether by hydrofoil or car ferry; some are operated by Trenitalia. Some ferries also serve other islands, such as Capri, Ischia, and Malta. The Adriatic Coast has ferry service; most ports serve foreign destinations, but a few ferries serve other Italian Adriatic ports. Check port cities of departure and arrival online under "porto di" and the city name to see additional options, passenger lines, and timetables. For information and reservations, contact:

Caronte&Tourist (Salerno to Sicily) *800 627 414.* www.carontetourist.it
Grandi Navi Veloci – *010 20 94 591.* www1.gnv.it
Grimaldi Lines – *081 496 444.* www.grimaldi-lines.com
SNAV – *081 42 85 555.* www.snav.it
Tirrenia – *892 123.* www.tirrenia.it
Trenitalia – www.trenitalia.com
Alilauro – *081 49 72 238.* www.alilauro.it

By Train

Trenitalia, the state railway network (*www.trenitalia.it*), travels the length and breadth of Italy. Ticket machines usually have

Genoa port

© Gunter Menz/Fotolia.com

25

English-language displays and accept credit cards. Whenever possible, reserve a seat or you may wind up huddled in the aisle. Also, be aware that Italy has 10 different services, from the posh Frecciarossa to the Eurostar (ES), to the slow, local Intercity (I) and Regionale (R) train services. Mix-ups could result in costly fines and upgrades. Abbreviations indicate a train's type on the display boards and schedules (printed on large yellow and white posters).Super Economy is the least expensive ticket, available for a limited number of seats without refund, change or access to an alternate train. Economy allows for one ticket change prior to departure; no refunds for cancellations or for alternate trains from that booked. The 10 Journey Carnet allows a 20 per cent discount on Frecciarossa and Frecciargento high-speed trains. Biglietto Base is the least expensive ticket that allows for a change prior to departure; Biglietto Flessibile costs 25 per cent more than Base, but tickets can be changed even after departure time. Groups of 2-5 passengers may also qualify for discounts. Bicycles can be taken on trains (usually all local services) for a supplement. Italo it's a private rail line was inaugurated. Red high-speed trains connect Milan, Bologna, Florence, Rome, Naples and Venice.Trenitalia in Italy honours the Eurail and InterRail passes (though a *supplemento*, an additional fee, may be charged for some services). For additional discounts, including family and group (sometimes a minimum of two) consult the train websites. **Trenitalia** – *89 20 21 or 199 89 20 21*. www.trenitalia.com

Italo Treno – *06 07 08 or 892020*. www.italotreno.it

By Coach/Bus

While much of Italy is accessible by train, buses often offer additional destinations, sometimes more direct routes and budget fares. Bus travel is generally comfortable and efficient. However, there is no national bus company, which can make finding the correct bus company difficult. Usually the easiest and quickest way is to contact the destination tourist office for bus company information. The following is a selection of the many bus companies in operation in Italy: **SITA** (www.sitabus.it) has an extensive network, operating in Tuscany, Veneto, Campania, Puglia, and Basilicata.

For getting around Lazio beyond Rome, try **COTRAL**, 800 174 471 (06 72 05 72 05 from mobile), www.cotralspa.it. Other operators: **Marozzi bus** (www.marozzivt.it), **BusItalia** (www.fsbusitalia.it), **FlixBus** (www.flixbus.it), **GencoBus** (www.gencobus.it), **ARST** (arst.sardegna.it), **AST** (www.aziendasiciliana trasporti.it) **Italobus** (www.italotreno.it).

By Car

Italian roads are excellent, and there is a wide network of motorways (*autostrade*). The Italian motorway website can be found at www.autostrade.it.

Highway code

The minimum driving age is 18. Traffic flows on the right. Drivers and front-seat passengers must wear seat belts, also mandatory in the back where they are fitted.

Speed limits

© meskolo/Fotolia.com

Children under 12 must travel in the back seat, unless the front seat is fitted with a child restraint system. Full or dipped headlights should be switched on in poor visibility and at night; use sidelights only when a stationary vehicle is not clearly visible.

In the event of a breakdown, a red warning triangle must be displayed in the road; these can be hired from the ACI (Automobile Club Italia) offices at the frontier (deposit refunded).

Drivers should watch out for unfamiliar road signs and take great care on the road (there's much truth in the joke that Italian drivers prefer using their horn to their brakes!). At crossroads, cars coming from the right have priority. Flashing lights indicate a driver is not slowing down. Severe penalties are applicable for drunk-driving offences.

Speed limits

In built-up areas, 50kph/31mph; on country roads, 90kph/55mph; on motorways, 90kph/55mph for vehicles up to 1 000cc and 130kph/80mph for vehicles over 1 100cc.

Parking

Car parks with attendants are common. The crime rate is high, so the extra expense is often worthwhile, especially in the south (Naples is most notorious). Obviously, check rates before parking to avoid unpleasant surprises.

Many large towns limit traffic in their historic town centres (only authorised vehicles may enter), indicated by large rectangular signs saying *ZTL*. Parking outside town is advisable anyway, as Italy's old, narrow streets usually have no pavements.

Road signs

Motorways (*autostrade* – subject to tolls) and dual carriageways (*superstrade*) are often indicated by green signs; ordinary roads by blue signs; tourist sights usually by brown or yellow signs. A national road, Strada Statale, is indicated by SS, and a provincial road, Strada Proviniciale, by SP.

Road tolls

Tolls are payable on most motorways (*www.autostrade.it*), calculated according to the distance between the car axles and engine capacity.

At an unmanned booth, press the button for a ticket, which must be presented at the exit.

Motorway fees can be paid in cash (look for lanes with signs representing toll collectors), with the Via Card and by credit card (look for lanes with the Via Card sign and blue stripes on the road surface). The Telepass (*www.telepass.it*) is a toll pre-pay system that allows cars to pass through road tolls quickly. Unless you have a Telepass don't stray into the signed lane by mistake – it is usually on the far left.

Petrol

Gasolio = diesel
Senza piombo = premium unleaded (95 octane)
Super Plus or **Euro Plus** = super unleaded (98 octane)
Petrol stations are usually open 7am–7pm. Many close at lunchtime (between 12.30pm and 3pm), on Sundays and public holidays. Self-service stations have machines that don't give change. Sometimes a start button or lever activates the flow; however, look around.

Maps and Plans

Michelin Map 735 at a scale of 1:1 000 000 covers the whole country. At 1:400 000, Michelin Map 561 covers the northwest, 562 the northeast, 563 the centre, 564 the south, 565 Sicily and 566 Sardinia; at 1:200 000, 553 covers Bolzano and Aosta to Milan; at 1:100 000, 115 covers the westernmost stretch of the Italian Riviera. The Michelin Atlas Italy (1:300 000) contains a complete index of towns, 80 plans of the largest cities and covers all of Italy; it is also available in mini format. Folded maps 38 (1:10 000) and 46 (1:15 000) cover Rome and Milan. The Touring Club Italiano (TCI), Corso Italia 10, Milan, 02 85 26 304 www.touringclub.it), publishes a regional map series at 1:200 000. www.touringclub.it. Motorists should also consult **www. ViaMichelin.com** to prepare for their journey. The service enables travellers to select their preferred route (fastest, scenic, etc.) and to calculate distances.

Motoring organisations

Road rescue services – In case of breakdown, contact ACI (Automobile Club Italia), 116 (24hrs). This breakdown service (tax levied) is operated by the ACI for foreign motorists. The ACI also offers a telephone information service in English (and other languages) for road and weather conditions as well as for tourist events: 803 116, www.aci.it.

Car rental

There are car rental agencies at airports, railway stations and in all large towns and resorts throughout Italy. The main agencies are Avis, Hertz, Eurodollar, Europcar, Maggiore, Budget and Sixt. Fly-drive schemes or train-and-car packages are available. European cars usually have manual transmissions, but automatic cars are available on request. Many companies won't rent to drivers under 21 or 23 – or will insist upon large cash deposits. An International Driving Permit could be required for non-EU nationals; both the **American Automobile Association** (www.aaa.com) and **Royal Auto Club – RAC** (www.rac.co.uk/news-advice/) issue these.

BASIC INFORMATION
Communications
The telephone service is organised by TIM ITALIA (www.tim.it).

Mobile Phones
Telecom Italia Mobile (TIM) (www.tim.it), Vodafone (www.vodafone.it), Wind (www.wind.it), and 3 (www.tre.it) are the major mobile companies in Italy.

Internet
Many hotels provide a public PC, permit modem hook-ups or have wireless access. Try the following for free access via a laptop: Libero (www.libero.it), Tiscali (www.tiscalinet.it) and Telecom Italia (www.tim.it). Easy Internet is a reliable connection café; its main outlets are open 24 hours (www.easy.com).

Phonecards
Phonecards (schede telefoniche) are sold in denominations of €3 and €5 and are supplied by CIT offices and post offices as well as tobacconists (signs bearing a white "T" on a black background). Often, users must insert a code or tear off a pre-cut corner to activate the card. Also useful for foreigners are New Welcome cards, available in denominations of €5 and €10.

Public phones
Phone boxes (Digito telephone) may be operated by phonecards (sold in post offices and tobacconists) and by phone credit cards or coins. To make a call: lift the receiver, insert payment, await dialling tone, then punch in the required number.

Telephoning
When making a call within Italy, the area code (e.g. 06 for Rome, 055 for Florence) is always used, from outside and within the city you are calling. For international calls dial 00 plus the country code:

- ✆ **44** for the UK
- ✆ **61** for Australia
- ✆ **1** for Canada
- ✆ **64** for New Zealand
- ✆ **1** for the USA

If calling from outside the country, the intern.l code for Italy is **39**. Dial the full area code, even when making an international call (eg when calling Rome from the UK, dial 00 39 06, followed by rest of number).

Useful numbers
The following calls are subject to a charge:

- ✆ **1254** Directory Enquiries.
- ✆ **170** Operator Assisted International Calls.

Electricity
The voltage is 220AC, 50 cycles per second; the sockets are for two-pin plugs. Pack an adapter to use for hairdryers, shavers, computers, etc.

Emergencies
✆ **113 General Emergency Services** (soccorso pubblico di emergenza); to be called only in cases of real danger.
✆ **112** International emergency number; in Italy, **Police** (carabinieri).

☎ 115 Fire Brigade
(vigili del fuoco).

**☎ 118 Emergency Health
Services** (emergenza sanitaria).

☎ 1515 Forest Fire Service.
Environmental Emergencies.

☎ 803 116 Automobile Club
d'Italia Emergency Breakdown
Service.

Mail/Post

Opening hours

Post offices are open 8.15am–
1.30pm on weekdays, 8.15am–
12.30pm on Saturdays. Some
branches in city centres and
shopping centres are also open
afternoons. For information, t
www.poste.it. Stamps are also sold
at tobacconists (*tabacchi*) which
display a black *valori bollati* sign.

Stamps

Stamps for letters or postcards, up
to 20 grams: Zone 1 (Europe inc UK)
is €1; Zone 2 (Americas) is €2.

Money

Currency

The unit of currency is the euro,
which is issued in notes (€5, €10,
€20, €50, €100, €200 and €500)
and in coins (1 cent, 2 cents, 5
cents, 10 cents, 20 cents, 50 cents,
€1 and €2). Correct change is
something of a commodity in Italy.
Many bars are unable to break a
€20 or €50 note.

Banks

Banks are usually open Mon–Fri
8.30am–1.30pm and 2.30–4pm.
Some branches are open in city
centres and shopping centres
on Saturday mornings Travellers'
cheques have declined in use and
may be more difficult to change.
Money can be changed in post
offices (except travellers' cheques),
money-changing bureaux and
at railway stations and airports.
Commission is always charged.

Credit Cards

Much of Italy remains a cash-based
society. Payment by credit card
is possible in most major shops,
hotels, restaurants and petrol
stations. The *Michelin Guide Italia*
and *Michelin Guide Europe* indicate
which credit cards are accepted
at hotels and restaurants. Money
may also be withdrawn from a
bank, but may incur interest and
charges. Some companies now
add a 1–3 per cent conversion fee

Euro, notes and coins

to credit purchases; avoid using these cards abroad. Finally, inform the company of your itinerary, so a "suspicious activity" block doesn't freeze the account.

Taxes and tipping

Italy adds on a variable tax – averaging 22 percent – to most goods and services. The *Imposta sul Valore Aggiunto* (IVA) mostly lurks unseen, part and parcel of the bill. Visitors from non-EU countries can claim back the IVA on each item over €155. Italians tip about five percent in a pizzeria or humble trattoria, or just round up to the nearest euro. The rate should rise in more expensive restaurants, but never top 10 per cent. €0.50 tips are appropriate for bar service. Taxi drivers expect around €0.75, as do cloakroom attendants; porters €0.50–€1 per bag.

Newspapers

The main Italian newspapers (available throughout Italy) are *Il Messaggero* and *Il Giorno*. The two national newspapers are *Corriere della Sera* and *La Repubblica*. The *Osservatore Romano* is the official newspaper of the Vatican City. Foreign newspapers are available in the cities and large towns. *Wanted in Rome* magazine keeps expatriates connected in the capital, with another version in Milan.

Pharmacies

Crosses (typically in green, white or red neon) mark pharmacies (chemists). When closed, each will advertise the name of the duty pharmacy and doctors on call.

Pharmacy sign

©Norman Pogson/Fotolia.com

Public Holidays

Offices and shops are closed in Italy on the following days: **1 Jan, 6 Jan, Mon after Easter, 25 Apr, 1 May, 2 June, 1 Nov, 8 Dec, 25–26 Dec**. Holidays are also observed in cities on local feast days honouring patron saints, including: **25 Apr** (St Mark) – Venice, **24 June** (St John the Baptist) – Florence, Turin, Genoa, **29 June** (Sts Peter and Paul) – Rome, **4 Oct** (St Petronio) – Bologna and **7 Dec** (St Ambrose) – Milan.

Time

Italy lies in the Central European Time Zone and is one hour ahead of Greenwich Mean Time (GMT +1).

MOST FAMOUS PLACES

Historic ruins and Renaissance relics are most commonly cited as Italy's main attractions. Yet the cultural and natural diversions in the boot-shaped country are far from homogeneous. In Italy, travellers can ski the Alps, bask on miles of beaches and explore ancient civilisations – sometimes all within the same day. It is easy to understand why Italy is one of the world's most visited and beloved destinations.

Milan, Lombardy and the Lakes *(pp36–53)*

Affluence is evident in Lombardy, from the stunning villages of the region's Lake District (Regione dei Laghi) to Milan, where Italy's chic designers, bright business minds and savvy media players maintain a very visible presence.

Though Lombardy is the epitome of modern Italy, it is not without its heritage trail, which marches right through Milan, by way of the Duomo and Leonardo da Vinci's *Last Supper*, to the photogenic and refined cities of Lombardy's countryside. The Franciacorta area near Brescia draws increased attention for its bubbly wines, produced using classic methods of fermentation.

Duomo, Siena

Genoa and Portofino *(pp54–61)*

A sliver of a region, Liguria possesses almost everything that a tourist could wish for on a trip to Italy, including alpine vistas, warm Mediterranean breezes and colourful coastal villages that make the heart sing. Liguria's coast curves along the Gulf of Genoa, named for the capital, which has an illustrious maritime past. Exploring Genoa's busy harbour or hiking the Cinque Terre are popular pastimes.

The Alps – Valle d'Aosta and Piemonte *(pp62–65)*

The north western regions of the Valle d'Aosta and Piemonte are a study in contrasts. The Valle d'Aosta is defined by mountains,

Portofino, Liguria

© Dan Breckwoldt/iStockphoto.com

Grand Canal, Venice

© G. Glinsk/Fotolia.com

Todi, Umbria

© Silvano Audisio/Bigstockphoto.com

while the geographical highlight of Piemonte is the fertile Po River Plain. Basking in the shadow of Mont Blanc, the Valle d'Aosta shares many traditions with its French neighbours. On the other hand, Turin, Piemonte's regional seat, was the first capital of a unified Italy.

Tucked firmly into the Dolomites, the dual autonomous provinces of Trentino and Alto Adige/

Vineyards near Alba, Piedmont

© J. Arnold/ hemis.fr

Südtirol make up this region. Spectacular mountain passes have made Trentino-Alto Adige/ Südtirol a pristine skiers' paradise. However, its relative isolation over the centuries has preserved a pervasive Germanic culture, from towns names in both German and Italian, to linguistic pockets of medieval German. The Iceman, in Bolzano's archaeological museum, is a favourite attraction. Barolo is the most famous red wine from Piemonte, but there are many wines to taste, often made with grapes unique to specific areas.

Venice, Verona and around *(pp66–83)*

Connected via canals and alluring bridges, Venice, the capital of the Veneto, is instantly recognisable and boasts a unique culture derived from its days as one of the Mediterranean's most prominent seafaring powers. The Veneto and Friuli-Venezia Giulia, a small region that was once a part of Austria's domain, possess cities of quiet charm. Verona and Padua thrive in

ITALY'S MOST FAMOUS PLACES

33

arts and commerce. Superb wines range from the fragrant whites of Friuli, to bubbly Prosecco, and hefty red Amarone and Valpolicella near Verona.

Tuscany and Umbria *(pp84–103)*

Home to the Renaissance art jewel of Florence, Pisa's famous Leaning Tower and the vineyards of Chianti, Tuscany is perhaps Italy's most well-known region. Its dizzying collection of must-see sights goes beyond the well-known diversions to include Renaissance cities like Lucca surrounded by gracious farm villas, medieval enclaves in Siena and San Gimignano, and natural wonders such as thermal baths. Indeed, all of Tuscany begs to be explored. Of the wines, Chianti is the most famous, produced in its Classico version in eight designated zones, while other Chianti is produced outside but still following strict guidelines. Montalcino is famous for its Brunello, Montepulciano for its Vino Nobile, and Scansano for Morellino. However, Tuscany has many wines produced throughout the region. Its simple hearty cuisine is based on grilled meats including wild boar, soups, and grains.

Landlocked and deep green, Umbria is a quiet region of hill towns and mountain forests, from which both saints and artists have drawn inspiration. The main attraction is Assisi, the peaceful town where the great basilica to St Francis beckons millions of both devoted pilgrims and art lovers each year. Umbria's pleasant capital Perugia, a strategic town since Etruscan times, has an impressive cache of art and artefacts in its museums and university. The dark red wine, Sagrantino di Montefalco, continues to draw international interest to Umbria.

Bologna and Emilia-Romagna *(pp104–113)*

A rich meat-based cuisine has steered many a tourist to Emilia-Romagna, busy with industry from food to Ferraris. Balsamic vinegar is aged in towns around Modena, while prosciutto ham and Parmesan cheese is perfectly cured in Parma's microclimate. Bologna, the regional seat, has a lovely historic centre of medieval towers and Renaissance squares. Ravenna, a former capital of Byzantium, astounds with its trove of ancient mosaics.

Rome *(pp114–127)*

It would take more than a lifetime to explore Rome, the ancient city that serves as the capital of both Italy and the region of Lazio. Rome and its treasures largely overshadow Lazio's other highlights, which include UNESCO

Villa d'Este, Tivoli, Lazio

© Davide Romanini/Dreamstime.com

Isola di Sant'Antioco, Sardinia

© Moreno Novello/Fotolia.com

heritage sites in Tivoli, Etruscan ruins, and volcanic lakes. The centre of Rome offers wonders from the mighty Colosseum and Forum, to the sublime Pantheon, and even a foreign nation, the Vatican. Its glorious piazzas are still a set for daily gossip, its narrow streets still occupied by artisans.

Naples and the Amalfi Coast *(pp128–149)*

Campania epitomises the balmy, Mediterranean retreat. Glamorous seaside getaways on the Amalfi Coast and Isle of Capri have long attracted the elite. The Bay of Naples is a heart-stopping stunner of deep blue waters framed by the volcanic Mount Vesuvius. The volcano destroyed nearby Pompeii, Italy's most visited archaeological site after the centre of Rome. Naples, the capital and cultural heart, is a fun and fast-paced jumble of Baroque art, regal buildings and superb cuisine.

Sardinia *(pp150–155)*

Accessible from many ports along the Tyrrhenian Coast, Sardinia is the second-largest Mediterranean isle.

Sardinia's unique island culture has a pocket of Catalan heritage. Much of Sardinia seems untamed; in the interior and even some of the coast. Conversely, the Emerald Coast attracts the elite to its exclusive resorts. Cagliari, the capital, is a busy port.

Sicily *(pp156–175)*

The great island of Sicily, the Mediterranean's largest isle, is prized by travellers for its extensive Greek and Roman ruins, which lie in situ at Agrigento, Segesta and Taormina, among others. Modern Sicilian life is centred around Palermo, its melting pot capital whose energy matches that of Mount Etna, the active volcano on the opposite side of the island and its highest point. Sun-drenched and spoiled for sights, Sicily is always in season. Sicily and Naples offer some of Italy's best cuisine, which reflects the various influences of rulers, conquests, and trade; from Arab, French, and Spanish, to dishes inspired by the bounty of the sea and the land's rich volcanic soil.

Greek temple in Agrigento, Sicily

© anzeletti/iStockphoto.com

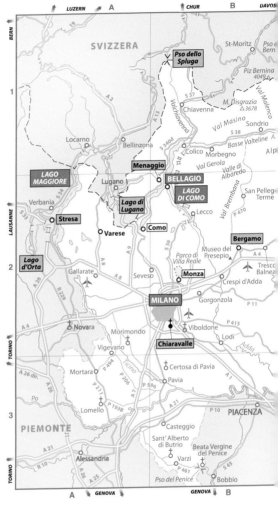

LOMBARDY AND THE LAKES

Lombardy is among Italy's largest and wealthiest regions. Diverse industries, including fashion, textiles, agriculture, chemicals, steel, plastics, and publishing, account for approximately one-quarter of Italy's GDP. Lombardy's capital, Milan, holds about 10 per cent of Italy's wealth, as its ritzy shopping testifies. Beyond Milan, Stendhal once called Bergamo "the most beautiful place on Earth," while the court in Mantua was once famous throughout Europe. The green Po Delta

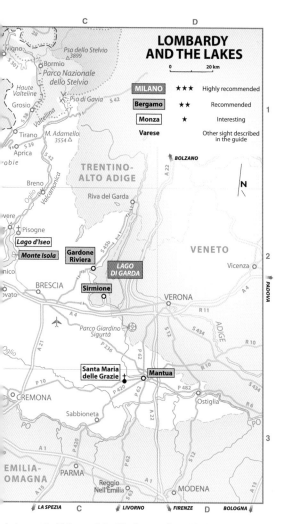

LOMBARDY AND THE LAKES

0   20 km

MILANO	★★★	Highly recommended
Bergamo	★★	Recommended
Monza	★	Interesting
Varese		Other sight described in the guide

between the Ticino and the Mincio, together with the Adda, feed lakes Maggiore, Como and Garda. The Regione dei Laghi villages centre around Lakes Como, Lugano and Maggiore. To the north of Lombardy are alpine passes. Farm production varies from worms that turn mulberries into silk, to rice, dairy, and wine. Lombardy wines include Franciacorta and Oltrepò, made according to Champagne methods, as well as reds like Barbera, Lambrusco, and Pinot Nero.

In the art world, Leonardo da Vinci painted his superb *Last Supper* in Milan, while Michelangelo Merisi hailed from the town of Caravaggio.

MILAN★★★

Milan is Italy's second city in terms of population, politics and cultural affairs. But Lombardy's capital leads in commercial, industrial and banking activities, which have made Milan, set in the heart of northern Italy at the foot of the Alps, the country's financial heartland. The enterprising spirit and the city's history have made Milan one of the country's most dynamic towns.

THE CITY TODAY

Milan prides itself on its knack for innovation. The design capital of Italy is the financial and marketing base for mega-brands such as Prada, Gucci, Versace and Giorgio Armani. Determined that luxury goods have a market even during an economic downturn, Milan has numerous urban renewal projects in progress awarded to high-profile international architects.

MiCo (Milano Congress) is its recent 18,000-seater convention centre,

Practical Information

Getting There

◆ **By Car and Train** – Motorways connect Milan to Venice, the Lakes, Genoa and the south. Milan's majestic central railway station has good metro links.

◆ **By Air** – Linate Airport, 8km/4.9mi from the centre, has buses to Piazza San Babila (bus ATM 73, 42 min, €1.50, www.atm.it). **Air Bus Linate**–Centrale (ATM coach from Stazione Centrale, 25 min, €5 or €9 A/R, ticket on board) and by coach from Stazione Centrale (Starfly www.starfly.net, 30min, €5, ticket on board). **Malpensa Airport**, 45km/28mi out of town, has rail (40min, 02 72 49 49 49, www.malpensaexpress.it, €13 or €20 A/R,) and bus links (50min, 02 58 58 31 85, www.malpensashuttle.it, €10 or €16 A/R and Stie, www.stie.it, €10). Taxis from Malpensa can be expensive and delayed in traffic. **Orio al Serio** (the airport at Bergamo) is 50 km/31 mi from Milan, with buses to central Milan (1hr, www.terravision.eu, €5; www.orioshuttle.com, €5).

Getting Around

◆ **By Public Transport** – Public services are punctual and fast (especially the underground lines). Public transportation systems are run by **ATM** (*02 48 607 607; www.atm.it*).

◆ **By Car** – From Mon–Wed (7.30am–7.30pm), Fri (7.30am–6pm) central Milan, Area C, is a limited traffic zone; access is regulated by daily Ecopass permits (€5), 02 48 68 40 01 or 02 02 02. Pay parking: yellow lines are for residents only, blue lines allow a limited length of time (check signs), parking coupons are purchased from tobacconists and newsagents.

◆ **By Taxi** – Pick ups at a taxi rank or 02 85 85, 02 40 40 or 02 69 69.

◆ **By Bicycle** – BikeMi is the city's bike-sharing project, 02 48 607 607, www.bikemi.com.

◆ **By Car** – Car sharing is common in Milan. Car2Go (www.car2go.com), E-vai (www.e-vai.com), Enjoy (enjoy.eni.com), DriveNow (www.drive-now.com/milano).

Duomo

the largest trade show space in Europe (www.micmilano.it). Sustainability projects include the reclamation of an Alfa Romeo industrial area for an urban park. Expansion and renovation of Teatro alla Scala was completed in 2004. Food is Italy's second largest industry, and in 2015 was the central theme for the Universal Exposition (Expo), "Feeding the Planet, Energy for Life," held in Milan.

A BIT OF HISTORY

Milan has a turbulent history; it is probably Gallic (Celtic) in origin, but was subdued by the Romans in 222 BC and expanded. Diocletian made Milan the 3C seat of the Western Empire. In 313, in the **Edict of Milan**, Constantine gave freedom of worship to the Christians. In 375 **St Ambrose** (340–96), a prestigious doctor of the Church, became the city's bishop.

Following the 5C and 6C barbarian invasions, in 756 Pepin, King of the Franks, conquered the area; his son Charlemagne wore the Iron Crown of the Kings of Lombardy from 774. In 962 Milan again became Italy's capital.

In the 12C Milan allied with other cities in the Lombard League (1167) to thwart its conquest by Emperor Frederick Barbarossa. In the 13C the **Visconti**, **Ghibellines** and aristocrats seized power, building Milan's cathedral and Pavia's Monastery. His daughter, Valentina, married Louis, Duke of Orleans, the grandfather of Louis XII of France. The Sforza next ruled Milan: the court of **Ludovico il Moro** (1452–1508) attracted Leonardo da Vinci and Bramante. Louis XII of France proclaimed himself the legitimate heir to the Duchy of Milan, setting out to conquer the territory in 1500. His successor François I was thwarted by Emperor Charles V. From 1535 to 1713 the Spanish ruled. During the plague, 1576–1630, the Borromeo family performed humanitarian work. Under Napoleon, Milan was capital of the Cisalpine Republic (1797), then the Kingdom of Italy (1805). Milan became capital of the Venetian-Lombard Kingdom in 1815.

MILAN

39

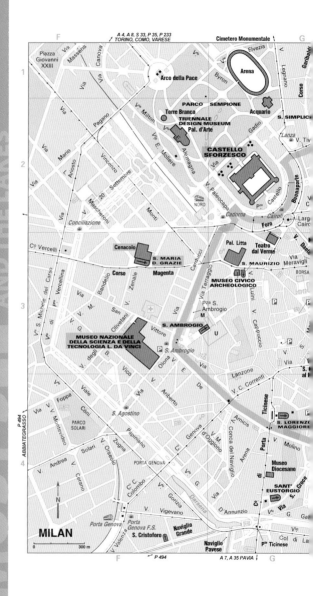

MILAN

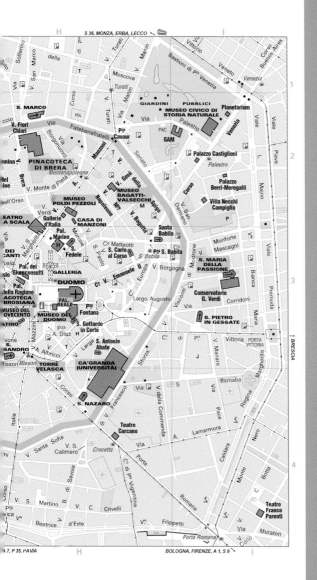

BOLOGNA, FIRENZE, A 1, S 9

A 7, P 35, PAVIA

BRESCIA

MILAN

HIGHLIGHTS

Duomo★★★

Interior open daily 8am–7pm.
Clothes must be appropriate for
a place of worship; no large bags
and suitcases (the Cathedral does
not have a bag checkroom); no
photography or video cameras.
Exterior: Duomo Info Point (Piazza
del Duomo 18; 02 72 02 33 75; www.
duomomilano.it). Here you can buy
tickets to the roof, and to visit the
baptistry and treasury; Combined
Ticket €15 (visit to the roof with
elevator) or €11 on foot).

Best seen in the light of the setting
sun, this Gothic marvel of white
marble, bristling with belfries,
gables, pinnacles and statues,
stands at one end of an esplanade
teeming with pigeons – largely
responsible for the building's
deterioration.

Building began in 1386, continued
in the 15C and 16C under Italian,
French and German master masons
and was finished between 1805 and
1809, on Napoleon's orders.
Inside, the imposing nave and
aisles are separated by 52 high
pillars (148m/486ft). Seek out

the mausoleum of Gian Giacomo
Medici in the south arm of the
transept, the curious statue of
St Bartholomew in the north arm,
the crypt (cripta) and treasury
(tesoro). On the way out, you
can see the entrance to the early
Christian baptistery (battistero).
Don't miss a walk on the roof
among the numerous pinnacles
and multiple white-marble statues
(2 245 in all).

Museo del Duomo★★

Piazza Duomo 12. Open Tue–Sun
10am–6pm; last admission 1hr
before closing. €6. Closed 1 Jan,
1 May, 15 Aug and 25 Dec.
02 72 02 34 53. www.museo.
duomomilano.it.

Housed in the royal palace built
in the 18C by Piermarini, the
museum shows the various stages
in the building and restoration
of the cathedral. Also of note are
the splendid **Aribert Crucifix★**
(1040), the original support for
the Madonnina (1772–3), and the
wooden **model★** of the cathedral.
Cross over to the **Galleria Vittorio**
Emanuele II★, laid out in 1877.

Museo del Novecento

© G. Gnoni/Sime/Photononstop

Museo del Novecento★★
Via Marconi 1. Open Mon 2.30–7.30pm, Tue, Wed, Fri and Sun 9.30am–7.30pm, Thu and Sat 9.30am–10.30pm; last admission 1hr before closing. €10 (entrance is €6 during the last two hours prior to closing and every Tuesday from 2pm). 02 88 44 40 61. www.museodelnovecento.org.
Located in the Arengario, an interesting modern building constructed in the 1930s, the museum displays a range of 20C artwork. The exhibits are organized chronologically, giving visitors an overview of Italian art movements from the beginning of the 1900s to the 1980s, and include works by Boccioni, Balla, Carrà, de Chirico, Burri, Fontana and Kounellis, as well as Giuseppe Pellizza da Volpedo's "The Fourth Estate." The world's largest collection of Futurist art is also on display. The large windowed façade offers a beautiful view over Piazza Duomo.

Palazzo Reale
Piazza Duomo 12. Open Mon 2.30–7.30pm, Tue, Wed, Fri and Sun 9.30am–7.30pm, Thu and Sat 9.30am–10.30pm; last admission 1hr before closing. €12. 02 88 44 5181. www.palazzorealemilano.it.
Located on Piazza Duomo opposite the entrance to Galleria Vittorio Emanuele, Palazzo Reale was renovated and redesigned halfway through the 18C by Piermarini (1743-1808) at the behest of the Austrian court. Originally home to the city's municipal offices, today the building is used as a cultural centre and exhibition space, and hosts most of Milan's most important temporary exhibitions.

Castello Sforzesco
© Johndavid34 / Fotolia.com

Pinacoteca Ambrosiana★★
Piazza Pio XI 2. Open Tue–Sun 10am–6pm. €15. Closed 1 Jan, Easter and 25 Dec. 02 65 97 728. www.ambrosiana.eu.
This 17C palace was an early public library, and boasts Leonardo's **Codice Atlantico** drawings.

Castello Sforzesco★★★
Piazza Castello. Open daily 7am–7.30pm (in winter 6pm). Museums open Tue–Sun 9am–5.30pm. €5. 02 88 46 37 00. www.milanocastello.it.
This huge brick quadrilateral castle, the former seat of the Sforza Dukes of Milan, houses the seven sections of the **municipal art collection**: Ancient Art; Furnishings and Wood Sculpture; Applied Arts and Musical instruments; Egyptian section of Archaeology; Prehistory; City of Milan. Some 96 drawings scholars attributed to Caravaggio are on display here. Da visitare il Museo Pietà Rondanini-Michelangelo!

Triennale Design Museum★
Viale Alemagna 6. Tue–Sun 10.30am–8.30pm. €8, €10 for entrance to the museum and all

exhibitions. 02 72 43 41. www.
triennaledesignmuseum.it.
This museum takes a scientific
but entertaining approach
to Italian design. Themed
presentations change every year,
hosting **exhibitions** and events
that highlight contemporary
Italian design, urban planning,
architecture, music and the applied
arts. The museum's permanent
collection includes a large
number of hallmark objects from
contemporary Italian design, like
the Lambretta scooter, Bialetti's
moka espresso maker and the
luscious lip-shaped Bocca Sofa.

Palazzo Bagatti Valsecchi★★

Via Gesù 5. Open Sept–Jul Tue–Sun
1–5.45pm. Closed hols. €9. 02 76
00 61 32. www.museobagatti
valsecchi.org.
At the end of the 19C, the brothers
Fausto and Giuseppe Bagatti Vals-
ecchi richly decorated the interior
of their home in the Renaissance
style, mixing genuine 15–16C
pieces and high-quality replicas.

Museo Poldi Pezzoli★★

Via Manzoni 12. Open Wed–Mon
10am–6pm. Closed public hols.
€9. 02 79 48 89. www.museopoldi
pezzoli.it.
Attractively set out in an old
mansion, the museum displays
collections of weapons, fabrics,
paintings, **clocks**★ and bronzes.
Among the paintings are works by
the Lombard school, **portraits**★★
of Luther and his wife by Lucas
Cranach, the famous **Portrait of a**
Woman★★★ by Piero del Pollaiolo,
a **Descent from the Cross**
and a **Madonna and Child**★★
by Botticelli.

Teatro alla Scala★★

Traditionally recognised as being
the most famous opera house
in the world, La Scala surprises
people seeing it for the first time
because of the simplicity of its
exterior, which gives no hint of the
magnificence of its auditorium.
Built from 1776 to 1778 with six
levels of boxes, it can seat 2 000
people. The **Museo Teatrale alla**
Scala★ (*Largo Ghiringhelli, 1; open*
9am–5.30pm, €7. Closed public hols.

Teatro alla Scala

© M. Silva/age fotostock

02 88 79 24 73, www.teatroallascala.org) presents Toscanini and Verdi memorabilia. From the museum, you can visit boxes and see the auditorium. The theater's simple and sober façade betrays little of the lavish decorations inside the theater, where red velvet, gold leaf gold leaf and ornate stuccos reign.

Gallerie d'Italia★

Piazza della Scala 6. Open 9.30am–7.30pm (Thu until 10.30pm); last admission 1hr before closing. Closed Mon, 1 Jan, 1 May, 25 Dec. 800 16 76 19. www.gallerieditalia.com. Housed within the magnificent neoclassical **Palazzo Anguissola**, this collection of 19C Italian art includes beautiful bas reliefs by Canova as well as works by Boccioni and others.

Pinacoteca di Brera★★★

Via Brera 28. Open Tue–Sun 8.30am–7.15pm (Thu 8.30am–10.30pm). €10. 02 72 26 32 64/ 229. www.brera.beniculturali.it. Renaissance masterpieces include The Wedding of the Virgin by Raphael, Madonna and Child by Bellini, Dead Christ by Mantegna, also works by Van Dyck, Rembrandt, Rubens, and frescoes taken from local churches. A 20C collection of art was added in the 1970s.

Basilica di Santa Maria delle Grazie★★

Piazza Santa Maria delle Grazie. Open daily 7am–noon and 3.30–7.30pm (summer 7am–noon and 4–7.30pm). legraziemilano. it. This Renaissance church erected by the Dominicans from 1465 to 1490 was finished by Bramante. The interior (restored) is adorned with frescoes by Gaudenzio Ferrari in the fourth chapel on the right, and with the impressive **dome★**, gallery and cloisters all by Bramante. The best view of the **east end★** is to be had from Via Caradosso.

Cenacolo (The Last Supper)★★★

Open Tue–Sun 8.15am–6.45pm, by reservation only. €10 reservation. 02 92 80 03 60. legraziemilano.it/il-cenacolo/.

Basilica di Santa Maria delle Grazie

© Philippe Orain/Michelin

MILAN

45

In the former refectory of the monastery is **The Last Supper★★★** by **Leonardo da Vinci**, painted 1495–98 at the request of Ludovico il Moro. A skilful composition, it creates the impression that the painted space is a continuation of the room itself. Christ is depicted at the moment of the institution of the Eucharist: his half-open mouth suggests that he has just finished speaking. Around him there is a tangible sense of shock and premonition of imminent disaster with its intimation of Judas' betrayal. The technique used (Leonardo chose egg tempera, possibly mixed with oil, and placed the image on the coldest wall in the room), dust, WWII bomb damage and, more recently smog, have all contributed to the need for considerable restoration work (it has been restored 10 times, most recently in 1999). Today it better displays its original colours and use of chiaroscuro. Opposite is a **Crucifixion★** (1495) by Montorfano, somewhat overshadowed by *The Last Supper*.

Museo Nazionale della Scienza e della Tecnologia Leonardo da Vinci★★
Via San Vittore 21. Open Tue–Fri 9.30am–5pm, Sat and hols 9.30am–6.30pm. Closed 1 Jan, 24–25 Dec. €10. 02 48 55 51.
www.museoscienza.org.
This vast museum exhibits interesting scientific objects, documents, and art relating to science and nature. The **Leonardo da Vinci Gallery** shows models of the artist's inventions. Other sections deal with acoustics, chemistry, telecommunications and astronomy. Large pavilions have displays relating to railways, aircraft and shipping.

Basilica di Sant'Ambrogio★★★
Piazza Sant'Ambrogio 15. Open 10am–12 and 2.30–6pm (Sun and hols 3–5pm). 02 86 45 08 95.
www.basilicasantambrogio.it.
The basilica, founded at the end of the 4C by St Ambrose, is a magnificent example of 11–12C Lombard-Romanesque style with its pure lines and fine **atrium★** adorned with capitals. The crypt behind the chancel holds the remains of St Ambrose, St Gervase and St Protase. A magnificent Byzantine-Romanesque **ambo★** (12C) stands to the left of the nave. The precious gold-plated **altar front★★** is a masterpiece of the Carolingian period (9C). In the chapel of San Vittore in Ciel d'Oro (*end of the south transept*), the remarkable 4–5C **mosaics★** date to soon after the death of Ambrose. Access to Bramante's portico is from the north transept.

Basilica di San Lorenzo Maggiore★★
Corso di Porta Ticinese 35. Open Mon–Sat 9am–6.30pm, Sun 9am–7pm. 02 89 40 41 29.
www.sanlorenzomaggiore.com.
Founded in the 4C and rebuilt in the 12C and 16C, the basilica has kept its original octagonal plan. In front of the façade is a majestic **portico★** of 16 columns, all that remains of the Roman town of Mediolanum. The Byzantine-Romanesque interior has galleries exclusively reserved for women. From the south *atrium* go through the 1C Roman doorway to the

Basilica di Sant'Ambrogio

© V. Valletta/AGF RM/age fotostock

4C **Cappella di Sant'Aquilino★**, which has paleo-Christian mosaics. Further on, the **Porta Ticinese**, a vestige of the 14C ramparts, leads to the artists' quarter.

Chiesa di Santa Maria della Passione★★
Via Conservatorio 14. Open 7am–noon, Sun and hols 9–noon and 3–6.15pm. 02 76 02 13 70.
This, one of Milan's largest churches after the Duomo, occupies a pretty square next to the Conservatorio. Built in 1482, its Baroque façade was added in the 18C. Inside, its many works of art include a very fine Last Supper by Gaudenzio Ferrari in the left transept, along with works by Daniele Crespi, Bernardino Luini and Bergognone, who also painted the frescoes that decorate the sacristy.

Chiesa di Santa Maria presso San Satiro★
Via Torino 17. Open Tue–Sat 9.30am–5.30pm, Sun 2–5.30pm. 02 87 46 83.

With the exception of its 9C bell tower and 1871 façade, both the church and the baptistry are the work of Bramante. He resolved the church's lack of space with clever trompe l'œil décor in gilded stucco and created a marvellous false choir.

Ca' Granda-Ex Ospedale Maggiore★★
Now occupied by the university, this former hospital was built in 1456 for Francesco Sforza to a design by Filarete. Modified several times since, its lengthy brick façade is adorned with pairs of windows, arches and sculpted busts in medallions. The inner courtyard was designed by Richini.

Torre Velasca★★
Piazza Velasca 5.
This 1956 pink skyscraper is an emblem of Milan. Designed by Belgioioso, Peresutti and Rogers, its top nine floors project outwards, giving the reinforced concrete tower its mushroom shape.

ADDITIONAL SIGHTS

MUDEC
Via Tortona 56. Open Tue–Sun 9.30am–7.30pm (Thu and Sat–10.30pm). €5 (€12 for exhibitions). 02 54 917. www.mudec.it.
Born of an industrial archaeological recovery effort conducted in the ex-Ansaldo factory area in Milan's Tortona neighbourhood, MUDEC is an exhibition centre for municipal ethnography and temporary exhibitions.

Armani Silos
Via Bergognone 40. Open Wed–Sun 11am–7pm. €12. 02 91 63 00 10. www.armanisilos.com.
Built in 1950 to store grain, this space hosts a selection of creations by the famous designer, divided into themes addressing aesthetics and history.

Fondazione Prada
Largo Isarco 2. Open Wed–Mon 10am–7pm (Fri and Sat 10am–8pm). €10. 02 54 917. www.fondazioneprada.org.

Spread out in an articulated architectural configuration that combines pre-existing buildings with three new constructions (Podium, Cinema and Torre), the foundation was formerly a 1910 distillery. Today it's an open space for contemporary art and cinema culture.

Pirelli HangarBicocca
Via Chiese 2. Open Thu–Sun 10am–10pm. 02 66 11 15 73. www.hangarbicocca.org.
Pirelli HangarBicocca is a non-profit foundation established in Milan in 2004 through reconversion of an industrial building. The institution is dedicated to the production and promotion of contemporary art.

EXCURSIONS

Abbazia di Chiaravalle★★
7km/4.3mi SE. Leave by Porta Romana and head towards San Donato. Via Sant'Arialdo 102. Open Tue–Sat 9am–noon and 3–5pm; guided tours Sat and Sun (€12 Abbazia + Antico Mulino + Cappella). Closed public hols. 02 84 93 04 32. www.monasterochiaravalle.it.
The early Gothic abbey, founded by St Bernard of Clairvaux in 1135, is dominated by a polygonal **bell tower★**. Visit the delightful cloisters.

Monza★
21km/13mi N.
A textile town in the hilly Brianza area dotted with lakes, villas and gardens, Monza has an attractive cathedral and a Neoclassical royal villa; its **gardens★★★** host the Grand Prix Formula One race.

Abbazia di Chiaravalle

@Hect/istockphoto.com

BERGAMO★★

Bergamo is situated on the northern edge of the Lombardy Plain at the confluence of the Brembana and Seriana valleys. Its strong artistic heritage graces this thriving industrial centre. The lower modern town contrasts with the delightful historic upper town. 51km/31mi from Milan.

A BIT OF HISTORY

The Gauls seized the settlement in 550 BC calling it Berghem; it was renamed Bergomum when the Romans took over in 196 BC. An independent commune from the 11–13C, it then joined the Lombard League. The town suffered during the struggles between the Guelphs (followers of the Pope) and the Ghibellines (followers of the emperor). Bergamo fell to the Visconti family; the Republic of Venice; Austrian rule in 1814; and final liberation by Garibaldi in 1859.

The artist **Lorenzo Lotto** worked here, composer Donizetti (1797–1848) was born here. Arts range from the lively Bergamasque, a pipe-dance, to Commedia dell'Arte, which originated in Bergamo.

CITTÀ ALTA★★★

The road to the upper city is steep, so you may prefer the funicular.

Stendhal once called **Piazza Vecchia★**, "the most beautiful place on Earth". Palazzo della Ragione, Italy's oldest town hall, dates from 1199, but was rebuilt in the 16C. It has graceful arcades and a Lion of St Mark over a central balcony symbolising Venetian rule. The Palladian-style Palazzo Scamozziano is opposite.

The **Cappella Colleoni★★** (1470–6) is a jewel of Lombard-Renaissance architecture, while the **Basilica di Santa Maria Maggiore★** dates from the 12C and contains nine Florentine **tapestries★★** (1580–6) relating the life of the Virgin.

CITTÀ BASSA★

Piazza Matteotti is central to the business and shopping area. The **Accademia Carrara★★** has 15–18C paintings. In the **ld Quarter★**, **Via Pignolo★** winds among 16–19C palazzi and churches.

Città Alta

BERGAMO

MANTUA★★

Mantua is set in a flat fertile plain, in southeastern Lombardy. To the north three lakes are formed by the slow-flowing River Mincio. This prosperous town has important mechanical and petrochemical industries, and is the number-one hosiery producer worldwide.

Practical Information

Getting There

Access roads are the A 22 and S 236 from Brescia.

A BIT OF HISTORY

Virgil recounted that Mantua was founded by Monto, though its origins likely are Etruscan, 6–5C BC. It passed from the Gauls to the Romans in the 3C BC. In 70 BC **Virgil**, the great poet and author, was born here. His *Aeneid* recounts the wanderings of Aeneas, the Trojan prince, whose settlement would form Rome. Virgil's beloved Mantuan countryside, its soft misty light, and pleasant rural life is evoked in his *Eclogues* (*Bucolics*) and *Georgics*.

In the Middle Ages Mantua was the theatre of civic strife, gaining independence in the 13C. Ruled by the enlightened Gonzaga family, patrons of the arts and letters, Mantua became a foremost intellectual and artistic centre 15–16C. Veronese artist **Pisanello** (1395–1455) decorated the Ducal Palace. The famous Gonzaga court lured humanist Politian (1454–94), architect Leon Battista Alberti (1404–72) and the Paduan painter **Andrea Mantegna** (1431–1506). **Giulio Romano** (1499–1546), Raphael's pupil, worked on the Ducal Palace and cathedral and the Palazzo Te. Manzoni's novel, *I Promessi Sposi*, describes events under Hapsburg rule.

PALAZZO DUCALE★★★

Piazza Sordello 40. Open Tue–Sun 8.15am–7.15pm (Camera degli Sposi by reservation only). Closed hols. €12. 0376 22 48 32. www. mantovaducale.beniculturali.it
The imposing Ducal Palace comprises buildings from various periods: the Magna Domus and the Palazzo del Capitano erected in the late-13C by the Bonacolsi, Lords of Mantua from 1272–1328; the Castello di San Giorgio, a 14C fortress with inner sections built 15–16C by the Gonzaga. The Camera degli Sposi **apartments★★★** are beautifully decorated.

PALAZZO TE★★

Viale Te 13. Open Mon 1–6.30pm, Tue–Sun 9am–6.30 pm (7.30pm in summer). Closed 25 Dec. 12€. 0376 32 32 66. www.palazzote.it.
This large country mansion was built on the plan of a Roman house by Giulio Romano for Federico II from 1525 to 1535. It combines Classical features and melodramatic invention: the amazing "broken" entablature in the main courtyard is a major achievement of the Mannerist style. The **interior** was ornately decorated by Giulio Romano and his pupils.

PIAZZAS

Of note is the medieval **Piazza Sordello★**, the centre of old Mantua, and the **Piazza delle Erbe★**, which is lined with palazzos.

THE LAKES ★★★

Narrow and long, these lakes are all of glacial origin and their banks are covered with luxuriant vegetation that flourishes in the particularly mild climate. A fairy-tale land of blue waters with a spectacular mountain backdrop, the area has always been a favourite haunt of artists and travellers. Alpine scenery contrasts with Mediterranean, villas boast lakeside gardens, flowers bloom throughout the year and small lakeside villages offer fresh fish and a variety of local wines. Each lake has its own specific character.

Practical Information

Getting Around

The best way to see the lakes is from a boat:

LAGO MAGGIORE – Excursions run from Arona to Locarno (lunch available on board), from Stresa or Laveno for the Isole Borromee and Villa Taranto and night cruises in summer. Car ferry between Laveno and Intra. *Toll free in Italy 800 55 18 01. www.navigazionelaghi.it.*
The delightful **Borromee Islands** are situated in the middle of the lake. *0323 305 56. www.borromeoturismo.it.*

LAGO D'ORTA – Regular departures from Orta to Isola San Giulio. *345 51 70 005. www.navigazionelagodorta.it.*

LAGO DI LUGANO – Lake cruises includes lunch, dinner and the "Grande Giro del Lago" cruises. *0041 91 222 11 11. www.lakelugano.ch.*

LAGO DI COMO – Boats run from Como to Colico, Tremezzo, Bellagio or Menaggio. From Tremezzo to Dongo, Domaso and Colico. Hydrofoil from Como to Tremezzo, Bellagio and Menaggio. Car ferries: between Bellagio, Varenna, Menaggio and Cadenabbia. *Toll free in Italy 800 55 18 01. www.navigazionelaghi.it.*

LAGO D'ISEO – Tours of the lake's three islands available in summer; Iseo, Sale Marasino, Monte Isola. Isola, regular ferries year round. *035 97 14 83. www.navigazionelagoiseo.it.*

LAGO DI GARDA – Desenzano to Sirmione and Gardone;and Peschiera to Garda and Gardone. *www.navigazionelaghi.it.*

Bellagio on Lake Como

LAGO MAGGIORE★★★

Lake Maggiore is the most famous of the Italian lakes, in part for its legendary beauty, majestic and wild, and also for the Borromean Islands. It is fed by the River Ticino, which flows from Switzerland; its waters change from a jade green in the north to a deep blue in the south. Exotic plants grow in the sheltered environment.

Isole Borromee★★★ – A large area of the lake was given to the princely Borromeo family in the 15C. In the 17C Charles III established a residence on Isola Bella, named after his wife, Isabella. On hot days, palace residents found cooler air in the caves. Boat trips are available to Isola dei Pescatori, which has retained its original charm, and to lush Isola Madre and its flowers and exotic plants.

Cannero Riviera★★ – The houses of the resort rise in tiers above the lake amid olive trees, vineyards and orange and lemon groves.

Laveno Mombello – A cablecar climbs to the summit of **Sasso del Ferro★★** for a fine panorama.

Pallanza★★ – This wonderful flower-filled resort has **quays★★** sheltered by magnolias and oleanders with lovely views of the lake. On the outskirts of the town on the Intra road is the **Villa Taranto★★** with its gardens of azaleas, heather, rhododendrons, camellias and maples.

Stresa★★ – This pleasant resort, which has always attracted artists and writers, has an idyllic location on the west bank of Lago Maggiore facing the Isole Borromee. The ski slopes are on **Mottarone★★★**, with a magnificent panorama of the lake, Alps and Monte Rosa Massif and a botanical garden.

LAGO D'ORTA★★

Lake Orta, one of the smallest Italian lakes, is separated from Lake Maggiore by the peak "Il Mottarone" in the northeast. It is delightful, with wooded hills and an islet, Isola San Giulio.

Chiesa della Madonna dal Sasso★★ – From the church terrace there is a magnificent view of the lake and its setting.

Orta San Giulio★★ – This small resort on the tip of a peninsula has alleyways lined with old houses and elegant iron balconies.

Isola San Giulio★★ – On this tiny jewel of an island stands the **Basilica di San Giulio**, said to date to the 4C, when St Julius visited.

Varallo – This industrial and commercial town in the Val Sesia is famous for its pilgrimage to the **Sacro Monte★★** with its 43 chapels.

LAGO DI LUGANO★★

Lugano has less of the grandeur of the other lakes, plus a mild climate and steep mountain countryside. Most of **Lake Lugano** is in Swiss territory.

Lanzo d'Intelvi★ – Set in the heart of a pine and larch forest, this resort (907m/2 976ft) is also a ski centre in winter. Some 6km/3.7mi away is the **Belvedere di Sighignola★★★**, also known as the "balcony of Italy" because of its extensive views.

Varese – 8km/5mi west of modern Varese rises the **Sacro Monte★★**, with its 14 chapels and pilgrimage church of the Virgin. From the summit there is a **view★★**. 10km/6.2mi to the northwest is the long mountainous ridge, **Campo dei Fiori★**, which raises its forest-clad slopes above the plain. There is a vast **panorama★★**.

LAGO DI COMO★★★

Lake Como, of all the Italian lakes, has the most variety; pretty villages, ports, villas, exotic gardens and mountain views.

Bellagio★★★ – Bellagio occupies a magnificent site on a promontory dividing Lake Lecco from the southern arm of Lake Como. Seek out the lakeside **gardens★★** of **Villa Serbelloni** and **Villa Melzi**.

Cadenabbia★★ – This delightful resort occupies an admirable site opposite Bellagio. A handsome avenue of plane trees links the resort with the Villa Carlotta and Tremezzo. From the Capella di San Martino, there is a good **view★★**.

Cernobbio★★ – This location is famous for the **Villa d'Este**, the opulent 16C residence, now a hotel.

Strada del Passo dello Spluga★★ – The Splügen Pass Road is one of the boldest and most spectacular in the Alps. The **Campodolcino– Pianazzo section★★★** is grandiose as it hairpins up the mountainside.

Como★ – The town was the birthplace of naturalist Pliny the Elder and his nephew, the writer Pliny the Younger. Begun in the late-14C, the **Duomo★★** was completed during the Renaissance. Adjoining the façade is the **Broletto★★**, or 13C town hall.

Menaggio★★ – Favoured by a cool summer breeze, this is one of the lake's smart resorts.

Tremezzo★★★ – A mild climate and a beautiful site combine to make Tremezzo a favourite place to stay. The terraced gardens, **Parco Comunale★**, are peaceful. The 18C **Villa Carlotta★★★** occupies an admirable site facing the Grigne Massif.

Varenna★ – The Villa Monastero has alluring **gardens★★**.

LAGO D'ISEO★

Though **Lake Iseo** is not very well known, its wild scenery, high mountain backdrop and peaceful villages all lend charm.

Monte Isola★★ – From the church of the Madonna della Ceriola, crowning this green island, there is a vast **panorama★★**.

Valcamonica – The Valcamonica follows the River Oglio as far as Lago d'Iseo. Over a stretch of 60km/37.3mi are UNESCO World Heritage prehistoric and early Roman **rock carvings★★**.

LAGO DI GARDA★★★

Lake Garda, the largest of the lakes, is considered one of the most beautiful. The Dolomites to the north shelter the lake from the cold winds, creating a very mild climate.

Gardone Riviera★★ – A small resort with long hours of sunshine and a wide choice of hotels. At 1km/0.6mi from the town is the eccentric **Vittoriale★** estate, which belonged to the poet Gabriele D'Annunzio (1863–1938).

Limone sul Garda★ – Terraced lemon groves stretch along the shores. From Limone a **panoramic route★★** climbs up to the Tremosine Plateau.

Malcesine★ – This attractive town stands on a promontory at the foot of Monte Baldo, dominated by the outline of the Castello Scaligeroa. From the summit of Monte Baldo (cablecar) there is a **view★★★**.

Punta di San Vigilio★★ – This headland has a romantic setting.

Sirmione★★ – The houses cluster around the 13C castle, **Rocca Scaligera★★** at the tip of the Sirmione Peninsula. Beyond is the vast Roman villa of the poet Catullus, the **Grotte di Catullo★★**.

GENOA AND PORTOFINO

Liguria, furrowed by deep, narrow valleys at right angles to the coast, had a maritime civilisation before the Roman era. The steep slopes of the inner valleys are dotted with hilltop villages. The rocky, indented coastline has enjoyed heavy coastal traffic since ancient times, with many small deep-water ports. The Roman Empire added olive groves and vineyards, now complemented by vegetables, fruit (melons and peaches) and flowers grown on an industrial scale as well as on terraces.

The Riviera di Ponente (**Western Riviera**) west of Genoa is sunnier and more sheltered than the Riviera di Levante (**Eastern Riviera**), but the latter has a more luxuriant vegetation. The chief towns are Imperia, Savona and Genoa (shipyards, steel production, oil terminal and thermal power station) and La Spezia (naval base, commercial port, thermal power station and arms manufacture).

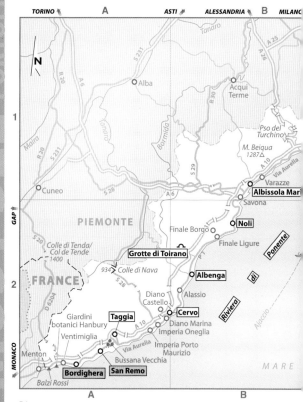

Portofino

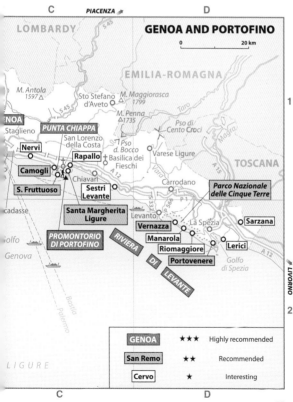

GENOA AND PORTOFINO

0   20 km

LOMBARDY

PIACENZA

EMILIA-ROMAGNA

M. Antola 1597 △

Sto Stefano d'Aveto
M. Maggiorasca 1799

M. Penna △1735

Pso di Cento Croci

TOSCANA

NOA

Staglieno

PUNTA CHIAPPA

San Lorenzo della Costa

Nervi

Rapallo

Pso d. Bocco

Varese Ligure

Basilica dei Fieschi

Camogli

Chiavari

Carrodano

S. Fruttuoso

Sestri Levante

Parco Nazionale delle Cinque Terre

cadasse

Santa Margherita Ligure

Levanto

PROMONTORIO DI PORTOFINO

Vernazza

La Spezia

Sarzana

RIVIERA

Manarola

Riomaggiore

Lerici

olfo

Genova

DI

Portovenere

Golfo di Spezia

LEVANTE

Bastia

Polmerw

LIGURE

GENOA	★★★	Highly recommended
San Remo	★★	Recommended
Cervo	★	Interesting

INTRODUCTION

LIVORNO

GENOA ★★★

The capital of Liguria, Italy's greatest seaport and the birthplace of Christopher Colombus, Genoa "la Superba" boasts a **spectacular** location★★. Stretched across the slopes of steeply tiered hillside, the port is overlooked by the colourful façades of a host of buildings. It is a city full of character and contrasts, where splendid palaces stand alongside the humblest alleyways.

Practical Information

Getting There and Around

Genoa (*Genova*) is connected by motorways to Milan (148km/ 91,9mi), Turin (172km/ 106,8mi), the Rivieras, and by tunnel through the Alps. The port has five passenger terminals: three for ferries and two for cruise ships. The city is enclosed by a mountain range curving around 30km/18.6mi of coastline. The historic centre surrounding the port is a maze of alleyways (*carruggi*); the modern part of the city is crossed by wide avenues. Genoa's well-organised public transport includes buses, an underground line, funiculars, lifts and a ferry service.
GenovaPass permits travel on all forms of public transport. €4.50 for a 24hr pass. www.amt.genova.it.
Volabus – This hourly bus links Cristofo Colombo airport with the city centre, stopping at both Brignole and Piazza Principe railway stations (*€6 allows up to 1hr on all public transport; 010 60151; www. airport.genova.it*). Ferry and cruise ships info at *www.porto.genova.it. Information: 848 000 030; www.amt.genova.it.*

Tours

A day out by train – This is one of the locals' favourite Sunday outings. A trip into the country on a historic 1929 narrow-gauge railway that runs up into the hills between Genoa and Casella making frequent stops at villages on the way. The train is ideal for walkers (stops by request) and there's plenty of info on footpaths. In summer it has 8–10 departures daily from Genoa Piazza Manin station; one-way takes around an hour (*848 00 00 30; www.ferroviagenovacasella.it*).
Genoa City Tour – Daily departures from Piazza Caricamento (in front of the Acquario) every 30min (10am–5pm). Duration 50min, recorded tour (earphones). *€12. 010 53 05 237; www.genoacitytour.com.*

Sightseeing

Card Musei – Includes entry to 25 museums in Genoa as well as discounts on certain attractions including the Acquario and exhibitions at the Palazzo Ducale. *€15 for a 48hr pass /€25 including use of public transport; www.museidigenova.it.*

A BIT OF HISTORY

By the 11C the Genovese fleet ruled supreme over the Tyrrhenian Sea, having vanquished the Saracens. With around 70 ships, all built in the city's dockyards, Genoa was a formidable power much coveted by foreign rulers.
In the Crusades Genoa established trading posts on the shores of

Porto Antico, Genoa

the eastern Mediterranean and following the creation of the Republic of St George in 1100, seamen, merchants, bankers and moneylenders worked together to keep Genoa a notch above the rest. Previously allied with Pisa against the Saracens (11C), the two cities fought over Corsica (13C) and in the 14C Genoa became a rival of Venice for trading rights in the Mediterranean.

In the 14C Genoa's trade with the Orient flourished and the Bank of St George was founded in 1408. The merchants became ingenious moneylenders and instituted such modern methods as bills of credit, cheques and insurance.Continual struggles between rival families led to the decision (1339) to elect a *doge* for life. In the 15C foreign protection was sought.

The great admiral **Andrea Doria** (1466–1560) distinguished himself against the Turks in 1519 and gave Genoa its aristocratic constitution and its status as a mercantile republic in 1528. Indignant at François I's unjust treatment of him, Doria entered into the service of Charles V. Following Doria's death and the development of rival ports on the Atlantic coast, Genoa fell into decline. Louis XIV destroyed the harbour in 1684. In 1768, by the Treaty of Versailles, Genoa surrendered Corsica to France. In 1848, under Giuseppe Mazzini, it became one of the cradles of the Risorgimento.

Fine Arts in Genoa – The 16–17C coincided with intense artistic activity, seen in the building of new *palazzi* and in the arrival of foreign artists, especially Flemish. In 1607 Rubens published a work on the *Palazzi di Genova* and in 1621–27 Van Dyck painted the city's nobility. Puget lived at Genoa (1661–67).

The Genovese School favoured dramatic intensity and muted colours; it includes such artists as Luca Cambiaso (16C), Bernardo Strozzi (1581–1644), the fine engraver Castiglione, and especially Alessandro Magnasco (1667–1749), whose sharp and colourful brushwork were a precursor of modern art.

The Genovese architect Galeazzo Alessi (1512- 72) was the equal of Sansovino and Palladio in the nobility and ingenuity of his designs.

PORT★★★

Boat tours: *40min tour of port daily, from Aquarium; 1day excursions to San Fruttuoso, Portofino; 1day whale-watching cruises. 010 26 57 12, www.liguriaviamare.it.*

The historic Porto Antico has been delightfully restructured, with a marina, bars, restaurants and the famous aquarium. The Bigo, designed by Renzo Piano to resemble cranes, has a panoramic lift and excellent bird's-eye view★. Genoa's Porto Nuovo is marked by La Lanterna lighthouse, symbol of the city.

Acquario★★★

Open Jan– Feb and Nov –Dec 9.30am–8pm; Jul–Aug 8.30am–10.30pm; rest of the year 8.30 or 9am–8 or 9pm (last entry 1hr 30min before closing). €25. 010 23 45 678. www.acquariodigenova.it.

Genoa's vast, well-organised aquarium has state-of-the-art displays and reconstructions of underwater environments.

PALAZZO DUCALE★

Piazza Matteotti 9. 010 55 74 000. www.palazzoducale.genova.it.

Behind the monumental façade of Palazzo Ducale (1778) is a lovely chapel★ with frescoes by G.B. Carlone with historical city scenes.

STRADA NUOVA (VIA GARIBALDI)★★★

In the mid-16C a number of patrician families built their residences on this street away from the historic centre. It is one of the loveliest in Italy and a UNESCO World Heritage Site. Three of the palazzi form a single museum: Palazzo Rosso, Palazzo Bianco and Palazzo Tursi [*open Tue–Fri 9am–7pm (winter 6.30pm), Sat–Sun 10am–7.30pm (winter 9.30am–6.30pm); €9; 010 55 721 93; www.museidigenova.it*].

Palazzo Tursi★★– The palazzo (no. 9) boasts a lengthy façade and terraced gardens. It passed to Giovanni Andrea Doria in 1596, and to the Savoy family in 1820.

Palazzo Bianco – (no. 11) houses a gallery with works by Caravaggio, Veronese, Rubens and van Dyck.

Palazzo Rosso – This palazzo (no. 18) has a sumptuous interior with art that includes works by van Dyck, Dürer and Veronese.

VIA BALBI★

This street is lined with palaces. The **Palazzo Reale★★** (Royal Palace) is at no. 10. Built (1643–50), the building has stunning frescoes and art works by Tintoretto, van Dyck and Guercino among others. The imposing 17C university building, **Palazzo dell'Università★**, at no. 5 has a beautiful courtyard and a majestic staircase.

CATTEDRALE DI SAN LORENZO★★

The 12C cathedral with 16C additions has a splendid Gothic façade★★, in the Genovese style.

GALLERIA NAZIONALE DI PALAZZO SPINOLA★★

Piazza Pellicceria 1. Open Tue–Sat, 8.30am–7.30pm (1st Sun of the month 1.30–7.30pm, free entrance). €4; €6.50 with Palazzo Reale. 010 27 05 300. www.palazzospinola.beniculturali.it.

This 16C palace has preserved its original 17C (*1st floor*) and 18C (*2nd floor*) interior design.

PROMONTORIO DI PORTOFINO★★★

This rocky, rugged promontory is a highlight of the Italian Riviera.
The coastline is dotted with villages in sheltered bays. Some of Italy's
most glamorous resorts retain the age-old appeal of simple fishing
ports. A nature reserve (parco naturale) protects the fauna and flora.
Numerous footpaths criss-cross over the headland – ideal for
discovering the secret charms of this region.

PORTOFINO★★★

*By sea: From Santa Margherita,
Rapallo and San Fruttuoso.
€5.50–€16.50 (round trip). 0185 28
46 70. www.traghettiportofino.it.
From Camogli to San Fruttuoso:
€10 (round trip). 0185 77 20 91.
www.golfoparadiso.it.*
To reach the delightful village
of Portofino, famous cove of
the jet set, drive through **Santa
Margherita Ligure★★** (*5km/3mi*),
another elegant seaside resort and
popular watersports centre. From
here the **Strada Panoramica★★** has
lovely views of the rocky coast.
Steps from the picturesque port-
side piazza of Portofino lead up
to the church of San Giorgio and
the footpath to **Castello Brown**
(formerly di San Giorgio) and the
walk to the lighthouse★★★ (*1hr
on foot there and back*) through
olives and pines for breathtakingly
lovely **views★★★** of Portofino and
the Gulf of Rapallo. The sun setting
over the sea is especially lovely.
The pathway continues to the
lighthouse and a view that extends
to La Spezia.

Parco Naturale Regionale di Portofino

The enitre Portofino Promontory
is a regional park. Explore its
dense network of trails and unique
natural environment of Apennine
and Mediterranean vegetation
– chestnuts grow alongside
olives. Discover the fascinating
underwater panorama in dive sites.

SAN FRUTTUOSO★★

*Footpaths from Portofino,
Portofino Vetta, Camogli and
Punta Chiappa (1hr 30min–
2hrs 30min). Boat services
operate along the coast. www.
sanfruttuoso.eu/toc.*
This tiny village at the head of a
narrow cove can only be reached on
foot or by sea. There is a beautiful
13–14C abbey, Abbazia di San
Fruttuoso, and an underwater
statue of Christ in the bay.

PORTOFINO VETTA★★

Lovely coastal views from the
hilltop (450m/1 476ft).

BELVEDERE DI SAN ROCCO★★

More wide panoramas from
the church terrace, this time to
Camogli and the western coast as
far as Genoa. A path leads to **Punta
Chiappa★★★** (1h15 each way by
steps and footpath to the right of
the church). Unforgettable views.

CAMOGLI★★

Tall houses crowd around a small
harbour in this picturesque
Portofino fishing village.

LIGURIAN RIVIERA★

The enchanting Italian or Ligurian Riviera is, like the French Riviera, a tourist paradise. The mild climate makes it popular year round; its resorts have excellent amenities and a wide range of hotels dot the coast. The hinterland is marvellous for walkers. Food specialities to taste include olive oil, pesto (basil sauce), very thin focaccia made from chick pea flour, and fish prepared in delightful ways. Local wines are red or white; the Cinque Terre, where grapes are harvested in difficult conditions, is famous for its Moscato passito (sweet) wine.

RIVIERA DI PONENTE★

Via Aurelia is the busy, winding main road of the riviera, parallel to the A 10 motorway. Of Roman origin it has some remarkable coastal viewpoints and passes resorts with villas and luxuriant gardens. Climate and position make the riviera a specialist in the flower industry.

Bordighera★★ – The villas and hotels of this resort are scattered among flower gardens. The old town still has fortified gateways.

Sanremo★★ – The capital of the Riviera di Ponente boasts coastal Liguria's longest hours of sunshine, with spas, a marina and cultural events. Sanremo is the main Italian flower market, exporting all sorts of blooms worldwide.

Taggia★ – Set amid vineyards and olive groves, dominating the Argentina Valley, this 15–16C arts centre features fine **works★** by Louis Bréa (*Virgin of Pity* and the *Baptism of Christ*) in the church of **San Domenico** (*www. conventosandomenicotaggia.org*). Imperia has the Museum of the Olive (*0183 29 57 62. www.museodellolivo.com.*).

Cervo★ – In this gorgeous village clinging to the coast, Piazza dei Corallini has the **San Giovanni Battista** church with a Baroque **façade★**, summer site of a prestigious chamber music festival.

From Marina di Andora, head inland to **Andora Castello**, an isolated site with ruins.

Albenga★ – A short distance inland, with a medieval **old town★** clustered round the **cattedrale**. The octagonal 5C baptistery has a paleo-Christian mosaic.

Grotte di Toirano★ – The Neolithic period caves have striking stalagmites and stalactites. Footprints, torch-marks and bearprints give testimony to former dwellers' presence.

Noli★ – A fishing village with traditional houses, 13C towers and a Romanesque church with a huge wooden statue of Christ.

Albissola Marina★ – The tradition of ceramics production dates to the 13C. The 18C Villa Faraggiana, set in a lovely **park★**, has extravagant interiors; its superb **ballroom★** has stucco and fresco decoration.

RIVIERA DI LEVANTE★★★

This stretch of coast has more character and is wilder than the Riviera di Ponente. Rugged cliffs and promontories, sheltered coves and tiny fishing villages, together with the pinewoods and olive groves inland, all lend it charm. Don't miss the beautiful villages of the Cinque Terre.

Nervi★ – This attractive seaside resort with multicoloured houses

Bay of Silence, Sestri Levante

was fashionable in the early 20C. The *passeggiata* **Anita Garibaldi★** is a pleasant coastal walk with fine views from the Alpi Marittimi to Portofino. Three Villa gardens make up the **public parks**.

Rapallo★ – A sophisticated seaside resort on a bay east of the Portofino Peninsula. Lungomare Vittorio Veneto is a palm-shaded seafront **promenade★**.

Sestri Levante★ – Busy shipyards, and also a seaside resort along the famous **Bay of Silence★** (Baia del Silenzio). In May, Sestri's Andersen Festival is dedicated to childhood *(www.andersenfestival.it)*.

Cinque Terre★★ – The spectacular beauty of the Cinque Terre (Five Lands – **Riomaggiore★**, **Manarola★**, Corniglia, **Vernazza★★** and **Monterosso**) combines natural and man-made features: the coastline and countryside together with vineyards and fishing villages. A panoramic **footpath★★** links the villages. The area is a UNESCO World Heritage Site.

Portovenere★★ – A lovely little seaside town with picturesque seafront houses and views over the water to Palmaria Island *(boat trips available)*. The church of San Pietro dates back to the 6C. From here there are fine **views★★** of the **Bay of Poets**, so named for Byron and Shelley who spent time here.

Lerici★ – An attractive port and resort dominated by an imposing medieval castle.

Sarzana★ – The busy town of Sarzana was once a base of the Republic of Genoa, and the numerous historic buildings bear witness to its past importance. The **Cattedrale** has a marble **altarpiece★** (1432) by Riccomani and a **Crucifixion★** (1138) by Guglielmo.

The **Fortezza di Sarzanello★** *Oct–Mar Sat–Sun and hols 10.30am–1pm and 3.30–5.30pm; Apr–mid Jun Sat–Sun and hols 10.30am–1pm and 3–7pm; mid Jun–Jul Mon–Fri 10.30am–1pm, Sat–Sun and hols 10.30am–1pm and 5–8pm; Ago daily 10.30am–1pm and 5–8pm. Sept Mon–Fri 10.30am–1pm (closed Tue), Sat–Sun and hols 10.30am–1pm and 3.30–6.30pm. €4. 0187 62 20 80. www.fortezzadisarzanello. com]*, former home of Castruccio Castracani, is a curious example of military architecture with moats and curtain walls guarded by towers.

THE ALPS

The Alps form Italy's northern backdrop. Towards the west, Valle d'Aosta is anchored dramatically by Mont Blanc, Italy's highest peak. Its decidedly French influence from neighbours France and Switzerland is evident. Piemonte, which borders Valle d'Aosta to the south, is one of Italy's largest regions, in both area and inhabitants. Turin, the capital, became the first seat of the Kingdom of Italy in 1861.The Alps toward the east show strong Germanic influence, a result of tribal invasions during the Roman Empire. Trentino-Alto Adige/Südtirol is comprised of two autonomous provinces: Trentino in the south, and Alto Adige in the north. Linguistic divisions remain today. The entire region is dominated by massifs of the Dolomite mountain range. The Alps are popular for winter holidays, as well as for climbing and hiking in the summer.

TURIN★★★

Situated at the foot of the scenic Alps, this complex charming city has profound contrasts. Clever at reinventing itself, Turin briefly was the capital of the new Kingdom of Italy and later of the automobile industry, before changing again to become the "factory-city"; a centre for culture and design. The Savoy dynasty gave Turin an elegant, Parisian aspect in its wide boulevards and grandiose architecture. Protector for centuries of the Turin Shroud, Turin's esoteric character attracted Paracelsus, Nostradamus and Cagliostro. Nietzsche wrote his major works here, claiming "Turin is the first place where I am possible."

Practical Information

Getting There
100km/62mi from the French border, Turin is easy to travel in and around by car.

♦ **By Bus** – Intercity terminal, Corso Vittorio Emanuele 131H. *011 4338 100. www.autostazionetorino.it.*

♦ **By Train** – *89 20 21.* The main RR stations: **Porta Nuova**, Corso Vittorio Emanuele II 53. *www.torinoportanuova.it.* **Porta Susa**, Corso Bolzano.

♦ **By Air** – The airport is 16km/9.94 mi north of the city in Caselle. *www. aeroportoditorino.it.* **Buses** run from the airport to Turin with Sadem (*800 801 600, www.sadem.it*).

Torino + Piemonte card Transport plus entry to some 60 museums and other sites. *€35–51 for 2–5 days. Turismo Torino e provincia, 011 53 51 81, www.turismotorino.org.*

Getting Around
Walking is the best way to discover the compact historic centre; arcades lining the main streets offer protection from the weather.

♦ **By Public Transport** – GTT at Corso Turati 19 bis/c, *800 01 91 52* (freephone) or *011 63 07 230, www. gtt.to.it.* Tickets: the *biglietto urbano* (€1.50) is valid for 90 mins, a *biglietto giornaliero* (€5) allows unlimited travel all day, the *shopping* (€3) is valid for four hours, or *carnets* at various rates.

♦ **By Taxi** – Pronto Taxi: *011 57 37.* Radio Taxi: *011 57 30.*

THE CITY TODAY

This northern factory town, still linked with Fiat, is a fashionable centre for culture and innovation. Turin was given a massive face-lift for the 2006 Winter Olympics.

ECONOMY

Local industries made Turin the capital of Italian engineering and innovation. The **Italian motor industry** was born here in 1899 with Fiat, followed by Lancia, tyre and coach manufacturers. The Fiat factory, transformed by **Renzo Piano**, is now an avant-garde conference centre and auditorium. Publishing is a tradition, from books to newspapers (*La Stampa*). The performing arts also thrive with the RAI National Symphony Orchestra, *Teatro Regio*, *Settembre Musica* and the *Torino Film Festival*. Barolo, Barbera, and Barbaresco are Piemonte's famous red wines, but there are many others. Piemonte is renowned for its food produce, including rich cheeses, meats, rice, hazelnuts, chestnuts, cherries and chocolate.

A BIT OF HISTORY

Romans transformed the Celtic capital in the 1C into a military colony. Later a Lombard duchy, it passed under Frankish rule. From the 11C for nearly 900 years Turin's destiny was linked to the **House of Savoy**: Charles Emmanuel III during his long reign (1732–73) organised the Kingdom's administration and established etiquette at court similar to Versailles; in 1861 Victor Emmanuel II became the first King of Italy, with Turin the government seat. The House of Savoy reigned over Italy until the proclamation of an Italian Republic in 1946.

HIGHLIGHTS

Piazza San Carlo★★ – Fine town planning in this graceful square.
Palazzo Carignano★★ – Birthplace of Victor Emmanuel II (1820–78); **Museo del Risorgimento★★**.
Piazza Castello – Centre of politics, Royal Palace and **Teatro Regio**.
Palazzo Reale★ – Home to the Princes of the House of Savoy.
Duomo★ – The cathedral houses the **Holy Shroud★★★** in which Christ was said to be wrapped after Descent from the Cross.
Via Po★ – Beautiful 17–18C street with palaces and arcades.
Parco del Valentino★★ – Wooded park along the Po River.
Museo Egizio★★★ – One of the richest collections of Egyptian antiquities in the world; recently restored.
Galleria Sabauda★★★ – Gallery presenting the collections of the House of Savoy.
Museo del Cinema★★★ – A vast collection of the history of cinema.
Museo dell'Automobile Carlo Biscaretti di Ruffia★★★ – An extensive collection of cars, chassis and engines:
Museo di Arte Antica★★ – The museum of ancient art.
GAM – Galleria Civica di Arte Moderna e Contemporanea★★ – This fine art collection gives a good overview of Italian art, especially 19C and 20C Piemontese schools.

LANGHE AND MONFERRATO★★

South of Turin, the Langhe and Monferrato vineyards produce world-class wines. This verdant stretch is a gourmet's paradise. The hills and vineyards of Langhe-Roero and Monferrato became the 50th Italian UNESCO World Heritage site.

TURIN

THE DOLOMITES★★★

Situated between the Veneto and Trentino-Alto Adige/Südtirol, the fan of so-called "Pale Mountains" (*Monti Pallidi*) take on red tints at sunset. Their harsh, rocky contours embrace crystalline lakes and mysteries, which have become the very stuff of poetic legend. The Dolomites are Italy's winter playground and include the Dolomiti Superski, a network of 1 200km/3 937mi of ski slopes and over 400 lift facilities. But with an average of 300 days of sunshine and some mountains reaching an altitude over 3 000m/9 840ft, it is possible to enjoy the slopes year-round. Val Gardena is a popular tourist centre, while Cortina d'Ampezzo is one of the premier ski resorts in Europe.

STRADA DELLE DOLOMITI★★★

The main touring route is the great Dolomite Road, a world-famous example of road engineering.

Marmolada★★★ – Famous for its glacier and very fast ski runs. The **cablecar** from Malga Ciapela goes up to 3 265m/10 712ft offering admirable **panoramas★★★** of the Cortina peaks (Tofana and Cristallo), the Sasso Lungo, the enormous tabular mass of the Sella Massif and in the background the summits of the Austrian Alps including the Grossglockner.

Passo di Sella★★★ – Linking the Val di Fassa and Val Gardena this pass offers one of the most extensive **panoramas★★★** in the Dolomites, including the Sella, Sasso Lungo and Marmolada massifs.

Val Gardena★★★ – One of the most famous valleys in the Dolomites for both its beauty and crowds of tourists. The inhabitants still speak a language which was born during the Roman occupation: the Ladin dialect.

Passo Pordoi★★★ – The highest pass (2 239m/7 346ft) on the Dolomite Road lies between huge blocks of rock with sheer sides and shorn-off tops.

Cortina d'Ampezzo★★★ – Cortina, the capital of the Dolomites, is a winter-sports and summer resort with a worldwide reputation.

VAL PUSTERIA AREA

Val Pusteria, or Pustertal, is bordered to the south by the Dolomites and by the central Alps to the north. From the end of the 13C until the 16C it belonged to the county of Gorizia and formed part of the Strada d'Alemagna, a road that linked Venice and Germany.

Abbazia di Novacella★★ – The abbey was founded in 1142 and run by Augustinian monks.

Lago di Braies★★★ – This shimmering lake is the starting point of some arduous footpaths.

Tre Cime di Lavaredo★★★ – From the refuge at Auronzo, the Lavaredo shelter can be reached in half an hour. From there the Locatelli shelter takes another hour; this last stretch offers spectacular views.

Lago di Misurina★★ – This lake is set among a plantation of fir trees and is an excellent starting point for excursions from Tre Cime di Lavaredo to the Cristallo.

MERANO★★

Merano, situated at Val Venosta valley on the Adige, delighted "Sissi", Empress Elizabeth of Austria, with its spas and alpine scenery. Visitors still come for its thermal waters, good facilities, and the gardens of Castel Trauttmansdorff. Autumn brings the Gran Premio Ippico steeplechase and the Merano Wine Festival. Cablecars and chairlifts lead to winter-sports and summer excursions. German-Austrian influence is evident in its language as well as cuisine, from breads and meats to white wines like Müller-Thurgau, Sylvaner, Riesling and Traminer, although some good reds include Schiava, Lagrein, and Pinot Noir.

HIGHLIGHTS

Winter and summer promenades★★ – These winter and summer promenades run along the **Passirio River**. Inverno has shops, caffès and terraces. Passeggiata Gilf ends near a waterfall. The summer promenade, on the opposite bank, meanders in a park with pines.

Tappeiner promenade★★ – This walk (7km/4.3mi long) winds above Merano with views of the Tyrol.

EXCURSIONS

Avelengo★ – A scenic road leads to the Avelengo Plateau, dominating the Merano Valley.

Merano 2000✳ – Access by cablecar. This plateau hosts winter sports and is a base for summer hikes into the mountains.

Tirolo★ – This charming Tyrolean village is dominated by the 12C **Castel Tirolo**. **Castel Fontana** (also **Brunnenburg**) is a strange set of 13C fortifications later rebuilt. American poet, Ezra Pound worked on his *Cantos* here from 1958.

VAL PASSIRIA★

50km/31mi to the Rombo Pass; 40km/ 24.8mi to the Monte Giovo Pass.
The steep **Rombo Pass Road★** (Timmelsjoch) offers impressive views of the frontier mountain peaks. The **Monte Giovo Pass Road★** (Jaufenpass) climbs amid conifers; its descent has splendid **views★★** of snow-capped summits of Austria.

Submerged clock tower, Lago di Resia
© i-Stockr/iStockphoto.com

VAL VENOSTA★

From Merano, take the S 38 in the direction of Resia.
Covered in apple and apricot orchards, sunny Venosta Valley widens as it climbs towards the Resia Pass. Val Venosta's most famous inhabitant, Ötzi, lived 5 300 years ago; his body was preserved by the ice in the spot where he died, in Val Senales (*Ötzi is in the Archaeological Museum of Bolzano. www.iceman.it/en/*).

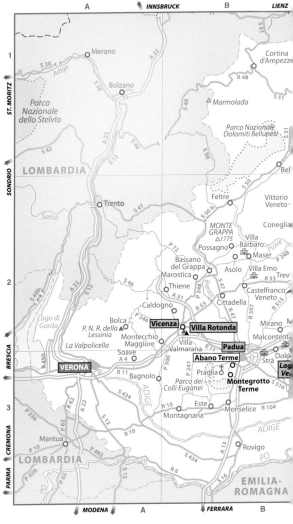

VENICE AND AROUND

The Veneto and Friuli-Venezia Giulia regions have powerful maritime histories. Veneto's capital Venice, once the seat of the powerful Venetian Republic, ruled large swathes of territory in the Adriatic and Mediterranean for more than 1 000 years and developed new trade routes to the Far East thanks to the exploration of Marco Polo.

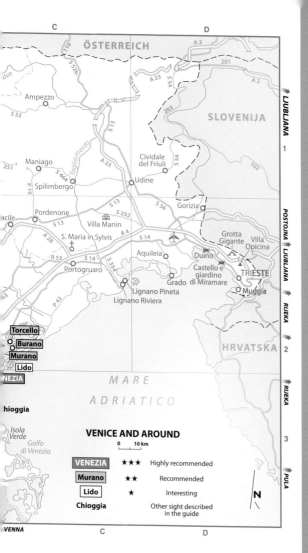

VENICE AND AROUND

0   10 km

VENEZIA	★★★	Highly recommended
Murano	★★	Recommended
Lido	★	Interesting
Chioggia		Other sight described in the guide

N

Trieste, Italy's easternmost city and the capital of Friuli-Venezia Giulia, was once part of the Austrian Habsburg's domain and the gateway to the East for the countries of central Europe. Both regions are known for their refinement, ranging from Palladian villas to delicious cuisine and sophisticated wines. Shakespeare's great love story between Romeo and Juliet was set in the splendid city of Verona.

VENICE ★★★

Venice is a legendary city, presiding regally over the lagoon for more than a thousand years. "La Serenissima" – "her most serene" – has a multitude of moods: labyrinthine streets, quiet canals, busy ports, lively wine bars (*bacari*), a lavishness from textiles to ballrooms, and broody landscapes à la *Death in Venice*. Painting has flourished here, alongside the exquisite glass art of Murano Island. Yet the true attraction is always Venice itself, which Lord Byron dubbed "a fairy city of the heart".

GONDOLAS

For centuries gondolas have been the traditional means of transport in Venice. An austere craft, its iron hook acts as a counterweight to the gondolier. The curved fin resembles the *doge's* hat and the prongs represent the *sestieri* or districts of the city: the opposite prong symbolises the Giudecca. The unique experience of a ride is justifiably costly. Six people may share a gondola. A 35 min journey without a musical accompaniment costs *day €80/night €100*. Each 20min after the initial 40min costs *day €40/ night €50*. For information contact the Istituzione per la Conservazione della Gondola e la Tutela del Gondoliere, *041 52 85 075. www.gondolavenezia.it*. For a budget gondola experience, a *traghetto* (gondola ferry) ferries passengers for €2 across points along the Grand Canal (San Marcuola, Santa Sofia, al Carbon, San Tomà, San Samuele, Santa Maria del Giglio and Dogana). A limited number of bridges cross the Grand Canal (Scalzi, Rialto, Accademia and Costituzione), so the *traghetti* are fundamental transport for Venetians.

THE CITY TODAY

The sea is the source of Venice's fortunes and its grief; in recent years, the water has become the city's primary foe. December 2008 saw the *acqua alta* (high water) peak above 1.5m/5ft, flooding buildings and *piazze*, halting transport and scaring away tourists. The MOSE project, which would create a system of mechanised gates to defend against the rising tides, has been controversial since its inception in 2003, with opponents claiming that the barriers will damage the fragile ecosystem of the Venetian Lagoon. In addition to MOSE (still under construction), a number of charities, including Save Venice (*www.savevenice.org*), have been established to help preserve Venice's artistic heritage. It is often said that the charm of Venice is more at risk from the tourist tidal wave than from sinking into the sea. The city is keen to encourage longer-stay visitors rather than day-trippers, who contribute little to the local economy.

A BIT OF HISTORY

Venice is built on 117 islands; it has 150 canals and 400 bridges. A canal is called a *rio*, a square a *campo*, a street a *calle* or *salizzada*, a quay a *riva* or *fondamenta*, a filled-in canal *rio terrà*, a passageway a *sottoportego*, and a courtyard a *corte*.

The Venetians – The Venetians are both proud and fiercely traditional, known for their commercial and practical skills. Masks and capes,

Gondolas, Isola di San Giorgio Maggiore in the background

Practical Information

Venice Card

Venezia Unica–City Pass
(€39.90 for adults over 30; €29.90 ages 6–29) is valid for 5 years and includes free entry to the Palazzo Ducale,10 museums and 16 Chorus churches, as well as further discounts at many sites, attractions, concerts and excursions. *041 24 24, www.veneziaunica.it.*
Rolling Venice card offers discounts for young visitors aged 14–29 (*www.actv.it*, €20). The paper can be purchased at the *www. veneziaunica.it* ticket desk for €6.

Sightseeing

Combined tickets – Museum Pass includes: museums on Piazza San Marco (Palazzo Ducale, Palazzo Correr, Museo Archeologico and Biblioteca Nazionale Marciana), Casa di Goldoni, Ca' Rezzonico, Palazzo Mocenigo, Ca' Pesaro, Museo di Storia Natural, Museo del Vetro (Murano) and Museo del Merletto (Burano) (€24, *valid for 6 months, 848 082 000*).

Getting There

Frequent buses run from Venice Marco Polo Airport about 10km/6mi (*20min*) from the city. *041 26 06 111. www.veniceairport.it.* The main road to Venice is the A 4. It is linked to Mestre by the **Ponte della Libertà**. The **Grand Canal** – 4km/2.5mi – divides central Venice. In Venice, all public transport is water-borne. Heavy traffic on the Grand Canal and the fact that stops are infrequently "door-to-door" mean that walking can sometimes be quicker. However, the experience of travelling along the Grand Canal by boat is a terrific way to begin a stay in Venice. The famous Venetian water-boats, the 🚤 **vaporetti**, have a well-organised and frequent timetable of services. Here are two of the most useful routes: **Line 1** Piazzale Roma, stops along the Grand Canal, including Ponte di Rialto and San Marco; terminates at the Lido.
Lines 41/42 Piazzale Roma and Murano, stops at Giudecca and San Zaccaria (adjacent to San Marco). *Single ticket €7.50 valid 1h. 12hr (€18), 24hr (€20) and multiple day – up to 7 days (€60) (www.actv.it).*

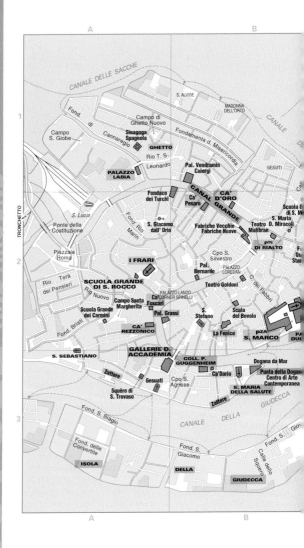

CANALE DELLE SACCHE

S. ALVISE

MADONNA
DELL'ORTO

CANALE

Campo di
Ghetto Nuovo

Sinagoga
Spagnola

Campo
S. Giobe

Fond. di Cannaregio

GHETTO

Fondamenta d. Misericordia

Rio T. S.
Leonardo

Pal. Vendramin
Calergi

GESUITI

PALAZZO
LABIA

Pal.
Fondaco
dei Turchi

Ca'
Pesaro

CANAL
GRANDE

CA'
D'ORO

Scuola G
di S. M

TRONCHETTO

S. Lucia

Fond. Rio
Marin

S. Giacomo
dall' Orio

Fabriche Vecchie
Fabriche Nuove

Teatro D. Malibran
S. Maria
D. Miracoli

Ponte della
Costituzione

PTE
DI RIALTO

Piazzale
Roma

I FRARI

Cpo S.
Silvestro

Pal.
Bernardo

PALAZZO
LOREDAN

F
Qu
Stan

Rio Terà
dei Pensieri

SCUOLA GRANDE
DI S. ROCCO

Rio Nuovo

Campo Santa
Margherita

Ca'
Foscari

PALAZZO LANDO
Ca'
CORNER SPINELLI

Teatro Goldoni

C. Dei Fabbri

Scuola Grande
dei Carmini

Pal. Grassi

S.
Stefano

Scala
del Bovolo

Fond. Briati

CA'
REZZONICO

La Fenice

PZA
S. MARCO

PA
DU

S. SEBASTIANO

GALLERIE D.
ACCADEMIA

COLL. P.
GUGGENHEIM

Dogana da Mar

Zattere

Ca'Dario

Punta della Dogan
Centro di Arte
Contemporanea

Gesuati

Cpo S.
Agnese

S. MARIA
DELLA SALUTE

Squèro di
S. Trovaso

Zattere

DELLA

GIUDECCA

Fond. S. Biagio

CANALE

DELLA

Fond. S.
Giacomo

Fond. S.
Gio

Calle dello
Squero

Fond. delle
Convertite

ISOLA

DELLA

GIUDECCA

once popular with the locals and
still worn in Venice at Carnival time,
add to their elusiveness. Skilled
courtesans, diplomats and spies
have given Venice a reputation
for intrigue and glamour.

Venice was founded in AD 811 by
the inhabitants of Malamocco, near
the Lido, fleeing from the Franks.
They settled on the Rivo Alto,
known today as the Rialto. In that
year the first *doge* was elected and

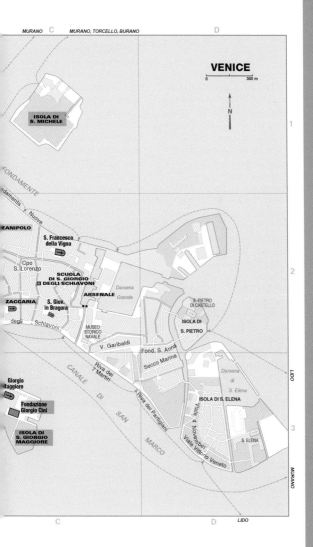

MURANO C   MURANO, TORCELLO, BURANO   D

VENICE

0   300 m

N

ISOLA DI
S. MICHELE

FONDAMENTE

damenta Nuove

ZANIPOLO

S. Francesco
della Vigna

Cpo
S. Lorenzo

SCUOLA
DI S. GIORGIO
DEGLI SCHIAVONI

Darsena
Grande

ARSENALE

ZACCARIA   S. Giov.
in Bragora

degli   Schiavoni

MUSEO
STORICO
NAVALE

V. Garibaldi

S. PIETRO
DI CASTELLO

ISOLA DI
S. PIETRO

Fond. S. Anna

Riva dei
7 Martiri

Secco Marina

CANALE

DI

SAN

Giorgio
Maggiore

Fondazione
Giorgio Cini

ISOLA DI
S. GIORGIO
MAGGIORE

Riva dei Partigiani

Darsena
di
S. Elena

ISOLA DI S. ELENA

Viale 4

Novembre

S. ELENA

Viale Vittorio Veneto

MARCO

LIDO

MURANO

C   D   LIDO

thus started the adventures of the Venetian Republic, known as "La Serenissima", which lasted 1 000 years. In 828 the relics of St Mark the Evangelist were brought from Alexandria; he remains the town's protector to this day.

The Venetian Empire – From the 9–13C Venice grew richer as it exploited its geographic position between East and West. Its maritime and commercial power conquered key markets in Istria and Dalmatia. The Venetians captured Constantinople in 1204. Trade in spices, fabrics and precious stones from markets in the East grew apace. **Marco Polo** (1254–1324) returned from China with fabulous riches. The 14C war with rival Genoa ended in victory for the Venetians in 1381. The first half of the 15C Venetian power was at its peak. They captured Verona, Vicenza, Padua, Udine, and then Brescia and Bergamo. The Adriatic became the Venetian Sea from Corfu to the Po. The capture of Constantinople by the Turks in 1453 started the decay, escalated when the discovery of America shifted trade. Meanwhile, Venice continued an exhausting struggle with the Turks.

The "Most Serene Republic" ended in 1797; Napoleon Bonaparte entered Venice and abolished a thousand-year-old constitution, then ceded the city to Austria. Venice and the Veneto were united with Italy in 1866.

PIAZZA SAN MARCO★★★

St Mark's Square is the heart of Venice, where the covered galleries of the **Procuratie** (procuratorships) shelter famous caffès (🍸 **Florian**, Quadri), and luxury shops.

The square opens onto the Grand Canal through the **Piazzetta San Marco**. The two granite columns crowned by "Marco" and "Todaro" (St Mark and St Theodore) were brought from the East in 1172.

Basilica★★★

Built throughout the 11C, the basilica of St Mark's was consecrated in 1094 and combines the Byzantine and Western styles.

The body of St Mark, stolen from Alexandria in 828, was miraculously recovered here. The plan of a Greek cross is crowned by a bulbous dome flanked by four smaller domes. The relics of **St Mark** rest under the high altar (*Open Mon–Sat 9.30am–5pm; Oct–Easter Pala d'Oro and Treasury 9.45am–4pm; Sun and hols 2–5pm. Basilica free. Pala d'Oro €2,50. Treasury €3. 041 27 08 311; www. basilicasanmarco.it).*

The ceiling mosaics depict the New Testament, starting with the dome of the apse with Christ as Pantocrator (Ruler of All) and ending with the Last Judgement in the area above the *atrium.*

The originals of the famous **gilded bronze horses★★** are on display at **Museo di San Marco** (*open daily 9.45am–4.45pm; €5; 041 27 08 311; www.museosanmarco.it).*

Campanile★★

Open mid-Jul–mid-Sept, 8.30am –9.30pm; Apr/Easter–Jun and mid-Sept–Oct, 9am–7pm; rest of the year 9.30am–3.45pm. €8. 041 27 08 311. www.basilicasanmarco.it.
A symbol of Venice, the bell tower (99m/325ft high) is a reconstruction of the 15C campanile, which collapsed in 1902.

The **panorama★★** from the top extends to the Grand Canal. At the base is the **Loggetta Sansoviniana** with statues of Minerva, Apollo, Mercury and Peace.

Palazzo Ducale★★★

Open daily 8.30am–7pm (5.30pm Nov–Easter); last adm. 1hr before closing. Closed 1 Jan and 25 Dec. €19 Museo Correr, Museo Archeologico Nazionale, Monumental Rooms of Biblioteca

Piazza San Marco

Marciana or Museum Pass. 041 27 15 911. palazzoducale.visitmuve.it. The palace was a multi-functional symbol of Venetian power and glory, residence of the *doges*, the seat of government and law courts, as well as a prison. It was built in the 12C but was transformed between the 13C and the 16C. A pretty geometric pattern in white-and-pink marble lends great charm to the two **façades**. The main entrance is the **Porta della Carta★★**. The gateway leads into the Porticato Foscari; opposite is the **Scala dei Giganti** (Giants' Staircase) dominated by statues of Mars and Neptune. At the top of Sansovino's **Scala d'Oro** (Golden Staircase), pass through a suite of rooms as follows: the **Sala delle Quattro Porte** (Room of the Four Doors), where the ambassadors awaited audience with the *doge*; an antechamber, **Sala dell'Antecollegio**, for diplomatic missions and delegations; **Sala del Collegio**, where the *doge* presided over meetings; the Senate Chamber, **Sala del Senato** or "**dei Pregadi**", where the members of the Senate submitted their written request to participate in the meetings; and **Sala del Consiglio dei Dieci** (Chamber of the Council of Ten), where the council met the powerful magistrates who used the secret police and spies to safeguard the institutions. Beyond **Sala della Bussola**, the waiting-room for those awaiting interrogation, and the armoury (armeria) is the **Sala del Maggior Consiglio** (Grand Council Chamber). In this vast room the legislative body appointed all public officials and the constitutional election of the new *doge* was held. These checks and balances kept any one man from seizing power. In the chamber hang portraits of 76 *doges* as well as Tintoretto's **Paradise**. Proceed to the **Sala dello Scrutinio** (Ballot Chamber); the **Prigione Nuove** (New Prisons) and the Bridge of Sighs (Ponte dei Sospiri). Further along are the Censors' Chamber (**Sala dei Censori**), the seat of the judiciary and the Sala dell'Avogaria.

Ponte dei Sospiri★★

The 16C **Bridge of Sighs** connects the Doges' Palace with the prisons and is so named as prisoners had their final enchanting glimpse of Venice from the window.

Museo Correr★★

Piazza San Marco 52. Open Mar–Oct 10am–7pm (ticket office closes at 6pm); Nov–Mar 10am–5pm (ticket office closes at 4pm). Closed 1 Jan and 25 Dec. €19 (ticket valid for all the musems of the Piazza San Marco). 848 082 000 or (+39) 041 427 30 892 (from abroad). www.museiciviciveneziani.it.
Venetian history and art lead to the Napoleonic wing and the library, and through the Procuratie Nuove. Access also to Venice's excellent Archeological Museum.

La Fenice★

Campo San Fantin 1965. Open daily 9.30am–6pm. €10 . 041 78 66 75. www.teatrolafenice.it.
The theatre was built in 1792 in a charming and isolated square. It burned down first in 1836, and again in January 1996. Venice decided to rebuild it "how it was, where it was". Among many other operas, Rossini's Tancredi and Verdi's Rigoletto and La Traviata had their premières there.

GRAND CANAL★★★

Palazzo Labia★★

Campiello San Geremia. By the Riva di Biasio vaporetto stop.
The residence of Spanish merchants, the Labia, late-17C.

Ca' d'Oro★★★

Open 8.15am–7.15pm (2pm Mon); last admission 30min before closing. Closed 1 Jan, 1 May and 25 Dec. €8.50 (€10 with Palazzo Grimani). 041 52 00 345. www.cadoro.org.
The exterior gilt has disappeared, but the mansion retains an elegant façade in the ornate Gothic style. The **Galleria Franchetti** displays a fine **St Sebastian★** by Mantegna.

Ponte di Rialto★★

The **Rialto Bridge**, the sixth version and the first in stone, was built by Antonio da Ponte (1591). Classic views of the Grand Canal.

Palazzo Grassi★

Campo San Samuele. Open during exh. only; Wed.–Mon 10am–7pm. Closed, 24–25 Dec and 1 Jan. €15 (€20 inc Punta della Dogana). 041 20 01 057.
Built in the 18C, this was the last great Venetian palace to be constructed before the fall of the Republic. It now hosts exhibitions.

Ca' Pesaro★

Sestriere Santa Croce 2076. Open Apr–Oct Tue–Sun 10am–6pm; rest of the year 10am–5pm. Closed 1 Jan, 1 May and 25 Dec. €10 (incl ticket with the Museo di Arte Orientale) or Museum Pass. 848 082 000 or 041 427 30 892 (from abroad). www.capesaro. visitmuve.it.
The **Museo d'Arte Orientale** (Museum of Oriental Art) and the **Galleria Internazionale di Arte Moderna** (International Gallery of Modern Art) are in this palace by Longhena.

Ca' Corner della Regina
Calle de Ca' Corner. 02 56 66 2611. www.fondazioneprada.or.
The home of Monte di Pietà bank until 1969, this building then hosted the ASAC (the Venice Biennale's historical contemporary art archives) from 1975 to 2010, and in 2011 became the Venetian headquarters for Fondazione Prada, hosting various cultural activities focused mainly on contemporary art and cinema (*Open during exhibitions or free by reservation at least 7 days in advance*).

Ca' Foscari★
San Tomà vaporetto stop.
This 15C palazzo is the main seat of Venice's university. A symmetrical façade with three superimposed groups of windows with multiple lights, creates harmonious rhythm with the single-light windows and the stretches of stonework.

Ca' Rezzonico★★
Dorsoduro 3136. Open 10am–6pm (5pm Nov–Mar); last admission one hour before closing. Closed Tue, 1 Jan, 1 May and 25 Dec. €10 or Museum Pass. 848 08 20 00 or (+39) 041 427 30 892 (from abroad). www.carezzonico.visitmuve.it.
The **Museo del Settecento Veneziano** (Museum of 18C Venice) has splendid furnishings.

Ca' Dario★
The late-15C palazzo has gained a sinister reputation for the suspicious deaths of a succession of owners and residents.

Collezione Peggy Guggenheim★★★
Dorsoduro 701. Open Wed–Mon 10am–6pm. €15. 041 24 05 411. www.guggenheim-venice.it.
This 18C palazzo, residence of collector Peggy Guggenheim until her death, has interesting 20C art.

Punta della Dogana
Dorsoduro 2. Open Wed–Mon 10am–7pm (last entrance at 6pm). Closed, 24, 25 Dec and 1 Jan €15 (€20 with Palazzo Grassi). 041 20 01 057. www.palazzograssi.it.
As a centre of contemporary art, the city's former customs house presents exhibitions of works from the Pinault Collection.

Le Zattere★
Walking along the Zattere quays is like looking out from a balcony onto the agitated Giudecca canal and Giudecca Island, with its historic buildings such as the Molino Stucky and the churches of the Zitelle and Il Redentore, the latter one of the most important religious buildings in Venice.

GHETTO★★
The Jewish quarter (*ghetto*), in the Canneregio district, was the first such in Western Europe. In dialect the term *geto* referred to a mortar foundry. The Museo Ebraico and synagogues are open to visitors. To identify which inhabited buildings house a synagogue, just look at the upper floors. the five windows and lanterns at the top of the roofs indicate the presence of a place of worship. (*www.museoebraico.it.*).

Santa Maria della Salute

GALLERIE DELL'ACCADEMIA★★★
Open 8.15am–7.15pm (2pm Mon), last adm.45min before closing.Closed 1 Jan, 1 May and 25 Dec. €12. 041 52 00 345. www.gallerieaccademia.org.
The Academy presents the most important collection of Venetian art from the 14C to the 18C. Masterpieces include a **Madonna Enthroned** and the **Virgin and Child between St Catherine and Mary Magdalene** by Giovanni Bellini; **St George** by Andrea Mantegna; **The Tempest** by Giorgione; a **Portrait of a Young Gentleman in His Study** by Lorenzo Lotto; a sinister **Pietà** by Titian; **Christ in the House of Levi** by Veronese; and the **Miracles of the Relics of the True Cross** by Gentile Bellini and Carpaccio.

CHURCHES

Santa Maria della Salute★★
Built to mark the end of a plague epidemic (1630), this landmark has modillions and concentric volutes.

In the **Wedding at Cana** (sacristy) Tintoretto painted himself as an Apostle (left).

San Zanipòlo★★
The square boasts an **equestrian statue**★★ of the mercenary leader Bartolomeo **Colleoni** by Verrocchio and contains the **Scuola Grande di San Marco**★ and the imposing Gothic church of Santi Giovanni e Paolo (contracted in Venetian dialect to Zanipolo), burial place for the *doges*.

Basilica di Santa Maria Gloriosa dei Frari★★★
Open 9am (1pm Sun)–6pm. Closed 1 Jan, Easter, 15 Aug and 25 Dec. €3 or Chorus Pass. 041 27 50 462. www.basilicadeifrari.it.
This great Franciscan church, Santa Maria Gloriosa dei Frari, has an imposing appearance and funerary monuments, including those of several doges, Canova and Titian. The sacristy has a stunning tryptich by Bellini. Of two works by Titian, one is **Assumption of the Virgin** on the high altar.

San Zaccaria★★

The interior of the Renaissance-Gothic Church of St Zachary is covered with paintings; the most important is Giovanni Bellini's **Sacra Conversazione**.

EXCURSIONS

La Giudecca

Formed by eight islands, Giudecca was once a place for the Venetian nobility to get away from the city. Today it offers a walk along the quay, from the canal that separates it from San Giorgio Maggiore to the Molino Stucky designed by German architects in the late 19C. On Giudecca Island, the Church of the **Santissimo Redentore★** designed by Palladio (*open Tue–Sat 10am–4.30pm. 041 27 50 462; €3; www.chorusvenezia.org*) is one of Venice's most famous and venerated temples, and the setting for one of city's most popular festivals (third Sunday in July).

Isola di San Giorgio Maggiore★★

The island is crowned by San Giorgio Maggiore, another church designed by Palladio, which houses important paintings by Tintoretto (in the choir and sacristy). It is essential to climb to the top of the bell tower, which gives the most beautiful **view★★★** over Venice. Close by, visit the **Fondazione Giorgio Cini** (*Only guided tours (1hr) Sat–Sun 10am–5pm; guided tours in English a 11am, 1pm, 3pm and 5pm (winter 11am, 1pm and 3pm). €10. 041 22 01 215. www. cini.it*) in San Giorgio monastery, where you can enjoy exhibitions, plays and concerts.

Murano★★

By the end of the 13C, the threat of fire prompted the Grand Council to move the glassworks to Murano. Its museum, **Museo del Vetro★** (*open 10am–6pm (Nov–Mar 5pm); closed 1 Jan, 1 May, 25 Dec; €10; 041 73 95 86; www. museovetro.visitmuve.it*), displays exquisite glassware. The Museum is under restoration in order to improve and enlarge the pre-existing spaces through the opening of a new building. **Santi Maria e Donato★★**, is a masterpiece of 12C Veneto-Byzantine art; the **mosaic floor★★** recalls St Mark's. The ferry to Murano also stops at the **Island of San Michele**, which has accommodated Venice cemetery since 1807. This is a beautiful graveyard with many tomb monuments, and the remains of Igor Stravinsky, Sergei Diaghilev, Josif Brodsky and Ezra Pound (*Summer Mon-Sun 7.30am–6pm; winter–4pm*).

Burano★★

Boldly coloured houses and a rich lace-making tradition render the island impressively picturesque. The Island of Mazzorbo, connected to Burano by footbridge, has a vineyard replanted with historic golden Dorona grapes.

Torcello★★

Despite being overgrown and scarcely populated today, the island was once more powerful than Venice. The 7C Cattedrale di Santa Assunta has lovely mosaics.

LAGUNA VENETA★★

The Venetian Lagoon is the largest in Italy. It was formed at the end of the Ice Age by the convergence of flooded rivers, swollen by melted snow from the Alps and Apennines. A habitat for waterfowl and fish, its delicate balance threatens Venice.

Practical Information

Getting There

The Laguna Veneta is bordered to the south by Chioggia and to the north by Trieste. The main access road is the A 4.

A BIT OF HISTORY

In 12C Europe torrential rains caused high tides and flooding. The River Brenta broke its banks and deposited silt, mud and detritus in the Lagoon. The Republic of Venice tried to defend itself by placing palisades along the coast, diverting the course of the rivers and building great dykes, but the lagoon continued to pose a threat. Over the ensuing centuries (15C–17C), major drainage programmes were implemented, affecting the Brenta, Piave, Livenza and Sile rivers. In 1896 the waters of the Brenta were diverted into the Bacchiglione. Despite these measures, Venice itself is at risk: it is slowly sinking.

NATURE

The Laguna Veneta survival depends on a subtle balance between excessive sedimentation (the emergence of new land) and erosion (deposits carried by the sea and rivers are so scarce that a stretch of lagoon can become sea).

HIGHLIGHTS

Grado★

At the time of the barbarian invasions the inhabitants of Aquileia founded Grado, which was, from the 5C to the 9C, the residence of the Patriarchs of Aquileia. Today Grado is a busy little fishing port and seaside resort with a growing reputation and wonderful old town with cobbled streets.

Quartiere Vecchio★

The picturesque old town has a network of narrow alleys (*calli*) running between the canal port and the cathedral. The Duomo di Santa Eufemia (6C) has marble columns with Byzantine capitals, a 6C mosaic pavement, a 10C ambo and a valuable 14C Venetian silver-gilt **altarpiece★**. Beside the cathedral a row of sarcophagi and tombs leads to the 6C basilica of Santa Maria delle Grazie, which has some original mosaics.

Aquileia★

When Romans outlined the town site with a plough (181 BC), an eagle (*aquila*) hovered overhead. Aquileia was a flourishing market and headquarters of Augustus during his conquest of Germanic tribes. It became one of Italy's most important patriarchates (554–1751), ruled by bishops. Archeological museum.

Chioggia

Chioggia is not one of the lagoon islands, but rests on two parallel islands, linked to terra firma by a long bridge. The 2011 film, *Io Sono Li* (Shun Li and the Poet), was set in the fishermen's world in Chioggia.

PADUA★★

An art and pilgrimage centre, Padua revolves around historic Piazza Cavour. Caffè Pedrocchi was a meeting-place of the liberal elite in the Romantic period.

A BIT OF HISTORY

Few traces exist of ancient *Patavium*, one of the most prosperous Roman cities in Veneto during the 1C BC owing to its river trade, agriculture and the sale of horses. In the 7C Padua (*Padova*) was destroyed by the Lombards. From the 11C to the 13C it became an independent city-state. The city's greatest period of prosperity came under the Lords of Carrara (1337–1405). The Venetian Republic ruled from 1405 until 1797, when Napoleon abolished the Venetian Constitution.

The City of St Anthony the Hermit – This Franciscan monk, born in 1195, died aged 36 near Padua. He was a forceful preacher and is generally represented holding a book and a lily.

A famous university – The University of Padua, founded 1222, is the second oldest in Italy after Bologna. Galileo was a professor and students included Copernicus and the poet Tasso.

Art in Padua – In 1304 **Giotto** came to Padua to decorate the Scrovegni Chapel, with a superlative cycle of frescoes.

In the 15C the Renaissance in Padua was marked by **Donatello**, another Florentine, in the city from 1444 to 1453. Also in the 15C, Paduan art flourished under the Paduan artist **Andrea Mantegna** (1431–1506), a powerful painter and an innovator in the field of perspective.

HIGHLIGHTS

Giotto Frescoes, Scrovegni Chapel★★★ – This cycle of 39 frescoes was painted c.1305–10 by Giotto on the walls of the **Cappella degli Scrovegni**. The chapel, built in 1303, illustrates the lives of Joachim and Anna (the parents of the Virgin), Mary and Jesus: the *Flight into Egypt*, *Judas' Kiss* and the *Entombment* are among the most famous.

Frescoes in the Chiesa degli Eremitani★★ – In the Cappella Ovetari of the 13C Church of the Hermits (*the second on the right of the Cappella Maggiore*) are fragments of frescoes by **Mantegna**. The Cappella Maggiore has splendid frescoes by **Guariento**, Giotto's pupil.

Basilica di Sant'Antonio★★ – Across the square in which Donatello erected an **equestrian statue★★** of the Venetian leader **Gattamelata**. The **interior★★** chapel, the **Cappella del Santo★★**, has the tomb/altar of St Anthony (Arca di Sant'Antonio).

Battistero★★ – The 12C baptistery adjoining the cathedral contains frescoes covering the entire scriptures, painted 1376–1378 by **Giusto de' Menabuoi**.

Museo Diocesano★★ – The vast bishops' hall★ in the Palazzo Vescovile (Bishop's Palace) is painted with *trompe l'œil* of the Bishops of Padua. The diocese is one of Italy's largest and oldest.

EXCURSIONS

Abano Terme‡‡‡ – These thermal baths in the Euganean Hills are rightly famous.

Montegrotto Terme‡‡ – Also in the Euganean Hills, with outstanding spa facilities.

VICENZA★★

Strategically located at the crossroads of the routes that link the Veneto with the Trentino, the proud and noble city of Vicenza is a busy commercial and industrial centre, producing textiles, steel, chemicals and leather, and is a world centre for goldsmiths and gold trading. Gastronomic specialities of Vicenza include *baccalà alla Vicentina* and salt cod served in sauce with polenta. Local wines include Colli Berici, Arcole, Gambellara and Breganze.

A BIT OF HISTORY

The ancient Roman town of *Vicetia* became an independent city-state in the 12C. After several conflicts with the neighbouring cities of Padua and Verona, Vicenza sought Venetian protection at the beginning of the 15C. During that prosperity, Vicenza benefited from many rich and generous art patrons, who embellished the city with an amazing number of palaces, and the countryside with wealthy working farm villas.

Andrea Palladio – Vicenza was given the nickname of "Venice on terra firma" due to an exceptionally gifted man, Andrea di Pietro, known as Palladio, who spent many years in the city. The last great architect of the Renaissance, Palladio was born at Padua in 1508 and died at Vicenza in 1580. He harmoniously combined classical architecture with the contemporary styles of his time. The city of Vicenza and the Palladian villas of the Veneto form a UNESCO World Heritage Site.

HIGHLIGHTS

Piazza dei Signori★★

This open-air meeting-place recalls the forums of Antiquity. Two columns bear effigies of the Lion of St Mark and the Redeemer. With the lofty **Torre Bissara★**, a 12C belfry, the **Basilica★★**

(1549–1617) occupies one whole side of the square. The elevation is one of Palladio's masterpieces. The 15C **Monte di Pietà** is adorned with frescoes. The **Loggia del Capitano★**, formerly the residence of the Venetian governor, which stands to the left, was begun to the plans of Palladio in 1571 and left unfinished.

Teatro Olimpico★★

This splendid building in wood and stucco was designed by Palladio in 1580 on the model of the theatres of Antiquity. The tiers of seats are laid out in a hemicycle and surmounted by a lovely **colonnade** with a balustrade crowned with statues. The **stage★★★** is one of the finest in existence (www.teatrolimpicovicenza.it).

Corso Andrea Palladio★

The main street of Vicenza and neighbouring streets are embellished by palaces designed by Palladio and his pupils.

EXCURSIONS

Villa La Rotonda★★

Via della Rotonda 45. Open 10am–noon and 3–6pm (winter 10–12.30am and 2.30–5pm), €5; interior open only Wed, Sat. €10. www.villalarotonda.it.
Palladio's famous villa is majestic and harmoniously constructed.

Arena

VERONA★★★

Verona stands on the banks of the Adige against a hilly backdrop. Its rich artistic and historical heritage ranges from its Roman amphitheatre, still used for prestigious summer performances, to its Renaissance art and architecture. Italy's largest wine fair is held annually in Verona.

A BIT OF HISTORY

A major Roman colony in ancient times, Verona reached its peak under the Scaligers who governed for the Holy Roman Emperor (1260–1387). It then passed first to Milan and then Venice from 1405. Occupied by Austria in 1814, Verona became a part of Italy in 1866. Influenced by northern art, artists of the Veronese school developed a Gothic style with combined flowing lines and meticulous detail. **Antonio Pisanello** (c.1395–c.1450), traveller, painter, medal-maker and draughtsman, was the greatest exponent, marking the transition between medieval and Renaissance art.

HIGHLIGHTS

Arena★★

Open Tue–Sun 8.30am–7.30pm (Mon 1.30-7.30pm). €10. 045 800 51 51. www.arena.it.
Verona's famous pink-marble amphitheatre, still used for opera, was among the largest in Roman Italy, seating 25 000. The **panorama★★** from the top offers views of the town, surrounding hills and, on a clear day, the Alps.

Castelvecchio and Ponte Scaligero★★

This splendid castle built by Cangrande II Scaliger (1354) contains the **Museo d'Arte★★**, which shows the development of Veronese art from the 12–16C with canvases by Pisanello, Giambono, Carlo Crivelli, Mantegna, Carpaccio, the Bellinis, Tintoretto, Tiepolo and Longhi.

Piazza delle Erbe★★

This lively, attractive square lined with bars and a small morning market, is on the site of the Roman forum. In the centre of the square are a fountain and a Roman statue representing the town and columns, including a Venetian column topped by the winged Lion of St Mark (1523). Attractive historic *palazzi*, some with frescoes, are here too, including the Baroque **Palazzo Maffei**. In Via Cappello (no. 23) is **Casa di Giulietta** (Juliet's House), a Gothic palace that perhaps belonged to the Capulet family of Shakespearean fame. The well-known balcony is in the courtyard.

Piazza dei Signori★★

The elegant piazza, almost an open-air drawing room, contains imposing buildings including the 12C **Palazzo del Comune** (town hall), dominated by the **Torre dei Lamberti** tower, and **Palazzo dei Tribunali**. Opposite, the **Loggia del Consiglio** is an elegant Venetian-Renaissance edifice. The late-13C **Palazzo del Governo** with its machicolations and fine Classical doorway (1533) by Sammicheli was initially a Scaliger residence, then that of the Venetian governors.

Arche Scaligere★★

The Scaligers built their elegant Gothic tombs between their palace and church. Their family coat-of-arms includes a ladder (*scala*). Over the door of the Romanesque **Santa Maria Antica** church is the tomb of the popular Cangrande I (d. 1329).

Duomo★

Open daily Mar–Oct 10am–5.30pm (Sun opens 1.30pm); Nov–Feb 10am–1pm and 1.30–5pm (1.30–5pm Sun and hols). €2.50; €6 for 4 churches. www.chieseverona.it.
The cathedral has a 12C Romanesque chancel, a Gothic nave and a Classical-style tower. The remarkable Lombard-Romanesque main doorway is adorned with sculptures and bas-reliefs by Maestro Nicolò. The altarpiece decorated with an *Assumption* by Titian is the first altar on the left. The marble chancel screen is by Sammicheli (16C).

Teatro Romano★

Open Mon 1.30am–7.30pm, Tue–Sun 8.30am–7.30pm. €4.50. 045 80 00 360. museoarcheologico. comune.verona.it.
The Roman Theatre dates from the time of Augustus but has been heavily restored. The arena is famous for its opera, ballet and concerts. **Convento di San Girolamo** *(access by lift)* has a small **Museo Archeologico** and a lovely view over the town.

Basilica di San Zeno Maggiore★★

Open daily Mar–Oct 8.30am–6pm (Sun opens 12.30pm); Nov–Feb 10am–1pm and 1.30–5pm (1.30–5pm Sun and hols. €2.5; €6 for 4 churches. 045 59 28 13. www.chieseverona.it.
St Zeno is one of the finest Romanesque churches in northern Italy. It was built on the basilical plan in the Lombard style in the 12C. Mantegna painted the famous altarpiece and its crypt was the legendary setting for the marriage of Romeo and Juliet.

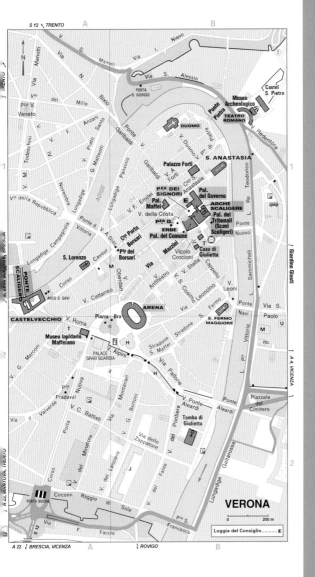

VERONA

Loggia del Consiglio.......... E

0   200 m

TUSCANY AND UMBRIA

The harmony of the beautiful Tuscan landscape of low-lying hills with graceful curves affording wide views of olive groves, vineyards and cypress trees, reinforces the great aesthetic sense of the Tuscan people. This region has the greatest concentration of Italy's artistic treasures, particularly in Florence, the capital and a model Renaissance city. Siena and San Gimignano are stunning examples of medieval architecture. Umbria, at the heart of the Italian peninsula, is landlocked between elegant Tuscany, the hilly Le Marche and Imperial Lazio. Etruscans built – and later civilisations enhanced – commanding cities atop promontories of volcanic tuff, of which Orvieto and Perugia, now the regional capital, were most prominent. Set admidst the deep greens of dense forests, the tranquil hill town of Assisi has the Basilica dedicated to St Francis and its famous frescoes by Giotto. Other artists left fine paintings in Umbria – Perugino, Pintoricchio, and Luca Signorelli.

Centre of Florence

TUSCANY AND UMBRIA

FIRENZE
Perugia

★★★ Highly recommended
★★ Recommended

0   40 km

rli

Rimini

Parco Naturale Monte San Bartolo

A 14

SAN MARINO

San Leo

Pesaro

MARE ADRIATICO

a Verna

Urbino

Corinaldo

Ancona
Portonovo

Riviera del Conero

1

Metauro

P 3

Sansepolcro

Jesi

Loreto

S 76

chiari

Frasassi

Esino

Monterchi

Fabriano

MARCHE

rezzo

Potenza

Macerata

ntecchio

Gubbio

UMBRIA

S 3

S. Severino Marche

Tolentino

Fermo

Cortona

Tevere

Ipogeo dei Volumni

Lago Trasimeno

S 75bis

ASSISI

△ M. Subiaso 1290

Perugia

Spello

P 77

Parco Nazionale dei Monti Sibillini

A 14

ntepulciano

Bevagna

Abba di Sassovivo

Ascoli Piceno

Cetona

Marsciano

Montefalco

Trevi

2

adicofani

Todi

Spoleto

Norcia

Arquata del Tronto

S 4

Tronto

ano

Paglia

L. di Alviano

Monteluco

Teramo

PESCARA

Orvieto

Cascata d.Marmore

Velino

L. di Campotosto

A 24

L. di Bolsena

Terni

ABRUZZO

S 4

L'Aquila

Pescara

L. di Vico

LAZIO

A 1

Tevere

S 4

A 24

A 25

ROMA

C

ROMA

ROMA

D

INTRODUCTION

85

FLORENCE★★★

One of Italy's most beautiful cities and one of the world's greatest artistic capitals, Florence is a testament to the Italian capacity for genius. The birthplace of Dante, the city was the cradle of a civilisation that nurtured the humanist movement and Renaissance architects, artists, scientists, mathematicians and thinkers in the first half of the 15C.

THE CITY TODAY

Florence has long depended on its legacy of the Renaissance to market itself, particularly to the millions of foreign tourists who swarm its streets and fill its coffers year after year. High prices and crowds have driven much of the native population to the suburbs. Some of the centre is closed to car traffic (Duomo and Santa Maria Novella) and major exhibits are now often held in outlying areas; an opportunity to see less explored districts and to once again rub shoulders with Florentines.

A BIT OF HISTORY

Italian genius flourished in Florence in a peacock display of brilliance. For three centuries, from the 13–16C, the city's exceptional artistic and intellectual activity left its mark on civilisation throughout Europe. During the Renaissance, a receptivity to the outside world, a dynamic open-minded attitude, and funding lured inventors, men of science and art to re-interpret and even surpass the achievements of the ancient world. **Dante** was not only a great poet but also a grammarian and

Practical Information

Getting There

◆ **By Air** – Amerigo Vespucci Airport (very small) serves major European capitals and is well connected by bus to the centre. *055 30 61 300. www.aeroporto.firenze.it.*
Florence lies at the foot of the Apennines in the Arno Valley. The city is situated where the A 1 and A 11 (Florence-coast route) meet.

Getting Around

Walking is by far the best way to explore the city. Autos and some car parks require permits. A good car park is at Fortezza da Basso; Santa Maria Novella station is costlier; beware incremental price increases, *www.firenzeparcheggi.it.*

◆ **By Buses** – ATAF *Tickets 90min, €1.20 (€2 on board); four tickets €4.70; tourist ticket 24hrs, €5; 3 days €12; 7 days €18; "Carta Agile," journeys, €10. www.ataf.net. 800 42 45 00.*
◆ **By Taxis** – *055 42 42, 055 43 90, or 055 47 98.*
◆ **Car Rental** – At the airport or in the city: Avis, Europcar, Hertz.
◆ **By Bicycle** – Cycling is a quick way of getting around Florence. Some hotels rent bicycles, or try Florence by Bike at Via San Zanobi 120r/122r (*www.florencebybike.it*).

Sightseeing

To avoid long queues visitors would be wise to buy tickets online for the Uffizi in advance. *055 29 48 83. www.uffizi.firenze.it (reservation necessary).*

Santa Maria del Fiore

historian, whose politics had him banished from Florence. **Giotto** was a painter, sculptor and architect. **Lorenzo the Magnificent**, a Florentine prince, incarnated the spirit of the Renaissance: a diplomat and pragmatic politician, a patron of the arts and poet that surrounded himself with the thinkers that created a new humanism. The Renaissance's most brilliant exponent may have been **Michelangelo**, painter, architect, sculptor and scholar; he typifies the Florentine quest for innovation and perfection.

Florence is set in the heart of a serenely beautiful **countryside**★★★ bathed by a soft, amber light. The low surrounding hills are clad with olive groves, vineyards and cypresses which appear harmoniously landscaped to please the human eye.

Such harmony is evident in the 13C campanile of La Badia by Arnolfo di Cambio, the campanile by Giotto, the façade of Santa Maria Novella by Alberti or the dome of Santa Maria del Fiore by Brunelleschi.

The beauty of these works seem a response to the beauty of the landscape and the light. The Florentine preoccupation with perspective throughout the 15C embraced the desire to re-create what the eye could see.

Great minds exchanged and pushed knowledge to the limits. Among the numerous wealthy families in Florence, it was the **Medici** leaders that exercised their influence most in the spheres of both fine arts and finance.

HIGHLIGHTS

Piazza del Duomo★★★

In the city centre, the cathedral, campanile and baptistry frame a beautiful square, demonstrating the traditions of Florentine art from the Middle Ages to the Renaissance.

Duomo (Santa Maria del Fiore)★★★

Open Mon–Sat 10am–5pm (earlier on Thu, 4.45pm Sat), Sun and hols 1.30–4.45pm (earlier on Thu, 4.45pm Sat). Crypt 10am–5pm.

Palazzo Vecchio, Piazza della Signoria

Cathedral free. €15, combined ticket for: cathedral, dome, baptistery, bell tower, crypt, museum.
055 23 02 885.
www.operaduomo.firenze.it.
One of the largest cathedrals in the Christian world, the Duomo is a symbol of the city's 13–14C power and wealth. It was begun in 1296 by Arnolfo di Cambio and consecrated in 1436.

The harmonious octagonal **dome★★★** by Brunelleschi took 14 years to build and to the present day remains the world's largest brick and mortar dome. To counteract the excessive weight he built two concentric domes, linked by props. Inside, the dome is painted with a huge fresco of the Last Judgement. The façade dates from the late-19C. The bareness of the interior contrasts sharply with the exterior's sumptuous decoration. The inner gallery offers an impressive view of the nave. Climb to the top of the dome (463 steps) to experience both its magnificent **panorama★★★** and its enormous scale, inside and out. The **Pazzi Conspiracy** took place

in the chancel, when the Pazzi, rivals of the Medici, assassinated Giuliano de' Medici and wounded his brother Lorenzo the Magnificent on 26 April 1478.

Campanile★★★
Open daily 8.30am–6.50pm (6 Jan: 1.20 pm). €15 (combined ticket: see Dome). 055 23 02 885.
www.operaduomo.firenze.it.
The tall slender white, red, and green marble bell tower (82m/269ft) complements the curves of Brunelleschi's dome. Giotto drew plans for it and began building in 1334.
The Gothic campanile was completed at the end of the 14C. The original bas-reliefs at the base of the campanile, designed by Giotto, are in the Cathedral Museum. The top (414 steps) offers a fine **panorama★★★**.

Battistero★★★
Open Mon–Sat, 8.15am–10.15 and 11.30am– 8pm, Sun 8.15am– 1.30pm. €15 (combined ticket: see Dome). 055 23 02 885.
www.operaduomo.firenze.it.

The **bronze doors**★★★ of the green and white marble baptistry, created by Andrea Pisano, Vittorio Ghiberti and Lorenzo Ghiberti are world famous. Michelangelo declared the east door (1425–52), facing the cathedral, worthy to be called the **Gate of Paradise**.
Interior – The interior is grand and majestic with its 25m/82ft diameter, its green-and-white marble and its paving decorated with Oriental motifs. The dome is covered with magnificent 13C **mosaics**★★★. On the right of the apse is the tomb of the anti-pope John XXIII, a work executed in 1427 by Donatello assisted by Michelozzo.

Museo dell'Opera di Santa Maria del Fiore★★
Piazza del Duomo 9. Open 9am–7pm. €15 (combined ticket, see Dome). 055 23 02 885. www.operaduomo.firenze.it
The museum exhibits works from the cathedral, campanile and baptistery. See models of Brunelleschi's dome, Michelangelo's famous unfinished **Pietà**, and admirable **bas-reliefs**★★ from the campanile.

Piazza della Signoria★★★
The political stage of Florence, past and present, has a wonderful backdrop formed by the Palazzo Vecchio, the Loggia della Signoria and, in the wings, the Uffizi Museum. Its many statues form an open-air museum.

Loggia della Signoria★★
The Loggia, built at the end of the 14C, was the assembly hall and later the guard room of the *Lanzi* (foot soldiers) of Cosimo I. Among its Classical and Renaissance statues is Cellini's Perseus.

Palazzo Vecchio★★★
Open daily Oct–Mar 9am–7pm, (Thu 2pm); Apr–Sept 9am–11pm (Thu 2pm). Last entry 1hr before closing. €10 (€14 combined ticket Palazzo Vecchio, Torre and tour of battlements). Closed hols. 055 27 68 325. www.museicivicifiorentini.comune.fi.it.
The Old Palace's powerful Gothic mass is dominated by a lofty bell tower opens into a **courtyard**★, restored in the 15C and to an interior of Renaissance refinement and splendour. The seat of government, the palace was taken over in the 16C by Cosimo I as his private residence; later abandoned it in favour of Pitti Palace it was renamed Palazzo Vecchio.
The apartments were decorated with sculptures by Benedetto and Giuliano da Maiano (15C) and paintings by Vasari and Bronzino (16C). The magnificent **studiolo**★★, was the study of Francesco de' Medici. In the Hall of the Five Hundred, a study is ongoing to see if Vasari's frescoes have covered earlier paintings by Leonardo da Vinci of The Battle of Anghiari.

Museo Gucci
Piazza della Signoria 10. Open daily 10am–8pm (Fri 10am–11pm). €7. 055 75 92 70 10. www.guccimuseo.com.
The museum extends over three floors, highlighting the 90-year history of this leather accessories company, a leader in the luxury goods market.

Galleria degli Uffizi★★★

*Open Tue–Sun 8.15am–6.50pm.
€8. Book in advance (add €4) to
avoid the long queues. Closed hols.
055 29 48 83. www.uffizi.it.*

One of the finest art museums in the
world, with collections assembled by
generations of Medici. The museum
follows the evolution of Italian art
from the 13–17C. The museum is
housed in a Renaissance palace
designed by Vasari in 1560, which
once housed the offices *(uffizi)* of
the Medici administration.
Among the artists displayed are
Giotto, Piero della Francesca, Beato
Angelico, Filippo Lippi, Botticelli,
Mantegna, Correggio, Leonardo,
Raphael, Michelangelo, Caravaggio,
Dürer, Rembrandt, and Rubens.

Ponte Vecchio★★

The oldest bridge in Florence,
originally lined with butcher shops,
switched to gold to reduce the
smell and add glitter. The **Corridoio
Vasariano**, a passageway linking
Palazzo Vecchio to the Pitti Palace
passes overhead and inside is lined
with self portraits of famous artists.

Palazzo Pitti★★

This 15C Renaissance building, of
rugged but imposing appearance,
pronounced rustication and many
windows, was built to the plans
of Brunelleschi for the Pitti family,
the rivals of the Medici. It was
Cosimo I's wife, Eleanora di Toledo,
who enlarged the palace by the
addition of two wings. The court
moved to the palace in 1560.

Galleria Palatina★★★

*Open Tue–Sun 8.15am–6.50pm
(last entry 45 min. before closing).
Closed hols. €8.50 combined ticket
with the Appartamenti Reali
and Galleria d'Arte Moderna.
055 23 88 614. www.uffizi.it.*

This gallery houses a marvellous
collection of paintings including
groups★★★ of works by Raphael
and Titian, the **Appartamenti
Reali★** (State Apartments) and
the **Galleria d'Arte Moderna★**
display mainly 19C and 20C Tuscan
works. The Silver Museum (**Museo
degli Argenti★★**) presents Medici
treasures and miniature portraits;
it also offers access to the Porcelain

Detail of The Birth of Venus *(1485) by Sandro Botticelli, Galleria degli Uffizi*

Museum, Costume Museum, and the gardens of Boboli and Bardini.

Giardino di Boboli★
Open daily 8.15am–7.30pm (6.30pm Apr, May, Sept, Oct; 5.30pm Mar; 4.30pm Nov–Feb). (last entry 1hr before closing). Closed hols. €7. 055 29 48 83. www.uffizi.it.
The Boboli Gardens were begun in 1549 when Cosimo I commissioned Tribolo to convert the hill behind the Pitti Palace into a vast garden. Together with Ammannati's courtyard and the terrace, it was to be the setting for the lavish pageants held by the Grand Dukes.
The park is a fine example of an Italian terraced garden with many different perspectives, interspersed with ramps, flights of steps and terraces and dotted with statues and fountains. The entrance is situated on the far side of the inner courtyard. The terrace is separated from the rear of the palace by the elegant Artichoke Fountain (Carciofo), built in 1641.

Palazzo e Museo Nazionale del Bargello★★★
Via del Proconsolo 4. Open daily 8.15am–2pm (1.20pm last admission). Closed hols. €8. 055 23 88 606. www.polomuseale. firenze.it/bargello.
Formerly the residence of the magistrate (*podestà*), then police headquarters (*bargello*), the palace's fine 13–14C medieval architecture centres around its majestic **courtyard★★** with a portico and loggia. This sculpture museum has masterpieces by Donatello, Cellini, Michelangelo, della Robbia, Giambologna and del Verrochio, and decorative arts.

Chiesa di San Lorenzo★★★
The Medici family **church★★**, where most were buried, was begun by Brunelleschi c. 1420. His great achievement is the **Old Sacristy★★**, decorated part by Donatello, as well as two **pulpits★★**.

Biblioteca Medicea Laurenziana★★
Piazza San Lorenzo 9. Open Mon–Fri 9.30am–1.30pm. 055 29 37 911. www.bmlonline.it.
Cosimo Medici's library was added to by Lorenzo the Magnificent. Charming 15C **cloisters★**. The vestibule has a magnificent **staircase★★** built by Ammannati to Michelangelo's designs. The **library** is also by Michelangelo.

Museo delle Cappelle Medicee★★
Piazza Madonna degli Aldobrandini 6. Open 8.15am–2pm. Closed hols. €8. 055 23 88 602. www.polomuseale.firenze.it.
The **Princes' Chapel** (17C–18C), grandiose but gloomy, is faced with semi-precious stones and is the funerary chapel for Cosimo I and his descendants. Michelangelo created the **Medici tombs★★★** for Giuliano and Lorenzo.

Palazzo Medici-Riccardi★★
Via Camillo Cavour 3. Open Thu–Tue 9am–7pm. Closed hols. €7. 055 27 60 340. www.palazzo-medici.it.
Michelozzo's 15C courtyard leads upstairs to the beautiful Chapel of the Magi with 15C frescoes, a colourful Renaissance pageant by Benozzo Gozzoli. A Medici residence, Lorenzo held court here 1459–1540.

Museo di San Marco★★
Piazza San Marco 3. Open daily Mon–Fri 8.15am–1.50pm (4.50pm. Sat–Sun and public hols). €4. 055 23 88 608. www.polomuseale.firenze.it.
Fra Angelico painted the Domenican chancel and monks' cells with edifying **frescoes★★★**, including an *Annunciation*.

Galleria dell'Accademia★★
Via Bettino Ricasoli 60. Open Tue–Sun, 8.15am–6.50pm. Closed hols. €8. 055 29 48 83. www.galleriaaccademiafirenze. beniculturali.it.
The **main gallery★★★** has the famous David by **Michelangelo**, as well as his four Prisoners and St. Matthew. The **picture gallery★** features 13–15C Tuscan masters including two Botticellis.

Opificio delle Pietre Dure★
Via degli Alfani 78. Open Mon–Sat 8.15am–2pm. Closed hols. €4. 055 26 51 348. www.opificio dellepietredure.it.
The museum holds works of the art of inlays of semi-precious stones that dazzle the eye with the intensity of their colours, purity, luminosity and detail. An ancient workshop has been fitted out on the upper floor.

Museo Archeologico★★
Piazza Santissima Annunziata 9b. Open Tue– Fri 8.30am–7pm (Mon, Sat and Sun 2pm). Closed hols. €4. 055 23 575. www.archeotoscana. beniculturali.it.
The museum has an important collection of Egyptian, Greek (**François Vase★★**), Etruscan (**Arezzo Chimera★★**) and Roman art. The mummies are in the quaint 19C Egyptian galleries.

Museo degli Innocenti
Piazza Santissima Annunziata 13. Open daily 10am–7pm (Thu 9.30am–10.30pm). €7. 848 08 23 80. www.istitutodeglinnocenti.it.
Inaugurated in June 2016, it details the essence of the institute throughout its six centuries of activity.

Chiesa di Santa Maria Novella★★
Piazza di Santa Maria Novella 18. Open Mon– Thu 9am–5.30pm (Apr–Sept 7pm), Fri 11am–5.30pm, Sat –5.30pm (Jul–Aug –6.30pm), Sun and hols 1–5.30pm (Jul–Aug noon–6.30pm). €5 (includes Cathedral and Cloisters). €5. 055 21 92 57. www.chiesasantamarianovella.it.
The Church of Santa Maria Novella and the adjoining monastery were founded in the 13C by the Dominicans. Frescoes and other works by a variety of artists.

Museo del Novecento
Antico spedale delle Leopoldine. Piazza Santa Maria Novella 10. Open Apr–Sept 9am–7pm (Thu 2pm, Fri 11pm); Oct–Mar 9am–6pm (Thu 2pm). Closed hols. €8.50. 055 28 61 32. www.museonovecento.it.
On a par with the best museums in the world, this institute is devoted to 19C Italian art, with a selection of some 300 works in 15 rooms, plus multimedia stations, video rooms and listening devices.

Palazzo Rucellai★★
Via della Vigna Nuova 18. Site is not open for visits.
The mansion, built between 1446 and 1451 by Bernardo Rossellino to plans by Leon Battista Alberti, was constructed for Giovanni Rucellai,

Basilica di Santa Croce

a member of a leading Florentine family. The mansion is the first example since Antiquity of a façade articulated by three orders.

Basilica di Santa Croce★★
Guided tour Mon–Sat 9.30am–5pm, Sun and hols 2–5pm. €8. Basilica, Cloister, Pazzi Chapel and museum. 055 24 66 105.
www.santacroceopera.it.
The church and cloisters of the 13–14C Santa Croce face one of the town's oldest squares. The **interior** is vast (140m x 40m/460ft x 130ft) and is paved with 276 tombstones. Michelangelo, composer Rossini (d. 1868), Lorenzo Ghiberti (d. 1455)and Galileo (d. 1642) are entombed here. The **Cappella dei Pazzi★★** by Brunelleschi is a masterpiece.

Museo della Fondazione Horne★
Via de' Benci 6. Open 9am–1pm. Closed Sun and hols. €7. 055 24 46 61. www.museohorne.it.
Herbert Percy Horne (1864–1916), English scholar and collector,

restored Palazzo Corsi to the atmosphere of a Florentine house during the Renaissance. Period furniture and art includes the Virgin and Child bas-relief by Sansovino, a St Stephen by Giotto, and the paintings of Dosso Dossi, Luca Signorelli, Masaccio, Pietro Lorenzetti, Benozzo Gozzoli, Domenico Beccafumi, Filippino Lippi and Simone Martini.
The first floor is distinguished especially by its leaded windows with lead rods and its lettuccio (bed). The tour concludes in the kitchen.

PASSEGGIATA AL VIALE DEI COLLI★★
2hrs on foot or 1hr by car.
East along the south bank of the Arno at the medieval tower in Piazza Poggi, take the winding street up to Piazzale Michelangelo for a splendid city **view★★★**. Uphill, the marvellous **setting★★** overlooking the town hosts the Florentine-Romanesque church of **San Miniato al Monte★★**.

LUCCA★★★

Situated in the centre of a fertile plain, Lucca has preserved a rich heritage of churches, palaces, squares and streets that give the town a charming air, unscathed by contemporary developments. The 16–17C ramparts (4km/2.5mi long) extend around the old town, including 11 bastions, linked by curtain walls, and four gateways. The province of Lucca is famous for its gracious villas (*see Michelin Green Guide Tuscany*).

Practical Information

Getting There
74km/46mi from Florence and 20km/12.4mi from Viareggio.

A BIT OF HISTORY

Lucca was colonised by the Romans in the 2C BC and has retained the plan of a Roman military camp, with the two principal streets perpendicular to one another. During the Middle Ages a system of narrow alleys and oddly shaped squares was added to the original network. The town became an independent commune at the beginning of the 12C and flourished until the mid-14C with the silk trade. In the early-14C the town's prosperity and prestige grew under Castruccio Castracani (d. 1328). Lucca's finest religious and secular buildings date from this period. Luccan architects adopted the Pisan style to which they added their characteristic refinement and fantasy. From 1550 onwards the town became an important agricultural centre and with this new prosperity came a renewed interest in building. The countryside was dotted with villas. In the early-19C, Elisa Bonaparte ruled the city for a brief period from 1805 to 1813. Following Napoleon's Italian campaigns he bestowed the titles of Princess of Lucca and Piombino on his sister.

Elisa showed a remarkable aptitude for public affairs and ruled her fief with wisdom and intelligence, encouraging the development of the town and the arts.

OLD TOWN

The atmospheric streets and squares of old Lucca have Gothic and Renaissance palaces, noble towers, old shops, sculptured doorways and coats of arms, wrought-iron railings and balconies.

HIGHLIGHTS

Duomo★★ – The cathedral, dedicated to St Martin, was rebuilt in the 11C, with changes in the 13–15C. The green-and-white marble **façade★★** is striking in its asymmetry. The upper section is the first example of the Pisan-Romanesque style (*see PISA*) as it developed in Lucca, with lighter, less rigid lines and inventive ornamentation. The campanile harmoniously combines the use of brick and marble. Works of art inside include examples by Nicola Pisano and Tintoretto.

Chiesa di San Michele in Foro★★ – The white 12–14C church on the site of the Roman forum has an exceptionally tall **façade★★**, a good example of Lucca-Pisan style.

Chiesa di San Frediano★ – This great church, dedicated to St Frigidian, was rebuilt in the original Lucca-Romanesque style in the 12C. The sober façade is faced with marble from the amphitheatre.

PISA★★★

Pisa's Campo dei Miracoli reflects past splendours and the enormous artistic influence it had from the 11–14C. Near the sea, set like Florence along the Arno River, Pisa is spacious and joyous with its yellow and pink houses. Be sure to take a meander past the famous Piazza del Duomo UNESCO World Heritage Site and into the city, too, almost totally encircled by walls and lively with its university, shops and restaurants.

A BIT OF HISTORY

Sheltered from raiding pirates, Pisa was a Roman naval base and commercial port until the end of the Empire (5C). A mighty independent maritime republic from the 9C, Pisa became the rival of Genoa and Venice, and the Pisans even waged war against the Saracens. Pisa reached the peak of its power and prosperity in the 12–13C, marked by the construction of fine buildings, including the famous leaning tower (begun in 1173) and the university. The 1284 defeat of the Pisan fleet at the **Battle of Meloria**, along with internal strife, broke Pisa's maritime empire. Pisa passed under Florentine rule, where the Medici took a special interest, as patron of the astronomer and physicist **Galileo** (1564–1642). The **Pisan-Romanesque style**, is most sublimely expressed in the cathedral's external decoration– the alternate-coloured marbles,

Practical Information

Getting There

Pisa is near the mouth of the Arno. Parco Naturale di Migliarino-San Rossore-Massaciuccoli is between Pisa and the sea.

♦ **Airport – Pisa International Airport** (Galileo Galilei) is served by a number of low-cost carriers (Ryanair, Easyjet, etc), as well as Delta and major European carriers. Well connected by bus to Florence, Siena, Lucca, Viareggio and to central Pisa. *050 849 300. www.pisa-airport.com.*

geometric patterns, its play of light and shadow, its strong mix of Islamic and Christian influences– reflect the reach of the maritime Republic. Sculptors **Nicola Pisano** and his son **Giovanni Pisano** (1250–c.1315) helped make Pisa a centre for Gothic sculpture.

Piazza del Duomo

PIAZZA DEL DUOMO (CAMPO DEI MIRACOLI)★★★

Cathedral): Open daily 10am–6pm (Apr–Sept 8pm). Battistero, Museo delle Sinopie e Camposanto: open daily 9am–6pm; Museo dell'Opera del Duomo closed for repairs at the time of writing. Last entry 30min before closing. €5, €7 joint ticket for two museums, €8 joint ticket for three museums. 050 80 50 11/12. www.opapisa.it.

In and around this famous square, also known as "Campo dei Miracoli" (Field of Miracles), are four buildings that form one of the finest architectural complexes in the world. It is advisable to approach on foot from the west through the Porta Santa Maria for the best view of the Leaning Tower.

Duomo★★

www.opapisa.it.

Construction of this splendid cathedral began in 1063 under Buscheto; Rainaldo designed the façade. The light and graceful **west front★★★** has four tiers of small marble columns; its facing alternates light- and dark-coloured marble. The plan is a Latin cross. The **bronze doors★** cast in 1602 are by Giambologna. The south transept door has very fine Romanesque bronze **panels★★** (late-12C) by Bonanno Pisano, depicting the Life of Christ. The **interior** (100m/330ft long) has 4 aisles, a deep apse, a three-aisled transept and a forest of columns.

Note the beautiful 1302–11 **pulpit★★★** by **Giovanni Pisano**.

Torre Pendente★★★

300 winding steps lead to the top. Open daily 9am–6pm (Apr–Sept 8pm). Last entry 30min before closing. €18 (includes Cathedral). Under-8s not allowed. 050 83 50 11. www.opapisa.it.

The **Leaning Tower of Pisa** is both a bell tower and a belfry. This white-marble tower (58m/189ft high) was begun in 1173 in a pure Romanesque style by Bonanno Pisano and completed in 1350. Built like the towers of Byzantium as a cylinder, the tower has six storeys of galleries with columns that seem to wind round in a spiral because of the slope of the building.

The tower slowly began leaning in 1178 and has continued to do so at a rate of between 1mm and 2mm a year (or half an inch over a typical decade). The movement is caused by the alluvial soil on which the tower is built; soil that is insufficiently resistant to bear the weight of the building. A number of restorations have had varying success in preventing its collapse.

Battistero★★★

www.opapisa.it.

The baptistry, begun in 1153, has two Pisan-Romanesque lower storeys, while the frontons and pinnacles above are Gothic. The majestic interior is full of light and has a diameter of 35m/115ft. The centre has a lovely octagonal **font★** (1246) by Guido Bigarelli. Its masterpiece is the admirable **pulpit★★** (1260) by Nicola Pisano.

Historic centre of Siena

SIENA★★★

Siena embodies the vision of a medieval city. With its yellowish-brown buildings (in the colour "sienna") the city, encircled by ramparts, extends over three converging clay hills. As a centre for the arts, Siena entices with its maze of narrow streets, lined with tall palaces and patrician mansions, which come together on the famous Piazza del Campo.

Practical Information

Getting There

Siena is 68km/42.3mi from Florence. Raccordo Autostrada Siena-Firenze links Siena with Florence.

A BIT OF HISTORY

Siena's greatest period of prosperity was the 13–14C, when it was an independent republic. The **Guelphs** versus **Ghibellines** conflict pitted Siena against its powerful neighbour Florence. The Battle of Montaperti (1260) was one of few where the Sienese Ghibellines defeated the Florentine Guelphs. During this time Siena acquired her most prestigious buildings, and a local school of painting evolved that played an influential role in the development of Italian art.

The mystical city of Siena was the birthplace in 1347 of **St Catherine**, who in 1377 helped to bring the popes back from Avignon to Rome. **St Bernardine** (1380–1444) helped victims of a plague and as a Franciscan preached throughout Italy. Weakened from 1348 onwards by the plague and by internal strife, by the early 15C Siena's golden era was over.

SIENESE ART

Sienese art followed Greek and Byzantine traditions. Graceful lines and the refinement of colour gave dazzling elegance. **Duccio di Buoninsegna** (c.1255–1318/19) combined inner spirituality with space and composition. **Simone Martini** (c.1284–d.1344 in Avignon), painter at the Papal Court in Avignon, was known throughout Europe. **Pietro** and **Ambrogio Lorenzetti** introduced great realism with minute delicate details. The sculptor **Jacopo della Quercia** (1371–1438) combined Gothic traditions with the Florentine-Renaissance style.

PIAZZA DEL CAMPO★★★

The scallop-shaped basin slopes down from the Palazzo Pubblico, with eight white lines radiating to create nine segments, each symbolising one of the forms of government that ruled Siena from the late-13C to the mid-14C.
At the upper end is the **Fonte Gaia** (Fountain of Joy). Twice annually the Piazza del Campo hosts the **Palio delle Contrade**, a costume procession followed by a dangerous horse race.

Palazzo del Comune (Pubblico)★★★

Open mid Mar–Oct 10am–7pm; Nov–mid-Mar 6pm. €9. €20 combined with Torre del Mangia and Museo S. Maria Scala (closed Tue). 0577 29 22 32. www.comune.siena.it.
The 13-14C Gothic city hall was the seat of Siena's governments and decorated by famous Sienese artists. The tower offers a superb **panorama★★** of chaotic rooftops and rolling countryside.

HIGHLIGHTS

Duomo★★★

Open Mar–1 Nov 10.30am–7pm (Sun and hols 1.30–6pm); 2 Nov–Feb 5.30pm (Sun and hols 1.30–5.30pm). €4-7. 0577 28 63 00. www.operaduomo.siena.it.
The black and white striped façade of the cathedral was begun in the 13C by Giovanni Pisano. Its unique 15–16C **paving★★★**, made by some 40 artists including **Beccafumi**, has 56 marble panels portraying mythological figures. The **pulpit★★★** was carved from 1266–1268 by **Nicola Pisano**. In front of the church, the

Complesso museale di Santa Maria della Scala (*www.santa mariadellascala.com*).

Museo dell'Opera Metropolitana★★

Open Mar–1 Nov 10.30am–7pm; 2 Nov–Feb 5.30pm. €7. 0577 28 63 00. www.operaduomo.siena.it.
The museum is in the extant part of a vast building started in 1339. The museum contains the *Maestà* (Virgin in Majesty) by Duccio.

Battistero di San Giovanni★

Open Mar–Oct 10.30am–7pm; 2 Nov–Feb 5.30pm. €4. 0577 28 63 00. www.operaduomo.siena.it.
This 14C baptistery is decorated with 15C frescoes.

Pinacoteca Nazionale★★

Via San Pietro 29. Open Tue–Sat 8.15am–7.15pm, Sun–Mon and hols 9am–1pm. €4. 0577 28 11 61. www.pinacotecanazionale.siena.it.
The 15C **Palazzo Buonsignori★** houses extensive 13–16C Sienese art including works by Duccio, Martini, Lorenzetti, Beccafumi.

Via di Città★, Via Banchi di Sopra

These flagstoned streets are bordered by remarkable **palaces★**.

Basilica di San Domenico★

St Catherine experienced her trances in this 13–15C Gothic conventual church.

EXCURSION

Abbazia di Monte Oliveto Maggiore★★

36km/22.4mi SE of Siena.
In this rose-coloured **abbey** don't miss the **Signorelli** frescoes.

SAN GIMIGNANO★★★

Rising up from the Val d'Elsa like a city of skyscrapers, San Gimignano is surrounded by rolling countryside dotted with vines and olive trees. Its 14 grey-stone towers set on a hilltop are enclosed within an outer wall. This small medieval town has been amazingly well preserved.

Practical Information

Getting There

From Florence or Siena take the Raccordo Autostrada Siena-Firenze to Poggibonsi (*13km/8mi from Poggibonsi*).

HIGHLIGHTS

Piazza della Cisterna★★

The herringbone pattern brick square has a 13C cistern, or well (*cisterna*). One of the most evocative squares in Italy with its tall towers and 13–14C mansions, it's a good spot to pause for *gelato* or the local white wine, Vernaccia.

Piazza del Duomo★★

The collegiate church, palaces and seven towers line this majestic square.

Collegiata★ (Santa Maria Assunta)

Open Apr–Oct 10am–7.30pm (Sat 5.30pm); Nov–Mar 10am–5pm. €4 (with Cappella di Santa Fina), €6 combined with Museo di Arte Sacra. 0577 28 63 00. www.duomosangimignano.it.
This 12C Romanesque church, extended in the 15C by Giuliano da Maiano, has splendid **frescoes★**: *Martyrdom of St Sebastian* (1465) by Benozzo Gozzoli; *Annunciation* by Jacopo della Quercia; Taddeo di Bartolo (14C) depicts **the Last Judgment★★** (1393); Barna da Siena depicts scenes from the Life of Christ. **Cappella di Santa Fina**, designed by Giuliano da Maiano, has an **altar★** by nephew Benedetto da Maiano and **frescoes★** (1475) by D. Ghirlandaio.

Palazzo del Popolo★

The 13–14C town hall has a tall **tower** with a city **view★★**; the Council Chamber features a remarkable **Maestà★** (Madonna and Child Enthroned, 1317) by L. Memmi; and **The Museo Civico★**.

EXCURSIONS

San Vivaldo★

17km/10.6mi NW. Open Apr–Oct Mon–Sat 3–7pm, Sun 10am; Nov–Mar 2–5pm. €5. 0571 69 92 67. www.sanvivaldointoscana.com.
Built in 1500, the chapels of the Franciscan monastery of San Vivaldo (d. 1320) re-create Jerusalem in miniature.

Certaldo

13km/8mi N.
This hilltop village features the **Casa Boccaccio** (*open Apr–Oct 9.30am–1.30pm and 2.30–4.30pm, Nov–Mar 9.30am–1.30pm and 2.30pm–4.30; closed Tue; €3; 0571 66 12 65; www.casaboccaccio.it*) former home and current museum of the great Italian writer **Giovanni Boccaccio** (1312–75), who wrote *The Decameron*; he is buried in the church of San Jacopo. **Palazzo Pretorio** was rebuilt 16C. The town also has nice ceramic and print shops.

ASSISI★★★

The walled city of Assisi, birthplace of St Francis, transmits an aura of tranquillity. The son of a rich Assisi textile merchant, Francis preached poverty, joy, humility, respect for nature and mysticism. The Franciscan Order of Minors founded by St Francis (c.1181–1226), inspired a new, religious, artistic movement and a turning point in Italian art. During the 13C the stark, austere churches were embellished with a new splendour to reflect the tender love of St Francis for nature and its creatures, as described in his canticles and the tales of St Bonaventure. From the end of the 14C famous masters came from Rome and Venice to Assisi to work on the Basilica of St Francis. The rigid traditions of Byzantine art were replaced by a more dramatic art imbued with a spiritual atmosphere. Cimabue and later Giotto were its most powerful exponents.

Practical Information

Getting There

Assisi spreads prettily across the slope of Monte Subasio and lies between Perugia and Foligno, on the SS 75.

HIGHLIGHTS

Basilica di San Francesco★★★

Piazza San Francesco. Basilica Inferiore (Lower Basilica) and Tomba: Open daily 6am–6.50pm. Basilica Superiore (Upper Basilica): Open daily 8.30am–6.50pm. 075 81 90 01. www.sanfrancescoassisi.org.
The basilica is an imposing vision at all hours. The complex consists of two churches, resting on a series of immense arches. The whole building, erected soon after the death of St Francis to the plans of Brother Elias, was consecrated in 1253. The interior **frescoes**, include a famous cycle by Giotto and his assistants depicting the life of St Francis.

Rocca Maggiore★★

The walls of this 12C fortress provide a spectacular **view★★★** of the Spoleto Valley below.

Via San Francesco★

This picturesque street is lined with medieval and Renaissance houses. At no. 13a the Pilgrims' Chapel (Oratorio dei Pellegrini) is decorated inside with 15C frescoes.

Piazza del Comune★

Note the **Tempio di Minerva★** (1C BC), a temple converted into a church, and the People's Captains' Palace (13C).

Duomo di San Rufino★

The 12C cathedral has a Romanesque **façade★★**. Inside is the baptismal font used for the baptism of St Francis, St Clare and Frederick II.

Chiesa di Santa Chiara★★

From the terrace in front of the church of St Clare there is a pretty view of the Umbrian countryside. The church was built from 1257–1265 (*www.assisisantachiara.it*).

PERUGIA★★

Perugia was one of the twelve Etruscan city-states in the 7C and 6C BC. The town has retained many lovely buildings from the Middle Ages. The Renaissance-era Collegio del Cambio houses frescoes by artist and master Pietro Vannucci, called Perugino, whose works are also in the Galleria Nazionale dell'Umbria and on the walls of Rome's Sistine Chapel. Umbria's capital and largest city today is an industrial and commercial centre and a vibrant university town.

Practical Information

Getting There

Perugia is perched atop a hill, in the heart of Umbria. The E 45 road links the town with Emilia Romagna.

HIGHLIGHTS

Piazza IV Novembre★★

This square in the heart of Perugia, one of the grandest in Umbria, has the chief buildings of the city's glorious past: the Priors' Palace, houses the Collegio del Cambio; Collegio della Mercanzia; and the Galleria Nazionale dell'Umbria, the cathedral; and the Great Fountain. Leading off the square is **Via Maestà delle Volte★** with its medieval houses and passages.

Galleria Nazionale dell'Umbria★★

Corso Vannucci 19. Open Tue–Sun 8.30am–7.30pm. €8. 199 15 11 23. www.gallerianazionaleumbria.it. The National Gallery of Umbria, in the Priors' Palace, displays Umbrian art from the 13C to the late-18C. Highlights: *Madonna* by Duccio, a **polyptych of St Anthony** by Piero della Francesca, and works by Fra Angelico, Perugino, Boccati and Fiorenzo di Lorenzo.

Fontana Maggiore★★

The Great Fountain (1278) has 25 panels sculpted by Nicola Pisano (lower) and son Giovanni (upper).

Palazzo dei Priori★★

The grand 13C Priors' Palace façade has a majestic outside staircase with a marble pulpit from which the priors harangued the people.

Chiesa di San Pietro★★

Through **Porta San Pietro★**, a majestic but unfinished 10C church, remodelled during the Renaissance, has 11 excellent canvases by Vassilacchi, a Greek contemporary of El Greco. Note the **carved tabernacle** by Mino da Fiesole and the marvellous 16C **intarsia choir★★**, a masterpiece of inlaid wood.

Museo Archeologico Nazionale dell'Umbria★★

Piazza G. Bruno 10. Open Tue–Sun 8.30am–7.30pm (Mon 10am–7.30pm). €5. 075 57 27 141. www.archeopg.arti.beniculturali.it. The National Archaeological Museum's prehistoric, Etruscan and Umbrian collections. The 3C BC **Cippo Perugino** (Perugia Stone), a travertine slab, is believed to be an Etruscan property contract.

Oratorio di San Bernardino★★

This Renaissance jewel (1461) by Agostino di Duccio is harmonious, has delicate multicoloured marbles, and sculptures.

ORVIETO★★

Orvieto rises dramatically from vertical cliffs of tuff; a remarkable **site★★★**. Once a major Etruscan centre, later Papal stronghold, Clement VII took refuge here in 1527 when Rome was sacked by King Charles. Vineyards below produce a pleasant white wine, Orvieto Classico.

Practical Information

Getting There

Orvieto is situated in southern Umbria, northwest of Lake Bolsena. The main access road is the A 1.

DUOMO★★★

Cappella di San Brizio: Open daily Nov–Feb 9.30am–1pm and 2.30–5pm, Mar–Oct 9.30am–6pm, Apr–Sept 9.30am–7pm. Closed Sun morning. €5 (ticket office in Piazza del Duomo 26). 0763 34 35 92. www.opsm.it.

The Romanesque-Gothic cathedral was begun in 1290 to enshrine the relics of the Miracle of Bolsena. Over 100 architects, sculptors, painters and mosaicists took part in the building, completed in 1600. Don't miss the frescoes by Luca Signorelli: his Last Judgment probably inspired Michelangelo's in the Sistine Chapel in Rome. **Palazzi Papali★** (**Museo dell'Opera**; *Nov–Feb 10am–1pm and 2–5pm, Apr–Sept 9.30am–7pm, Oct – Mar 10am–5pm. Closed Tue. €5 combined with Cappella di San Brizio; 0763 34 35 92. www. museomodo.it*) is boldest in structure and richest in colour among Italian-Gothic buildings. The original **façade★★★** (c. 1310–30) was by the Sienese Lorenzo Maitani, and developed by Andrea Pisano, Andrea Orcagna and Sanmicheli. Maitani was also responsible for the **bas-reliefs★★** (left to right): *Genesis, Jesse's Tree,* *Scenes from the New Testament* and the *Last Judgement*. Inside, the nave and aisles are roofed with timber. Gothic vaulting covers the transepts and the chancel.

UNDERGROUND ORVIETO

Piazza Duomo 23. Guided tours only. €6. 347 38 31 472. www.orvietounderground.it.

Orvieto lies on a bed of volcanic earth, with underground chambers (already present in Etruscan times) dug out of the hill. These caves (officially more than 1 000) hold medieval niches for funerary urns, the foundations of a 14C oil mill and a 6C BC well.

POZZO DI SAN PATRIZIO★★

Open daily, Nov–Feb 10am–4.45pm; Mar– Apr and Sept –Oct 9am–6.45pm; May–Aug 9am–7.45pm. €5. 0763 34 37 68.

St Patrick's Well (62m/203ft deep) was commissioned by Pope Clement VII de' Medici to supply the town with water in case of siege.

QUARTIERE VECCHIO★

This quiet quarter has retained its old houses, medieval towers and churches, including San Giovenale, decorated by 13C–15C frescoes.

GUBBIO★★

The small town of Gubbio, spread out over the slopes of Monte Ingino, has preserved its rich cultural and artistic heritage almost intact. Encircling ramparts, buildings of warm yellow stone roofed with Roman tiles, and towers and palaces outlined against a grim landscape, make it easy to imagine the harsh atmosphere of the Middle Ages.

Practical Information

Getting There
Gubbio lies off S 298, 40km/24.8mi from Perugia, in northeastern Umbria; it's a gateway to Le Marche.

OLD TOWN★★
Piazza Grande stands at the heart of the charming but austere Old Town, with its steep, narrow streets spanned by arches. The houses, flanked by palaces and towers, often double as ceramic artist's workshops. The façades sometimes have two doors; coffins were brought out through the narrower Door of Death. The most picturesque streets are Via Piccardi, Baldassini, dei Consoli, XX Settembre, Galeotti and those along the river, leading to Piazza 40 Martiri.

Palazzo dei Consoli★★
Piazza Grande. Open daily Mon–Fri 10am–1pm and 3–6pm (Sat–Sun 10am–1.30pm and 2.30–6pm); *Nov–Mar 10am–1pm and 2.30–5.30pm (Sat–Sun 10am–1.30pm and 2.30–6pm). €5. 075 92 74 298. www.museiunitigubbio.it.*
Overlooking Piazza Grande, this imposing Gothic building, supported by great arches rising above Via Baldassini, has a majestic façade that reflects the palace's internal plan. The stairway leads up to the vast hall *(salone)* where assemblies were held and which contains statues and stonework. The Museo Civico feataures the **Tavole Eugubine**, bronze tablets (2–1C BC) which are inscribed in Umbria's ancient language.

Palazzo Ducale★
Via F. da Montefeltro. Open daily 8.30am–7.30pm (closed Mon only Feb–Mar). €5. 075 92 7 872. www.comune.gubbio.pg.it.
The Ducal Palace, which dominates the town, was built from 1470 onwards for Federico de Montefeltro. The design is attributed to Laurana.

Palazzo dei Consoli

EMILIA-ROMAGNA

The western part of the region derives its name from the Via Emilia, a straight Roman road that crosses from Piacenza to Rimini. The south eastern half of the region is Romagna, once governed over by Ravenna, an outpost of the Byzantine Empire. Emilia Romagna has long been a breadbasket for Italy and is considered the country's gastronomic heart. Prosciutto di Parma, Parmesan cheese and balsamic vinegar from Modena are among the region's most famous products. Mortadella salami , meat sauces, and tortellini, among other dishes, originated in Bologna, the culinary capital.

Emilia Romagna is neatly divided into north and south by the Via Emilia (S 9), along which most of the region's major cities are situated. To the north, the vast Po Plain (Pianura Padana), which also touches Lombardy and Veneto, stretches the length of Emilia Romagna, making it one of Italy's most productive agricultural regions. Large areas are given over to vines and fruit trees, kiwis, peaches and plums

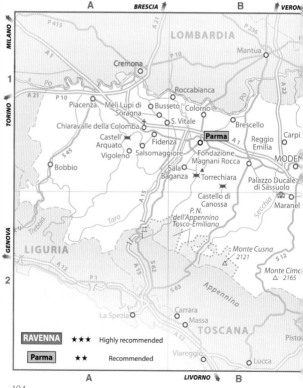

being particularly prolific. South of the Via Emilia are the slopes of the Apennine Mountains, separating Emilia Romagna from Tuscany and Marche. These mountains, the Tosco-Emiliano and Tosco-Romagnolo ranges, are home to wild boars and deer, which inhabit the thick beech, chestnut and conifer forests. The independent Republic of San Marino occupies a small perch of the Apennines at the border with Le Marche in a picturesque area.

The Po River runs into the sea in a wide delta between Ravenna and Venice; parts of this land are devoted to rice growing. Among the many lagoons are the Valli di Comacchio, well known for their eels. The Adriatic Coast also has long stretches of sandy beach. The cities of Ferrara and Parma are especially elegant with historic castles, palaces, first-rate museums and prestigious cultural events. Modena as the home of Ferrari, lures racing buffs and nearby Cremona is home to violin makers. This area is one of Italy's most prosperous regions.

BOLOGNA★★

The Emilian city of Bologna is often referred to as *dotta, grassa e rossa* (learned, fat and red). Wise it is indeed, thanks to its university – founded in 1088, it is considered the world's oldest – and an intense cultural life. The 'fat' refers to the city's gastronomic opulence and traditionally rich style of cooking. Its "redness", which over time has acquired political connotations, refers to the colour of its masonry. The city centre buzzes with activity and is dotted with towers and an incredible 37km/23mi of arcades.

A BIT OF HISTORY

The Etruscan settlement of *Felsina* was conquered in the 4C BC by the Boïan Gauls, whom the Romans then drove out in 190 BC. Their settlement, *Bononia* fell under the sway of the barbarians until the 12C. In the subsequent century, the city enjoyed the status of an independent commune and developed rapidly. A fortified city was built, and the university flourished. Against the Ghibellines and the emperor, Bologna

---

Practical Information

Getting There

Bologna is well placed for access to the Adriatic and Tuscan coasts, as well as the Dolomites. Situated at an important motorway interchange, the city has access to the A 1, the A 14 to the Adriatic and the A 13. It is also near the beginning of the A 22, the Brenner Transalpine route.

◆ **By Air** – Guglielmo Marconi **Airport** is situated 6km/3.7mi NW of the city in Borgo Panigale. *051 64 79 615. www.bologna-airport.it.*

◆ **By Car** – Situated 121km/75mi from Florence, 215km/133mi from Milan and 150km/93mi from Venice, Bologna is at a key intersection of a busy motorway network. Those intending to stay in the city for a while should park and use public transport to get around.

◆ **By Train** – The railway station is in Piazza Medaglie d'Oro, at the end of Via dell'Indipendenza. Buses nos. A, 25, 27 and 11 go to Piazza Maggiore

◆ **By Aerobus** – The public Aerobus connects the airport, the city centre and the railway station; during trade fairs it also runs through the *fiera* district (*aerobus.bo.it; €6*).

Getting Around

◆ **Public Transport** – Bologna has a wide public transport network. Purchase tickets at ATC offices, authorised vendors and automated machines. Tickets (*www.tper.it*): the City pass (€12) provides 10 journeys, can be used by one or more people at the same time; one-day tickets (€5); one-hour tickets (€1.30) are valid for 75min in the daytime. *051 29 02 90. www.tper.it.*

◆ **By Taxis** – CO.TA.BO. (Cooperativa Taxisti Bolognesi) *051 37 27 27. www.cotabo.it* and C.A.T. (Consorzio Autonomo Taxisti) radiotaxi *051 45 90. www.taxibologna.it.*

Visiting

Girotp City Tour – *051 37 94 52. www.cityredbus.com. €13.* An open-top tourist bus that covers the city's main highlights in around an hour. An easy way to get your bearings.

supported the Guelphs, partisans of communal independence. The latter won, defeating the Imperial Army of Frederick II at Fossalta in 1249.

In the 15C, following violent clan struggles, the city fell to the **Bentivoglio** family who ruled until 1506. The city then remained under Papal control until the arrival of Napoleon. The Austrians severely repressed several insurrections in the early-19C. Bologna was united with Piemonte in 1860.

The **Bologna school of painting** was an artistic movement founded by the brothers Agostino (1557–1602) and Annibale (1560–1609) with their cousin Ludovico (1555–1619) **Carracci**. They reacted against Mannerism with more "Classical" compositions that tried to express a simple spirituality.

Numerous artists – in particular the Bolognese painters **Francesco Albani**, **Guercino**, **Domenichino** and the celebrated **Guido Reni** – followed this movement, known as the **Accademia degli Incamminati** (Academy of the Eclectic), focusing on the study of nature. In 1595 Annibale Carracci moved to Rome to work on a commission for the Farnese family. His frescoes at Palazzo Farnese veer towards an almost Baroque illusionism.

CITY CENTRE★★★

The two adjoining squares, **Piazza Maggiore** and **Piazza del Nettuno★★★**, a harmonious ensemble, form the heart of Bologna together with **Piazza di Porta Ravegnana★★** nearby.

Fontana del Nettuno★★

This vigorous fountain is the work of Flemish sculptor Giambologna (1529–1608). The gigantic muscular bronze Neptune is surrounded by four sirens spouting water from their breasts.

Basilica di San Petronio★★
Piazza Galvani 5.
Open daily 7.45am–6pm.
www.basilicadisanpetronio.it.

The basilica, dedicated to St Petronius, was begun in 1390 to the plans of Antonio di Vincenzo (1340–1402) and ended in the 17C. The unfinished façade is remarkable

City centre

chiefly for the expressive reliefs over the **doorway★★** created by Jacopo della Quercia.

The **interior** is immense and has many **works of art★** including frescoes by Giovanni da Modena (15C) in the first and the fourth chapels. Near the basilica is the **Museo Civico Archeologico** and the 16C **Palazzo dell'Archiginnasio** (Piazza Galvani 1. *Mon–Fri 9am–6pm, Sat 7pm, Sun and hols 10am–2pm. www.archiginnasio. it*), home of an extensive library (10.000 manuscripts) and the 17–18C Anatomy Theatre (*Teatro Anatomico; open Mon–Fri 10am–6pm, Sat 7pm, Sun and hols 14pm*).

Santa Maria della Vita
Via Clavature 10. Tue–Sun 10am–7pm. 051 23 02 60. www.genusbononiae.it.
Stunning for its dramatic effect is the almost life-size terracotta sculptural group by Niccolò dell'Arca. His **Pietà★★**, or 'Lamentation of Christ' is an Italian masterpiece of the 15C, capturing the horror of the moment in its emotionally-charged figures.

Museo Civico Archeologico★★
Via dell'Archiginnasio 2. Open Tue–Fri 9am–3pm, Sat–Sun and hols 10am–6.30pm. €5. 051 27 57 211. www.iperbole. bologna.it/museoarcheologico.
The collection features Greek and Egyptian artifacts as well as ancient coins. The museum also has prehistoric, Roman and Etrusco-Italic sections, with a fine Roman copy of the head of Phidias' *Athena Lemnia*. Ornate funerary items (7C BC) were found in tombs of the

Verucchio necropolis near Rimini, a centre of the Villanovan culture.

Le Due Torri★★
These two leaning towers in Piazza di Porta Ravegnana belonged to noble families and are symbols of the continual conflict between the rival Guelphs and Ghibellines. The taller, **Torre degli Asinelli**, nearly 100m/330ft high, dates from 1109. The 486 steps to the top lead to an admirable **panorama★★** of the city (*Torre degli Asinelli: open daily summer 9am–7pm; rest of the year 9am–5pm; €3; www. bolognawelcome.com*). The second, **Torre Garisenda**, is 50m/164ft high and has a tilt of over 3m/10ft. The handsome 14C Palazzo della Mercanzia or Merchants' House, in the next square, bears the coats of arms of the various guilds and now houses the Chamber of Commerce.

OUTSIDE THE CENTRE

Strada Maggiore★
Along this elegant street, lined with some fine palaces (note Casa Isolani at no. 19, rare 13C architecture with a wooden portico), is the **Museo Civico d'Arte Industriale e Galleria Davia Bargellini** (*open Tue–Sat 9am–2pm, Sun 9am–1pm; free; 051 23 67 08; www.museibologna.it*), housed in a 1658 palace (at no. 44), which has collections of applied and decorative arts, and paintings from the 14–18C.

The 14C church of **Santa Maria dei Servi** is heralded by a Renaissance quadrisection **portico★**. Inside, in the third chapel on the right, there is a **Maestà★★** by Cimabue.

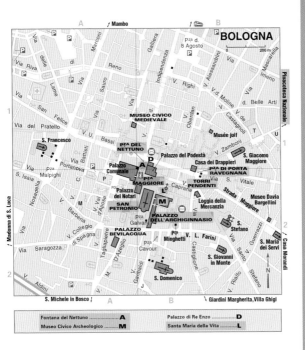

| Fontana del Nettuno | A |
| Museo Civico Archeologico | M |

| Palazzo di Re Enzo | D |
| Santa Maria della Vita | L |

Pinacoteca Nazionale★★

Via Belle Arti 56. Tue–Wed 9am–1.30pm, Thu–Sun and hols 2–7pm. €6. 051 42 09 411. www.pinacotecabologna. beniculturali.it. Closed hols.

An important collection, predominantly of the Bolognese school (13C–18C), here are the energetic **St George and the Dragon**★ by Vitale da Bologna and Giotto's *Madonna Enthroned and Child*. The **Carracci Room**★★ contains numerous masterpieces by Ludovico.

Basilica di Santo Stefano★

Via Santo Stefano 24. Open daily 8am–9pm. Donations welcome. 051 22 32 56.

The basilica comprises a group of buildings (originally seven)

overlooking the square with its Renaissance mansions. Entrance is through the **Church of the Crucifix** (Crocifisso), an old Lombard cathedral restored in the 11C and remodelled in the 19C. Turning left make for the atmospheric 12C **Church of the Holy Sepulchre** (Santo Sepolcro) and the shrine of Bologna's patron saint, St Petronius. The black cipolin marble columns were originally part of the ancient Temple of Isis (AD 100), converted to a baptistery and later into a church. The font, originally consecrated with water from the Nile, was reconsecrated with water from Jordan.

BOLOGNA

FERRARA★★

Ferrara's stunning historic centre is a UNESCO World Heritage Site. Already important in the Middle Ages, the city thrived as a cultural centre during the Renaissance. In this stylish and tranquil city, bicycles are a popular way to get around. Prestigious galleries and numerous events make Ferrara a major cultural centre in Italy. Lucrezia Borgia, who is buried here, arrived in Ferrara after her 1502 marriage to Alfonso d'Este. Film director Michelangelo Antonioni was born here.

Practical Information

Getting There
Near the Po Delta, off the A 13, which links Bologna with Padua.

A BIT OF HISTORY

Patrons of the Arts
Initially an independent commune, Ferrara belonged to the **Este** family from 1208 to 1598. Despite numerous family dramas, often bloody, the Estes embellished their native city with fine buildings and patronised both men of letters and artists. **Niccolò III** (1393–1441) murdered his wife Parisina and her lover but he begat **Lionello** and **Borso**, moulding them into efficient administrators and enlightened patrons. **Ercole I** (1431–1505), who was responsible for his nephew's murder, encouraged artists, as did his two famous daughters, Beatrice and Isabella d'Este. **Alfonso I** (1475–1534), the son of Ercole, became the third husband of Lucrezia Borgia, and **Ercole II** (1508–59) married Renée of France, the protector of the Calvinists. After the demise of **Alfonso II** (1533–97), Ferrara came under the rule of the Papacy and the Estes retired to the Duchy of Modena. The secular university was founded in 1391. Three epic poets

benefited from the Estes' largesse: **Matteo Maria Boiardo** (1441–94), **Ludovico Ariosto** and **Torquato Tasso** (1544–95).

The Ferrarese School
The leader of the Ferrarese school of painting was **Cosmè (Cosimo) Tura** (c.1430–95), borrowing a meticulous realism from the northern schools. Other artists include **Francesco del Cossa**, **Ercole de' Roberti**, **Lorenzo Costa**, **Dosso Dossi** and **Benvenuto Garofalo**.

OLD TOWN

Castello Estense★
Largo Castello 1. Open Tue–Sun 9.30am–5.30pm (Mar–Sept daily). Closed 25 Dec. €8. 0532 29 92 33. www.castelloestense.it.
This imposing castle, guarded by moats and four fortified gateways with drawbridges, was the seat of the Este family. The ground floor houses the spartan prison where Parisina and her lover were locked away. On the *piano nobile*, are the Ducal Chapel collection and apartments decorated with frescoes by the Filippi in the 16C.

Duomo★★
The 12C cathedral is in the Romanesque-Gothic Lombard style and presents a triple **façade★★** with a splendid porch.

The Last Judgement is depicted on the tympanum.

Medieval Streets

Via San Romano linked the market square (Piazza Trento e Trieste) and the port (now Via Ripagrande). Several houses have porticoes, an unusual feature in Ferrara. **Via delle Volte**, one of the town's symbols, has covered alleyways *(volte)* linking the houses of the merchants and their warehouses.

Along Via Mazzini are the **Sinagoghe**; three temples are for different rites, the Italian and German traditions and that from Fano in the Marches.

Casa Romei★

Via Savonarola 28-30. Open Thu–Sat 2pm-7.30pm, Sun–Tue 8.30am-2pm. Closed 1 Jan, 1 May, 25 Dec. €3. 0532 23 41 30.

This rare 15C bourgeois residence combines late Gothic decorative features and Renaissance elements.

Palazzina di Marfisa d'Este★

Corso Giovecca 170. Open Tue–Sun 9.30am-1pm and 3–6pm. €4. 0532 24 49 49. www.ferrarainfo.com.

Elegant residence (1559) where Marfisa d'Este entertained her friends, has remarkable ornate ceiling decoration.

Palazzo Schifanoia★

Via Scandiana 23. Open Tue–Sun 9am-6pm. €3. 0532 24 49 49. www.ferrarainfo.com.

This 14C palace is where the Estes relaxed (*schifanoia* means "away with boredom"). There are splendid frescoes in the Room of the Months

(**Salone dei Mesi★★**). The palace houses the **Museo Civico di Arte Antica**, which is part of the **Lapidario**.

RENAISSANCE TOWN

In 1490 Ercole I d'Este commissioned **Biagio Rossetti** to extend the town to the north. The extension (**Addizione Erculea**) built around two main axes – Corso Ercole I d'Este and Corso Porta Pia, Bragio Rossetti and Porta Mare – is a great Renaissance town featuring parks and gardens. This grandiose town-planning scheme made Ferrara the first modern city in Europe, according to the art historian Jacob Burckhardt.

Corso Ercole I d'Este★

This street, lined with splendid Renaissance palaces but lacking any shops, retains its original residential aspect. The focal point is the **Quadrivio degli Angeli**, emphasised by three palaces with a rich angular decoration, including the Palazzo dei Diamanti.

Palazzo dei Diamanti★★

The most distinctive of all the works by **Biagio Rossetti**, the marble façade of the palace has 8 500 diamond bosses that create a curious optical effect. Known internationally for the high quality of its temporary exhibitions, the first floor also houses the **Pinacoteca Nazionale★** (*Corso Ercole I d'Este 21; open daily 9am-7pm; €13; 0532 24 49 49; www.palazzodiamanti.it*), whose paintings represent the Ferrarese, Emilian and Venetian schools.

RAVENNA★★★

The sober exteriors of Ravenna's buildings belie the wealth of riches accumulated when Ravenna became the capital of the Western Empire and later an Exarchate of Byzantium. The mosaics that adorn the city's ecclesiastical buildings are breathtakingly beautiful in the brightness of their colours and powerful symbolism.

A BIT OF HISTORY

After the division of the Empire in AD 395 by Theodosius, Rome, already in decline, was abandoned in AD 404 by the Emperor Honorius, who made Ravenna the capital of the Roman Empire. Honorius' sister, **Galla Placidia**, governed the Western Empire. Barbarian invasions brought the Ostrogoth kings Odoacer (476–93) and **Theodoric** (493–526), who embellished Ravenna. The strategic location of Ravenna's port, Classis, led to trading with Byzantium, from 476 the Imperial capital. Ravenna came under Byzantine rule in 540 in the reign of the **Emperor Justinian** (482–565), exercising considerable influence over much of Italy.

THE MOSAICS

UNESCO World Heritage monuments, the oldest mosaics are in the Neonian Baptistery and the Tomb of Galla Placidia (5C). The Baptistery of the Arians, St Apollinaris the New, St Vitalis, and finally St Apollinaris in Classe (6C)combine the two great schools of the ancient world, the Hellenic-Roman and the Byzantine.

Basilica di San Vitale★★★

Consecrated in 547 by Archbishop Maximian, the basilica is an architectural masterpiece. The splendour, originality and light effects are typical features. The octagonal plan has two storeys of concave exedrae encircled by an ambulatory and a deep apse. The richly decorated interior is dazzling: precious marbles, splendidly carved Byzantine capitals, frescoes and especially the **mosaics** of the apse with their brilliant colours (www.turismo.ra.it).

Mausoleo di Galla Placidia★★★

This mid-5C mausoleum is embellished with mosaics. The sarcophagi in the mausoleum were made for Galla Placidia and family.

Basilica di Sant' Apollinare Nuovo★★

Erected between 493 and 526 by Theodoric, probably as a Palatine church, St Apollinaris is divided into a nave and two aisles articulated by beautifully crafted columns in Greek marble with Corinthian capitals. The north and south walls are decorated with a series of **mosaics** on a gold background distributed over three sections: the upper sections date from Theodoric's reign while the lower section was remodelled by Justinian, who eliminated any reference to Arianism .

Basilica di Sant' Apollinare in Classe★★

Near the sea, the basilica was begun in 534. The 6–7C **mosaics** show lovely colour harmony. Also note the marble columns and Christian sarcophagi (5C–8C).

PARMA★★

Parma is a town of refined charm and important markets. Its rich musical heritage – birthplace of conductor Toscanini – makes its audience among Italy's toughest critics. The town's gastronomic reputation is most famous for Parmesan cheese and dry-cured Parma ham. Piazza Garibaldi is its popular meeting-place.

Practical Information

Getting There
Parma is near the A 1, between the Po and the Apennines.

A BIT OF HISTORY
An Etruscan settlement was founded here in 525 BC; it became a Roman station on the Via Emilia in 183 BC. It declined but revived in the 6C under Ostrogoth King Theodoric. An independent commune in the 11–13C, it became a member of the Lombard League. After 1335, Parma was governed in turn by the Visconti, the Sforza and the French, then was annexed by the Papacy in 1513. The **Farnese** dynasty ruled from 1545 to 1731, then the city passed to the Bourbons and French influence (1748-1801). Stendhal lived and set *The Charterhouse of Parma* here. The Bourbons of Parma had their Versailles at Colorno, to the north.

The Parma School
Correggio (1489–1534), master of chiaroscuro, and **Il Parmigianino** (1503–40), are the key protagonists, whose works influenced artists well beyond Parma.

HIGHLIGHTS
Parma's historic core comprises the Romanesque **Episcopal Centre★★★** with its cathedral and baptistery, the Baroque church of San Giovanni, Palazzo della Pilotta (16–17C), and Correggio's Room.

Duomo★★
This Romanesque cathedral is flanked by a Gothic campanile. Its dome is decorated with famous **frescoes** by Correggio (1522–30). The remarkable rhythm of the *Assumption of the Virgin* shows mastery of perspective. The **Descent from the Cross** (1178) is by sculptor Antelami; 16C frescoes in the nave.

Battistero★★★
Italy's most harmonious medieval monument, attributed to Antelami, is a 16-sided polygon. The interior features the Labours of the Months in high relief, and admirable 13C **frescoes** with scenes from the *Life of Christ* and the *Golden Legend*.

Galleria Nazionale★★
Piazzale della Pilotta 5. Open Tue–Sat 8.30am–7pm, Sun and hols 2pm, first Sun of month 1.30–7pm (free entrance). €10 (including Teatro Farnese and Museo Archeologico Nazionale). 0521 23 33 09. www.gallerianazionaleparma.it.
Emilian, Tuscan and Venetian 14–16C paintings by Fra Angelico, Dosso Dossi, El Greco, Canaletto, Bellotto, Piazzetta and Tiepolo.

Teatro Farnese★★
For opening hours see Galleria Nazionale. €10. 0521 23 33 09. www.gallerianazionaleparma.it.
This 1619 wood theatre follows Palladio's style in Olympic Theatre in Vicenza.

ROME★★★

The "Eternal City" is a rich contrast of monuments that testify to its ancient glory, of opulent Papal courts, and infinite intrigues. Italy's capital did suffer from some uncontrolled expansion following the Second World War, but admired from the Janiculum Hill, Rome's seven hills still beckon with domes and towers that often guard rich, inventive interiors. Rome's piazzas and streets remain the social networks that they have been for millennia, bursting with news, as well as fountains: elegant Piazza Navona, the market at Campo de' Fiori, folksy Trastevere– all lively at night, too. Rome's monuments – famous the world over – are interwoven with artisans, luxury shops and daily Roman life: the Pantheon and Roman Forum, the massive Colosseum, St Peter's, Castel Sant'Angelo, Piazza Navona, the Spanish Steps, the Trevi Fountain and the Villa Borghese. A golden luminous atmosphere marvellously surrounds Rome and extends out into the Roman countryside; a choice for idylls full of cypresses, olives and pines.

Practical Information

Getting There

♦ **By Car** – As the saying goes, "all roads lead to Rome"; the city lies at the hub of a motorway network with the A 1, A 12 and A 24. Driving in Rome is not advisable: a special permit is required for the centre; parking is limited and expensive (two near Via Veneto: Villa Borghese and Via Ludovisi 60.)

♦ **By Train** – Stazione Termini or Tiburtina, both linked to Metro lines A and B, *www.trenitalia.com (89 20 21) or www.italotreno.it (06 07 08).*

♦ **By Air** – The main airport is Leonardo da Vinci (Fiumicino, *29km/18mi SW of Rome; www.adr.it*); transport is available from here to the centre by train to/from Stazione Termini (*Leonardo Express, €14*); and from Tiburtina, Tuscolana and Ostiense (line FL1, *€8*). Bus services are operated by Terravision (*€4*), and other companies. *www.terravision.eu.* Ciampino is Rome's second airport. *06 65 951.www.adr.it.*

Getting Around

♦ **By Taxi** – Taxis are at stands or on: *06 66 45, 06 49 94, 06 55 51, 06 35 70, 06 41 571.* Use only the official metered taxis, usually painted white.

♦ **By Bus, Tram or Underground** – ATAC (*06 57 003, www.atac.roma.it*). Tickets should be purchased before beginning the journey and validated in the machine in the bus. ATAC ticket options: BIT *valid for 100min; €1.50;* one-day (to midnight) *€7;* 3 day, *€18;* and CIS weekly periods, *€24.* The Roma Pass (*www.romapass. it*), valid 3 days, includes transport and two free museum entries plus discounts, *€38.50.*

Sightseeing

City information booths (PIT): Stazione Termini, Piazza Sonnino, Piazza Cinque Lune, Via Nazionale, and the corner of Via Minghetti (near Fontana di Trevi), Via dei Fori Imperiali and Largo del Colonnato (Piazza San Pietro). Information on cultural and tourist events in the capital. Open daily. *06 06 08. www.turismoroma.it/infoviaggio/pit.* **Internet** – The city's official website: *www.comune.roma.it.* **Archaeologia Card** (*€25, valid 7 days*) includes entrance to 9 museums and monuments.

Under the dome,
Basilica di San Pietro

A BIT OF HISTORY

Legend and Location

The legendary origins of Rome,
claim that Aeneas, son of the
goddess Aphrodite, fled from Troy
and landed at the Tiber, founding
Lavinium. Rhea Silvia the Vestal,
following her union with the
god Mars, gave birth to the twins
Romulus and Remus, who were
abandoned. Transported by the
Tiber, the twins came to rest at
the foot of the Palatine, and were
nursed by a wolf. Later, Romulus
killed Remus for violating the sacred
precinct. The city was ruled by a
succession of kings, alternately
Sabine, Latin and Etruscan. Rome's
seven hills, especially the Palatine,
was a strategic location on the
Salt Road (Via Salaria), inhabited
perhaps as early as the 10C BC.
Etruscans transformed Iron Age
huts into a town, with a citadel on
the Capitoline. The last Etruscan
king, Tarquin the Superb, was
ejected in 509 BC and the Consulate
was instituted. The Republican era
was an ambitious one of territorial
expansion and civil war. **Julius
Caesar** (101–44 BC) was appointed

consul and dictator for life, then was
assassinated on 15 March 44 BC.
Octavian, despite his inexperience
and youth, skilfully vanquished
rivals; in 27 BC the Senate granted
him the title **Augustus** and soon he
became the first Roman emperor, a
golden age. His successors were a
varied lot: those driven by madness
and cruelty (Caligula, Nero and
Domitian); the good administrator,
Vespasian; Trajan, the "best of
emperors" and a great builder; and
Hadrian, an indefatigable traveller
and warrior.

Christianity

The religion of Jesus of Nazareth
originated in Palestine and Syria,
and first reached Rome in the reign
of Augustus. The **Edict of Milan**
(313) allowed Christians to practise
their religion openly. The Bishop
of Rome, the pope, was Christ's
representative on Earth. As power
grew, the Pontiff and the Holy
Roman Emperor faced off. During
the Renaissance, popes waged
war and patronised the arts; artists
such as Raphael and Michelangelo
embellished the city for patrons Pius
II, Sixtus IV (Sistine Chapel and Santa

115

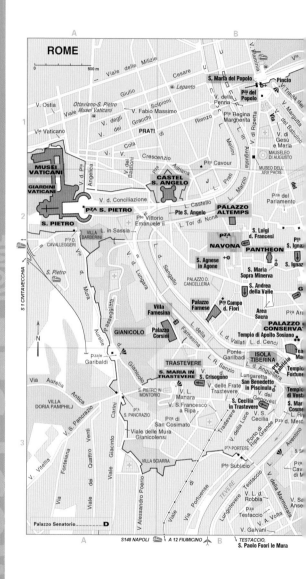

ROME

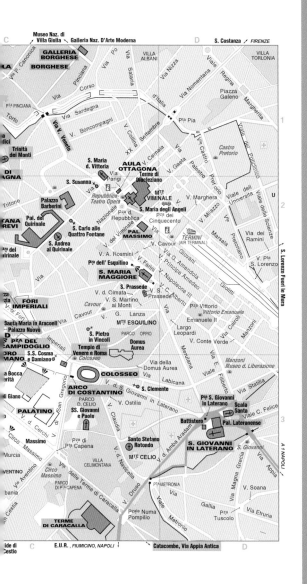

C — Museo Naz. di / Villa Giulia ↗ Galleria Naz. D'Arte Moderna   D   S. Costanza ↗ FIRENZE

GALLERIA BORGHESE

Via P. Canonica
Via Pinciana
Corso d'Italia
VILLA ALBANI
Via Po
Via Salaria
Via Nizza
Viale Regina Margherita
VILLA TORLONIA

PTA PINCIANA
Torto
Via Sardegna
V. Boncompagni
Via Nomentana
Piazza Galeno

dici
Trinità dei Monti

Via V. Veneto
V. Collina
XX Settembre
PTA Pia

S. Maria d. Vittoria
AULA OTTAGONA
Terme di Diocleziano

Castro Pretorio

DI AGNA
S. Susanna
Via Parigi

Tritone
Palazzo Barberini
Repubblica-Teatro Opera
MTE VIMINALE
S. Maria degli Angeli
PZA dei Cinquecento
V. Marghera
Viale dell' Università
Viale delle Scienze
U

TANA REVI
Pal. del Quirinale
S. Carlo alle Quattro Fontane
PAL. MASSIMO
TERMINI (AIR TERMINAL)
Via dei Ramini

PZA del irinale
S. Andrea al Quirinale
V. A. Rosmini
V. Cavour
Via G. Amendola
S. Lorenzo Fuori le Mura

PZA dell' Esquilino
V. Farini
V. S. Lorenzo

zia
FORI IMPERIALI
S. MARIA MAGGIORE
S. Prassede
V. Principe Amedeo
V. Napoleone III
Gioberti

Santa Maria in Aracoeli
Palazzo Nuovo
Cavour
V. d. Olmata
S. Prassede
Alberto
PZA Vittorio Emanuele

D
PAL. DEL CAMPIDOGLIO
V. S. Martino ai Monti
G. Lanza
Emanuele II
Via Manzoni

ORO
S.S. Cosma
MANO e Damiano
MTE ESQUILINO
PARCO OPPIO
Largo Leopardi
Via Carlo

Bocca
rità
S. Pietro in Vincoli
V. Conte Verde

di Giano
Tempio di Venere e Roma
Domus Aurea
Manzoni Museo d. Liberazione

PALATINO
Colosseo
COLOSSEO
Via della Domus Aurea
Viale
Via Statilia

V. d. Cerchi
ARCO DI COSTANTINO
V. d. S. Giovanni in Laterano
S. Clemente
Via Labicana
Viale C. Felice

Massimo
PARCO D. CELIO
SS. Giovanni e Paolo
V. Ostilia
PZA S. Giovanni in Laterano
Scala Santa
Pal. Lateranense

Murcia
Circo Massimo
PZA di PTA Capena
Santo Stefano Rotondo
Battistero
S. GIOVANNI IN LATERANO
S. Giovanni
A.1 NAPOLI

VENTINO
Aventino
PARCO DI PTA CAPENA
VILLA CELIMONTANA
MTE CELIO
V. d. Amba Aradam
Via Magna Grecia
Via Appia

bania
Via delle Terme di Caracalla
PTA METRONIA
V. Soana
Via Etruria

ide di Cestio
TERME DI CARACALLA
PZLE Numa Pompilio
Via Druso
Viale Metronio
Gallia
Via Tuscolo

C   E.U.R. , FIUMICINO, NAPOLI   Catacombe, Via Appia Antica   D

117

INTRODUCTION

Maria del Popolo), Julius II (Sistine Chapel ceiling), Leo X (chose Raphael as superintendent of the arts), Clement VII, Sixtus V (a great builder) and Paul III (Farnese Palace). The French, Spanish and Austrians ruled, prior to the Unification of Italy in 1871. Giuseppe Garibaldi led the revolt that led to the new State. Rome became its capital. The world wars and the rise of Fascist dictator Benito Mussolini brought hardship and horrors to Rome. Fear continued during the 1970s and 80s with terrorist attacks. Recent decades have seen calm and safety once again restored to this magnificent city.

Highlights

No other city in the world has such a wealth of Classical antiquities, medieval buildings, Renaissance palaces and Baroque churches. A minimum stay of two or three days is recommended. The following pages cover some 20 of the most worthy sights.

COLOSSEO/ FORO/PALATINO

Colosseo★★★ – Open daily 8.30am–1hr before dusk. €12 including Foro Romano and Palatino. Book in advance to bypass the crowds. 06 39 96 77 00. www.coopculture.it.

This amphitheatre, inaugurated in AD 80, is called the Flavian Amphitheatre after its initiator, Vespasian, first of the Flavian emperors. "Colosseum" probably refers to the colossal gilded bronze statue of Nero that once stood nearby or from its own colossal dimensions (527m/576yds in circumference and 57m/187ft high). Three superimposed Classical

orders (Doric, Ionic and Corinthian) crown this masterpiece. Ropes manipulated a linen awning to protect the spectators from sun or rain. Some 50 000 spectators watched fights between men and beasts, gladiatorial contests, and races in the arena.

Adjacent to the Colosseum, the **Arco di Costantino★★★** arch commemorates Constantine's victory over Maxentius in AD 315.

Foro Romano★★★ – *For schedule see Colosseo.* The religious, political and commercial centre of ancient Rome reflects the 12 centuries of history that created Roman civilisation.

The **Basilica Emilia** was the second basilica to be built in Rome (170 BC). On the Sacred Way, **Via Sacra★**, victorious generals marched in triumph to the **Curia★★**, where the Senate convened; inside are **Plutei di Traiano★★**, sculpted bas-relief panels showing Emperor Trajan, and sacrificial animals.

The Rostra was the **orators' platform★**. The imposing Triumphal Arch, **Arco di Settimio Severo★★**, commemorated in AD 203 the emperor's victories over the Parthians. At the foot of the Capitol stood some remarkable monuments: the late-1C **Tempio di Vespasiano★★** (Temple of Vespasian), near the Rostra, three elegant Corinthian columns remain; the **Tempio di Saturno★★★** (Temple of Saturn), which retains eight 4C columns; and the **Portico degli Dei Consentis★**, a colonnade with Corinthian columns (AD 367) dedicated to the 12 principal Roman deities. The **Colonna di Foca★** (Column of Phocas), AD 608, is in honour of the Byzantine Emperor Phocas, who presented

Colosseo

the Pantheon to Pope Boniface IV. The **Basilica Giulia★★**, which has five aisles, built by Julius Caesar and completed by Augustus, was the law court and exchange.

Three beautiful columns with Corinthian capitals remain of the **Tempio di Castore e Polluce★★★** (Temple of Castor and Pollux). The circular **Tempio di Vesta★★★** (Temple of Vesta) stands near the **Casa delle Vestalia★★** (House of the Vestal Virgins). The **Regia** was probably the residence of King Numa Pompilius, who succeeded Romulus. The **Tempio di Antonino e Faustina★★**), dedicated to Emperor Antoninus Pius and his wife, had the church of San Lorenzo in Miranda built within the temple. The **Tempio di Romolo** (son of Emperor Maxentius) has bronze doors and two porphyry columns. The grandiose **Basilica di Massenzio★★** (Basilica of Maxentius) was completed by Emperor Constantine. The **Arco di Tito★★** (Arch of Titus), 81 AD, commemorates his capture of Jerusalem. Next to the church of **Santa Francesca Romana★★**, the

Tempio di Venere e di Roma★★ (Temple of Venus and Rome) was erected by Hadrian 121–136. One of the largest, the west side was dedicated to goddess Rome; the east, dedicated to Venus, faces the Colosseum.

Palatino★★★ – *For schedule see Colosseo.* The **Palatine Hill** was chosen by Domitian for the Imperial Palace. In the **Domus Flavia★** (official State apartments) the emperor dispensed justice, had the throne room and the *lararium* (private chapel). The **Domus Augustana★★** (private Imperial apartments) rooms are set around two peristyles on two floors. The **Stadium★** held private games and spectacles for the emperor. The **Casa di Livia★★** (House of Livia) has fine vestiges of paintings. The **Orti Farnesiani** (Farnese Gardens), laid out in the 16C on the site of Tiberius' palace, afford **views★★** of the Roman Forum and town.

Fori Imperiali★★★ – *The visitor centre, Via dei Fori Imperiali.* Caesar, Augustus, Trajan, Nerva and Vespasian built these forums. Via dei Fori Imperiali, a 1932 Mussolini

Domus Augustana, Palatino

project, divides the forums.
The **Mercati di Traiano**★★
(*entrance Via IV Novembre 94;
open daily 9.30am–7.30pm; €14.
www.mercatiditraiano.it*) with
its semicircular façade, was a
distribution, supply and retail
market of c. 150 shops. The **Torre
delle Milizie**★ (⚭ *not open at
this time. www.comune.roma.it*)
is part of a 13C fortress. Finest
of the Imperial forums, the **Foro
di Traiano**★★★ (Trajan's Forum)
contains the **Colonna Traiana**★★★
(Trajan's Column), an unrivalled
masterpiece bas-relief of over 100
scenes; episodes of the war Trajan
waged against the Dacians. The
column is attributed to Apollodorus
of Damascus. The Augustan
Forum, **Foro di Augusto**★★ (*view
from Via Alessandrina*), has a few
columns from the Temple of Mars
the Avenger, with vestiges of the
stairway and of the forum wall. The
medieval House of the Knights of
Rhodes (Casa dei Cavalieri di Rodi),
was built above the ruins and rebuilt
in the 15C. In Caesar's Forum, the
Foro di Cesare★★ (*Via dei Fori
Imperiali, view from Via del Tulliano*),
are three lovely columns from the
Temple of Venus Genitrix.
Circo Massimo (*entrance piazza
di Porta Capena*). Open from
November 2016, this is the
archaeological area of what was
the largest building for shows and
competitions in ancient times.

CAPITOLINO★★★

The hill that symbolised the power
of ancient Rome now holds city
offices, the church of Santa Maria
d'Aracoeli, Piazza del Campidoglio
and its palaces, and gardens. The
Capitoline, once known as the
caput mundi (capital of the world)
enjoys a superb **view**★★★.
Piazza del Campidoglio★★★ –
Michelangelo refashioned this
exquisite square from 1536; it is
framed by three palaces and a
balustrade with statues of the
Dioscuri, and crowned by an
equestrian statue of Emperor
Marcus Aurelius. The **Palazzo
Senatorio**★★★, constructed in the
12C and modified in the late 16C, is
occupied by the mayor of Rome
and houses the Tabularium.
Musei Capitolini★★★ – *Open
daily 9.30am–7.30pm (ticket office
closes 6.30pm). €16 incl. Centrale*

Montemartini and temporary exhibitions (valid 7 days). 06 06 08. www.museicapitolini.org.

One of the finest collections of ancient sculpture and superb paintings from medieval times to the 18C. The **Palazzo Nuovo★★★** (*north*), designed by Michelangelo, houses ancient sculptures, including the Dying Gladiator (Gaul) and busts of the emperors. **Palazzo Senatorio**, Rome's city hall since 1144, houses the Tabularium. **Palazzo dei Conservatori★★★** (*south*) houses ancient sculpture including a bronze Hercules, an equestrian statue of Marcus Aurelius, ceramics, and the gallery of paintings.

PIAZZA VENEZIA

Piazza Venezia – This square hosts the very white monument to Victor Emmanuel II, the house of Napoleon's mother, the Venetian palace and considerable Rome city traffic.

Chiesa del Gesù★★ – The mother-church of the Jesuits, built 1568, has an interior lavished with Baroque gold, as well as Andrea del Pozzo's tomb of St. Ignatius Loyola.

CAMPO DEI FIORI AND GHETTO

Campo de' Fiori★★ – One of Rome's liveliest squares begins the day as a picturesque produce market. The statue of **Giordano Bruno**, a monk charged with heresy and burned at the stake here (*17 Feb 1600*), often serves as a meeting-point, especially for evening revellers into the wee hours.

Palazzo Farnese★★ – *Piazza Farnese 67. Tours in English; reserve at least 1 week in advance; €9. www.inventerrome.com.*
Most beautiful of the Roman

palaces, built by Alessandro Farnese (Pope Paul III, 1534), since 1635 this has been France's embassy in Italy (officially since 1875); it was designed in part by Michelangelo in 1546. Frescoes were painted (1593–1603) by **Annibale Carracci** assisted by his brother Agostino and pupils Domenichino and Lanfranco. The interior courtyard by Sangallo, Vignola and Michelangelo reflects Renaissance elegance. If you can't visit, walk around the palace to Via Giulia to glimpse the garden. The **Passeto Farnese**, that spans **Via Giulia★**, connects the palace to Santa Maria della Morte. The street fountain, **Fontana del Mascherone** (1626), was made from an ancient Roman mask and granite tub.
Ghetto and Isola Tiberina★★ – Rome's old Jewish quarter has the Synagogue (squared dome), the Arco d'Ottaviano which Augustus built for his sister, shops and restaurants. Via Ottaviana leads from a good Jewish bakery for sweets (unmarked, no.1) to Tiber Island, in ancient times occupied by mariners and a temple to Aeschulypius. The island's opposite bridge leads to Trastevere.

PIAZZA NAVONA★★★

Built on the site of Domitian's stadium (AD 86), one of Rome's largest squares retains its elliptical shape. Pleasant and lively, it has three Baroque fountains with Bernini's 1651 masterpiece in the centre, the **Fontana dei Fiumi★★★** (Fountain of the Four Rivers). The statues represent the four rivers – Danube, Ganges, Plata and Nile – symbolising the four known continents. Caffès, churches and palaces line the square. **Sant'Agnese in Agone★★** has a Baroque façade by Borromini, adjoining 17C **Palazzo Pamphilj**, now the Brazilian Embassy. The north end, Via di Tor Sanguigna, has remains of Domitian's Stadium. **Palazzo Altemps – Museo Nazionale Romano★★★** – *Piazza di Sant'Apollinare 44. Tue–Sun 9am–7.45pm. €8 (valid for Palazzo Massimo, Crypta Balbi, Terme di Diocleziano). 06 39 96 77 00. coopculture.it.* This magnificent 15C palace has ancient masterpieces including the **Ludovisi Throne★★★**, an enigmatic Greek sculpture of the Birth of Aphrodite (5C BC). Return to Piazza Navona, the west side leads to Via della Pace with the church **Santa Maria della Pace★** (17C façade by Pietro da Cortona). Inside, four Sybils were painted in 1514 by Raphael. Its cloisters are by **Bramante** (1444–1514). Also on Via della Pace is **Antico Caffè della Pace**, the atmospheric 1891 Victorian bar. Via di Parione leads to Via del Governo Vecchio; turn left to Piazza di Pasquino and its celebrated "talking" statue, **Pasquino** was the citizens' message board. The streets east of Piazza Navona lead to the Pantheon.

PANTHEON★★★
Mon–Sat 8.30am–7.15pm, Sun 9am–5.45pm, hols 9–12.45am. 347 82 05 204. www.pantheonroma.com.
The Pantheon, an ancient temple beautifully preserved, founded by Agrippa in 27 BC and rebuilt by Hadrian (118–125), was converted to a church in 608. The portico is supported by 16 monolithic granite columns, all ancient except for three on the left. The doors are original. The **interior★★★**, a masterpiece of harmony and majesty, is dominated by the **ancient dome★★★**, the diameter of which is equal to its height. The side chapels, adorned with alternately curved and triangular pediments, contain the tombs of the kings of Italy and of Raphael.

TREVI FOUNTAIN TO PIAZZA DEL POPOLO
Fontana di Trevi★★★ – *Watch your wallet in the heavy crowds.* **Nicola Salvi** designed the splendid Baroque fountain: Oceanus rides in a chariot drawn by seahorses and tritons.
Piazza di Spagna★★★ – The majestic 18C **Spanish Steps ★★★** lead up to the **Trinità dei Monti★** church. At the base is the **Fontana della Barcaccia★** (Boat Fountain) by Bernini's father, Pietro (17C), and Keats-Shelley House. Above, the French Academy at **Villa Medici★★**, built for the powerful Florentine Medici family, offers exhibits, films and concerts. Below, **Via dei Condotti**, lined with elegant shops, is home to the famous **Caffè Greco**. Via Margutta was full of artists' studios and was home to Federico Fellini.
Piazza del Popolo★★ – The **Piazza del Popolo**, designed by Giuseppe Valadier (1762–1839), embraces **Porta del Popolo★**, the 3C gate. **Santa Maria del Popolo★★** contains 15C **frescoes★** by Pinturicchio; **tombs★** by Andrea Sansovino; two **paintings★★★** by **Caravaggio** (*the Crucifixion of St Peter* and the *Conversion of St Paul*), and the **Cappella Chigi★** chapel designed by Raphael.

VIA VENETO AREA
Although no longer the centre of La Dolce Vita, the Via Veneto still

Fontana di Trevi

...ures well-heeled travellers with its grand hotels. To the north, **Villa Borghese**, a tranquil park with umbrella pines, is home to one of Rome's best museums, **Galleria Borghese★★★** (*www.galleria borghese.it*). It's also a good place for kids to run, or row on the pond. To the south, beyond Piazza Barberini is **Palazzo Barberini★★** (*www. galleriabarberini.beniculturali.it*), beautifully restored with a newly expanded museum space. Hans Holbein's Henry VIII keeps company with Raphael's La Fornarina, Caravaggios, and other greats.

TERMINI TO SAN GIOVANNI

The area of Rome's main train station is less pleasant, but has plenty of art treasures. Via Merulana connects the area's two main basilicas.
Palazzo Massimo alle Terme★★★ – *Largo di Villa Peretti 1. Tue–Sun 9am–7.45pm.€8 (valid for 4 musems). 06 39 96 77 00. www.archeoroma.beniculturali.it.* Roman antiquities include the numismatic collection★★, ancient sculptures, frescoes and mosaics. Among its many treasures are **Room of the Three Arches★★★** with Emperor Augustus, the Wounded Niobe★★★ (440 BC), the **Young Girl from Anzio★★**, and the Crouching Aphrodite★★★. Don't miss the frescoes from **Livia's Villa★★★** and paintings from the **Villa della Farnesina★★★**.
Basilica di Santa Maria Maggiore★★★ – Situated in **Piazza dell'Esquilino**, with its Egyptian obelisk, is a **view★★** of the 17C façade of one of the four major basilicas in Rome. Built by Pope Sixtus III (AD 432–40), he dedicated it to St Mary Major. The 1377 campanile (bell tower) is the highest in Rome. The **loggia** is decorated with 13C **mosaics★**. The **interior★★★** contains remarkable 5C **mosaics★★★** and the coffered **ceiling★** was gilded probably with the first gold from the New World.
Basilica di San Giovanni in Laterano★★★ – **Piazza di San Giovanni in Laterano** is marked by a 15C BC Egyptian obelisk, the

tallest in Rome. One of the four major basilicas in Rome, St John Lateran, the Cathedral of Rome, was the first basilica founded by Constantine prior to St Peter's in the Vatican, later rebuilt. The bronze door panels belonged to the *curia* of the Roman Forum. The grandiose interior has a 16C **ceiling**★★ and pretty **cloisters**★ by the Vassalletto (13C). The 4C **baptistery**★ has 5C and 7C mosaics and frescoes. The **Palazzo Lateranense** (Lateran Palace), rebuilt in 1586, was once the Papal palace. Nearby is the Holy Staircase, **Scala Sancta**.

TERME DI CARACALLA AND CATACOMBE

Terme di Caracalla★★★ – *Viale delle Terme di Caracalla 52. Open daily 9am–1hr before dusk. €6. 06 39 96 77 00. www.coopculture.it.*
These monumental baths built by Caracalla in AD 212 extend over more than 11ha/27 acres and could take 1 600 bathers at a time. The complex had main rooms (*caldarium*, *tepidarium* and *frigidarium*), a gym, libraries, and areas for sport and refreshment. In summer, opera and ballet are performed here.

Appia Antica and Catacombe★★★ – *The 118, 218, 660 and 664 buses pass some catacombs, as does the Archeobus. Cycle along the traffic-free Via Appia on Sun.*
Underground Christian cemeteries were built alongside the Via **Appia Antica**★★. In use from the 2C, long galleries radiate from an underground burial chamber (*hypogeum*). Symbolic carvings or paintings are precious early Christian art.
Catacombe di San Callisto★★★ (*Via Appia Antica 110; €8. 06 51 30 151. www.catacombe. roma.it*), **Catacombe di San Sebastiano**★★★ (*Via Appia Antica 136; 06 78 50 350*), **Catacombe di Domitilla**★★★ (*Via delle Sette Chiese 282; 06 51 10 342; Bus 714, 160*). *Guided tours only (45min), 9am–noon and 2–5pm. Closed: San Callisto, Wed; San Sebastiano, Sun; Domitilla, Tue. €8.*

ACROSS THE TIBER RIVER

Castel Sant'Angelo★★★ – *Lungotevere Castello 50. Open daily 9am–7.30pm. €10. 06 32 810. www.castelsantangelo.com.*
This imposing fortress was built in AD 128–139 as a mausoleum

Terme di Caracalla

for the Emperor Hadrian. A fine spiral ramp dating from Antiquity leads to the seven castle levels. The sculpture of the Archangel Michael, inserting his sword in its sheath, commemorates the end of a plague. Alexander VI (1492–1503) added octagonal bastions. In the 1527 sack of Rome, Clement VII took refuge and installed an apartment that was later embellished by Paul III; the **Popes' Apartment★** stands isolated at the summit of the fortress. The summit terrace has a splendid **panorama★★★** of the city. The Castel Sant'Angelo is linked to the east bank of the Tiber by the graceful **Ponte Sant'Angelo★**, adorned with copies of Baroque angels by **Bernini**. A long raised passageway (Il Passetto) links the fortress to the Vatican palaces.

THE VATICAN★★★

The Vatican City is bounded by a wall that makes up the greater part of the Vatican State as defined in 1929 in the Lateran Treaty, now reduced to only 44ha/109 acres and with 829 inhabitants. The Vatican State, with the Pope as Head of State and the Supreme Head of the Universal Church, has its own flag, anthem and issues its own stamps.
The Swiss Guard uniform is attributed to Michelangelo. The Pope grants **public audiences** on Wednesdays.

Piazza San Pietro★★★

This architectural masterpiece was begun in 1656 by Bernini. Two semi-circular colonnades frame the square and the façade of the basilica. Caligula had the 1C BC obelisk from Heliopolis placed in his circus; in 1585 it was moved here. The Vatican Post is on the piazza's south side.

Basilica di San Pietro★★★

Open daily 7am–7pm (Oct–Mar to 6.30pm); closed during papal audience (Wed morning).
In AD 324, Constantine ordered a basilica on the site where St Peter was buried after he had been martyred in Caligula's circus. By the 15C, the structure needed rebuilding, which ensued over two centuries. The plan was designed by Bramante and adopted by Michelangelo, then altered to a Latin cross at the behest of Paul V in 1606; Carlo Maderno added two bays and a façade to Michelangelo's square plan.
From 1629 the basilica was sumptuously decorated by Bernini in Baroque style.
The **façade** (115m/377ft long and 45m/148ft high) was completed in 1614 by Carlo Maderno; it is surmounted by colossal figures. The **portico**, Holy Door (right), is opened and closed by the Pope only during a Jubilee Year. The first chapel on the right displays the **Pietà★★★**, the powerful masterpiece carved by young Michelangelo 1499–1500. **Gregory XIII's Monument★** illustrates his Gregorian calendar. **Clement XIII's Monument★★★** is a fine 1792 Neoclassical design by Canova. The **Cattedra di San Pietro★★★** (St Peter's Throne) by Bernini (1666) in bronze encases a 4C episcopal chair.
The 13C bronze **Statue of St Peter★★** is attributed to Arnolfo di Cambio; pilgrims kiss its feet, shiny from being touched. **Innocent VIII's Monument★★★**

is a Renaissance work (1498) by Antonio del Pollaiuolo.

Urban VIII's Monument★★★, also by Bernini (1647), is a masterpiece of funerary art.

Paul III's Monument★★★ (16C) is by Guglielmo della Porta. The theatrical **baldacin★★★** by young Bernini crowns the pontifical altar (29m/95ft tall, height of the Farnese Palace) and was made using bronze plundered from the Pantheon roof.

The **dome★★★** designed by Michelangelo, was completed in 1593 by Giacomo della Porta and Domenico Fontana. From the **summit** (*access north side of basilica*), the terrace affords a **view★★★** of St Peter's Square, the Vatican City and Rome from the Castelli to the Janiculum to Monte Mario. You can climb up to the lantern. Open *daily 8am–6pm; Oct–Mar 5pm.€8 in lift plus 320 steps; €6 on foot (551 steps). 06 69 88 37 31. www.museivaticani.va.*

Musei Vaticani★★★
Entrance Viale Vaticano. Mon–Sat 9am–6pm. €16. 06 69 88 31 45. www.museivaticani.va.

Below: Vaults of the Sistine Chapel

The Vatican Museums occupy part of the palaces built by the popes from the 13C onwards. The **Museo Pio-Clementino★★★** (Greek and Roman antiquities) masterpieces include: the **Belvedere Torso★★★** (1C BC), greatly admired by Michelangelo; the **Venus of Cnidus★★**; the **Laocoon Group★★★**, a 1C BC Hellenistic work; the **Apollo Belvedere★★★**; **Perseus★★** by Canova; **Hermes★★★**, 2C; and the **Apoxyomenos★★★**, the athlete scraping his skin with a strigil. The **Museo Etrusco★**, on the second floor, has a 7C BC gold **fibula★★** adorned with lions and ducklings, the 5C BC bronze **Mars★★** and a 6C BC **chariot★★** (restored). The four **Stanze di Rafaello★★★** (Raphael Rooms), the private apartments of Julius II, were decorated by Raphael and his pupils from 1508 to 1524. The frescoes are remarkable: *The Borgo Fire, The School of Athens, Parnassus, The Expulsion of Heliodorus from the Temple, The Miracle of the Bolsena Mass* and *St Peter Delivered from Prison*. The **Pinacoteca★★★** has five **compositions★★★** by **Raphael**;

St Jerome★★ by Leonardo da Vinci and a **Descent from the Cross★★** by Caravaggio. On the first floor is the **Cappella Sistina★★★** (Sistine Chapel); its splendid vault, painted by **Michelangelo** from 1508–1512, illustrates episodes from the Bible with the Creation, the Flood and the Creation of Man. Above the altar, *The Last Judgement* was painted by Michelangelo in 1534. The upper walls were decorated by Perugino, Pinturicchio and Botticelli. The magnificent **Giardini Vaticania★★** gardens are adorned with fountains and statues.

TRASTEVERE

Literally "Across the Tiber", this busy neighbourhood is popular for casual dinners or drinks in the wee hours. The beautiful church of **Santa Maria in Trastevere★★** anchors its lively square. In a quiet area, Santa Cecila offers space for reflection, as well as mosaics and frescoes to admire. Don't miss the Renaissance frescoes at **Villa Farnesina** (*Mon–Sat 9am–2pm. €6. 06 68 02 72 68. www.villafarnesina.it*) painted by Rapahel and others in the banker Chigi's pleasure villa.

GIANICOLO

The lovely hill above Trastevere named after Janus offers a lovely walk on **Passeggiata del Gianicolo** with a breathtaking view of Rome's rooftops and on a clear day to the mountains east. The south begins near the grand Fontanone fountain, the north begins above **Ponte Mazzini** bridge. Further west, **Villa Doria Pamphili** park is landscaped more beautifully than Villa Borghese.

EXCURSIONS

Tivoli

See Michelin Green Guide Rome for detailed sight descriptions. Trains depart from Termini. By car, 32 km east on A24 or Via Tiburtina, the slower 3C BC consular road.
Tivoli's villas were important holiday resorts from Roman times through the Renaissance. Famous for its two contrasting gardens, its true glory is the Imperial Villa Adriana (Hadrian's Villa). Villa d'Este offers a spectacle of fountains, Villa Gregoriana is a bit wilder, with waterfalls.
Villa Gregoriana★ – *Largo Sant'Angelo. 0774 33 26 50. www. villagregoriana.eu*. This wooded park slopes to the River Aniene with the **Grande Cascata★★**. The **Tempio della Sibilla** is an elegant Corinthian-style temple.
Villa d'Este★★★ – *Piazza Trento 5. 199 766 166. www.villadestetivoli. info*. In 1550 Cardinal Ippolito Il d'Este built this villa with elaborate terraced **gardens★★★**. Statues, pools and fountains in Mannerist style enhance the natural beauty. A UNESCO World Heritage Site.
Villa Adriana★★★ – *Largo Marguerite Yourcenar 1. 6km/3.7mi SW of Tivoli. A detailed map of the site (at the ticket office). Open daily 9am–1hr before dusk. €8. 077 43 82 733. www.villaadriana. beniculturali.it*. Probably the richest building project in Antiquity, this was designed by Emperor **Hadrian** (AD 76–138). His travels around the Roman Empire are evident throughout: **Canopo★★★** evokes the Egyptian town of Canope with its of Temple of Serapis; also a theatre, baths, mosaics and idyllic spaces for reflection and pleasure.

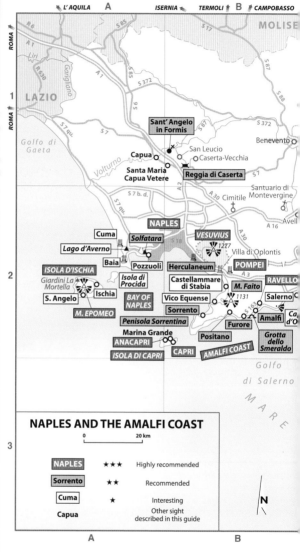

NAPLES AND THE AMALFI COAST

Campania owes its rich heritage to several civilisations, from the ancient
Greeks and Romans, to the French/Spanish Bourbons. Naples, a chaotic
but cultured metropolis, pulses in the shadow of Mount Vesuvius. Sunny,

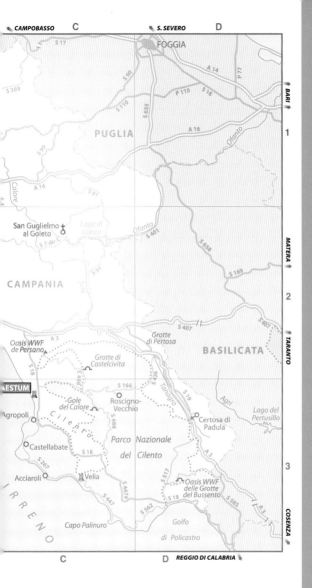

Campania offers spectacular settings. The Island of Capri, the hilltop village of Ravello on the Amalfi Coast and the ruins at Pompeii and Herculaneum, all boast sea views. Not surprisingly, its fertile volcanic soil yields products used in some of Italy's best cuisine.

NAPLES ★★★

Naples is an energetic universe of its own, imbued with fantasy and fatalism, superstition and splendour. Chaotic and heaving with traffic, yet elegantly rich with history, art and culture, it surrender its mysteries to anyone who scratches the surface. The Naples Bay is one of the most beautiful in the world. Poets and writers have rhapsodised its charms. UNESCO declared the historic centre of the city a World Heritage site.

NAPLES TODAY

Naples lives forever in the shadow of Mount Vesuvius, the volcano that destroyed Pompeii and the surrounding Roman enclaves more than 2 000 years ago. Smaller and with less frequent eruptions than Etna, the still-active mountain is considered more dangerous. Framed by the blue waters of the Bay of Naples, Vesuvius is a stunning backdrop and metaphor for the fatalistic hot-blooded energy of the city. The loud streets and the hurried pace of fast-talking denizens perhaps is the legacy of life on the edge of a cauldron. It is no wonder, then, that street food to eat on the go and pizza were perfected in this vibrant city.

A BIT OF HISTORY

Legend claims that the siren Parthenope gave her name to a town which had sprung up round her tomb, thus Naples is called the Parthenopaean City.

The Greek *Neapolis* was conquered by the Romans in the 4C BC. Virgil, Augustus and Tiberius wintered there, but the Neapolitans retained Greek customs during the Empire. Since the 12C, seven dynasties have reigned over Naples.

The Normans, Hohenstaufens, Angevins, Aragonese, Spanish and Bourbons.

The French Revolution of 1789 brought in French troops, and in 1799 a **Parthenopaean Republic** was set up, followed by a French kingdom (1806–15) under Bonaparte (Napoleon's brother) and afterwards Joachim Murat, who promoted excellent reforms. From 1815 to 1860 the Bourbons ruled despite two serious revolts.

ART IN NAPLES

The princes of the House of Anjou endowed Naples with many ecclesiastical buildings, influenced by the French-Gothic style. **"Robert the Wise" of Anjou** (1309–43) attracted poets, scholars and artists to his court in Naples. Boccaccio spent part of his youth in Naples. His friend Petrarch also lived here. In 1324 Robert the Wise brought the Sienese sculptor **Tino di Camaino** to adorn many of the churches with his monumental tombs. Roman artist Pietro Cavallini painted frescoes, as did Giotto whose works have disappeared.

The Neapolitan School (17C–early-18C)

Neapolitan painting flourished in the 17C. In 1607 the great innovator **Caravaggio** arrived. Bold and realistic, some of his models came from the mean streets, while chiaroscuro created dramatic effect with light. Among his followers were **Artemisia Gentileschi**, **José de Ribera**, **Giovanni Battista Caracciolo** and Mattia Preti. **Luca Giordano** instead used more light.

Practical Information

Getting Around.

The main access roads to Naples include the A 1, Autostrada del Sole, the A 3 for those arriving from the south and the A 16, linking Naples to the Adriatic. It is preferable to reach Naples by train or plane as traffic in the city is chaotic and few hotels have garages.

• **By Air** – Capodichino Airport (*081 78 96 111; www.gesac.it*), is 6km/3.7mi away from the city. Buses to Naples: Alibus arrives in Piazza Garibaldi and Stazione Marittima di Piazza Municipio, Molo Beverello (*€4*). Naples has a good network of public transport although bus transport does fall prey to traffic.

• **By Train** – The Cumana and Circumflegrea trains (Piazza Montesanto) connect Naples to Bagnoli and the Campi Flegrei. The Circumvesuviana (Piazza Garibaldi) swiftly connects Herculaneum, Pompeii, Castellammare, Vico Equense and Sorrento.

• **By Underground** – The Metropolitana FS crosses the city vertically from Piazza Garibaldi to Pozzuoli, while the collinare from Piazza Vanvitelli goes up to Piscinola/Secondigliano. A link goes from Piazza Vanvitelli to the Museo Archeologico.

• **By Funicular Railway** – Four Funicolare routes connect to the Vomero: the centrale (Via Toledo–Piazza Fuga); the Chiaia (Via del Parco Margherita–Via Cimarosa); and the Montesanto (Piazza Montesanto–Via Morghen). The Funicolare di Mergellina links Via Mergellina to Via Manzoni.

Tickets – "UNICO" tickets allow travel on buses, trams, the funicular railway and the underground (Metropolitana). *www.unicocampania.it.*

• **By Radiotaxi** – *Taxi Napoli 081 88 88, Consorzio Radio taxi 081 57 07 070, La Partenope 081 01 01.*

Sea connections – Ferry and hovercraft crossings to Capri, Ischia, Procida, the Amalfi Coast and Sorrento depart from the Molo Beverello and Mergellina ports. Boats depart from Molo Angioino for Sardinia and Sicily.

Tirrenia: *892 123. www.tirrenia.it.*
Alilauro: *Via Caracciolo 11, Napoli, 081 49 72 222. www.alilauro.it.*
Aliscafi SNAV: Stazione Marittima, *Napoli, 081 42 85 555. www.snav.it.*
Navigazione Libera del Golfo: *Molo Beverello, Napoli. 081 55 20 763. www.navlib.it.*

Sightseeing

The Campania>Artecard is available for 3 (*€21*), and gives free or discounted entry into many principal museums and archaeological sites in Naples and the Campania region, and discounts on other events and attractions. The card includes three days of free public transport. *800 600 601. www.campaniartecard.it*

The Baroque Period

Ferdinando Sanfelice (1675–1748) had a highly inventive and theatrical approach to staircases. **Luigi Vanvitelli** (1700–73) became the greatest 18C Neapolitan architect, entrusted with rivaling fabled Versailles at Caserta. In the 17C Naples began to specialise in the marvellous **Christmas mangers** (*presepi*).

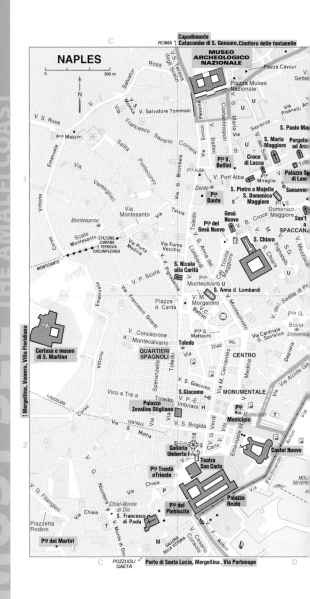

NAPLES

0   300 m

N

C   D

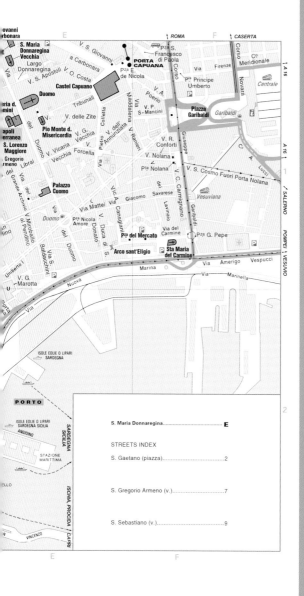

NAPLES

CITY CENTRE★★

Europe's largest historic centre is a world of contradictions. Glamorous palm-tree-lined boulevards hide dingy houses, while ornate palaces rise above trash-filled streets. The chaos, glamour and grunge create an atmosphere that is uniquely Neapolitan. Piazza vendors peddle, while scooters dash through alleyways between Baroque churches and Renaissance palaces.

Napoli Sotterranea★★

Associazione Napolisotterranea, Piazza San Gaetano 68. €9. 081 29 69 44. www.napoli sotterranea.org.

121 stairs lead 40m/131ft into Naples' underground, where Greeks scooped out caves from the tufa to build the city walls. During the Augustean era, the Romans constructed an aqueduct. A narrow passage leads to Greek cisterns. A 6 000-seat Roman theatre (1C–2C), was discovered in 2002; two arches are visible along Via Anticaglia. Following the decumanus (Via Tribunali), beyond Via San Gregorio Armeno is the church of **Santa Maria delle Anime del Purgatorio ad Arco** (*Via Tribunali 39; open Mon–Fri 10am–2pm; Sun 10am–5pm; Sat 10am–2pm; €5. 081 44 04 38. www.purgatorioadarco.it*), rich in macabre symbols of a fraternity that celebrated Mass for the souls in purgatory.

Palazzo Spinelli di Laurino★

Via Tribunali 362.

This 18C palace has an elliptical courtyard adorned with statues of the eight virtues; medallions in bas-relief depict mythological scenes. The church of Santa Maria Maggiore ("La Pietrasanta") has beautiful brick pavement and majolica (1764). The Renaissance **Cappella Pontano** (*Via Tribunali 16; open Mon–Sat 9am–1pm*) is near the beautiful 11C red-brick tower.

Piazza Bellini

One of the most enjoyable spots in the historic centre, Piazza Bellini is the gathering place for Fine Arts students and the literary crowd. Remains of the town's Greek walls (4C BC) are visible in the square. The Palazzo Firrao façade has statues that represent Kings of Spain, in the 15–17C.

Piazza Dante

This large semicircular square, modified in the 18C by Luigi Vanvitelli, bridges the old centre with the Spanish Quarter.

Quartieri Spagnoli

Built in the 16C to house the Viceroy's Spanish troops, Naples' Spanish Quarter is guarded by Certosa di San Martino. Streets from this labyrinth open into churches. The Spanish Quarter has a rough reputation. However, it is worth exploring; take precautions such as not walking alone at night, and keeping your purse or wallet out of sight. One of Naples' most exciting and intriguing places.

Galleria di Palazzo Zevallos Stigliano★

Via Toledo 185. Open Tue–Fri 10am–6pm (Sat and Sun 8). €5. 800 454 229. www.gallerieditalia.com/ it/napoli.

This magnificent 16C palace with an ornate entrance, was beautifully rebuilt in 1637. Here is the masterpiece **Martirio** di Sant'Orsola★ *(Martyrdom of St Ursula)*, painted by Caravaggio in 1610, weeks before his death.

Galleria Umberto I★
Via San Carlo.
This 1897 shopping gallery, with its mosaic pavement and marble reliefs, opens onto busy Via Toledo and is opposite the San Carlo Theatre. The glass and wrought-iron dome is supported by elegant female figures.

Piazza Trento e Trieste
This square is enclosed by the **Teatro San Carlo★★** Theatre, one side of the Royal Palace, the famous 🍽 **Gran Caffè Gambrinus**, and the Baroque church of San Ferdinando. Via Chiaia begins here.

Piazza del Plebiscito★
This semicircular "square" (19C) is enclosed by the royal palace and the Neoclassical façade of the church of San Francesco di Paola, modelled after the Pantheon in Rome. The equestrian statues of Ferdinand I and Charles III of Bourbon are by Canova.

Palazzo Reale★
Piazza del Plebiscito 1.
Open Thu–Tue 9am–8pm.
Closed hols. €4. 848 800 288.
www.coopculture.it.
The 17C palace was built by the architect Domenico Fontana. Eight statues of Kings of Naples adorn the façade. A huge staircase crowned by a coffered dome leads to the **apartments★**. The richly ornamented rooms have retained art, tapestries, paintings, furniture and fine porcelain. Note the splendid wood **door knockers★**

of *putti*, nymphs and animals are set off against a gilded background.

Piazza del Municipio
Facing the *lungomare*, the Piazza Municipio is on the site of an old Roman port. Remains of two Roman ships, excavated here, are displayed in the subway station.

Castel Nuovo (or Maschio Angioino)★
Piazza Municipio. Open Mon–Sat 9am–7pm. €6. 081 42 01 241.
This imposing castle, surrounded by deep moats, was built in 1282 for Charles I of Anjou, modelled on the castle at Angers.
A remarkable **triumphal arch★★** was designed by Francesco Laurana in 1467. The **Sala dei Baroni** has fine star shaped vaulting. The panoramic terrace offers beautiful views of the port and rooftops of Spaccanapoli.

PORT AND MARKET QUARTER
Founded by the Greeks who landed here in the 8C BC, the Angioino port was built in the early-14C by the House of Anjou and is one of Italy's busiest. The tram runs from the port to Santa Maria del Carmine.

CHIAIA AND THE LUNGOMARE★
The *lungomare* runs from the port of Santa Lucia to the little cove of Mergellina. Popular for a *passeggiata* – a stroll. Young lovers take refuge in the shady pine trees of the Villa Comunale. Piazza Sannazzaro is busy from late evening to the wee hours.

Porto di Santa Lucia★★
Santa Lucia juts out towards the sea with a tiny port. **Castel dell'Ovo**

135

[*Borgo Marinari, via Eldorado 3; open Mon–Sat 9am–6.30pm (in summer 7.30pm), Sun 9am–2pm; 081 79 54 593*] was the first castle in the city, built by the Normans, later a residence of the House of Anjou. Stunning views from its terrace. The jetty offers a splendid **view★★** of Vesuvius and the bay. In the evening Piazza Vittoria offers a **view★★★** of the twinkling lights the Vomero and Posillipo hillsides.

Via Partenope

Via Partenope is by the sea at Castel dell'Ovo. Great hotels, trendy bars and trattorias line the sunny avenue. The quays are lined with restaurants on stilts and the Borgo Marinaro (sea village).

Piazza dei Martiri

This pleasant piazza in the neighborhood of Chiaia pays tribute to those who fell during the revolt against the Bourbons. The tiny Calabritto has major names in Italian and French fashion. Beyond is Villa Comunale.

Mergellina★

Mergellina, at the foot of the Posillipo hillside, affords a splendid bay **view★★**; the Vomero hillside, crowned by Castel Sant'Elmo, slopes down towards Santa Lucia, then Castel dell'Ovo and Vesuvius.

VOMERO★

The best views of the city and the Gulf of Naples are from Vomero, with stepped alleyways and lush, green parks. In the centre is Piazza Vanvitelli, with big fashion streets, radiating from it. Vomero is a haven of peace above the Spanish area.

Certosa di San Martino★★

Largo San Martino 5. Open Thu–Tue 8.30am–7.30pm. €6. 848 800 288 or 06 399 67 050 (from mobile). www.coopculture.it.
This 14C monastery founded by the Anjou dynasty sits on the Vomero hill. The **Castel Sant'Elmo** was rebuilt by the Spaniards in the 16C and used as a prison. From the drill square (*access on foot or by lift*) the view spans the city and the bay. The **interior★★** of the church is lavishly Baroque and adorned with paintings by Caracciolo, Guido Reni and Simon Vouet. The treasury has frescoes by Luca Giordano and a Ribera painting. *La Pietà*. The **great cloister** is by Cosimo Fanzago. The section on festivals and costumes in the **museum★** features 18C and 19C Neapolitan **cribs★★** (*presepi*) in polychrome terra-cotta.

Villa Floridiana★

West of the city. Via Cimarosa 77. Open Wed–Mon 8.30am–7pm, Sat 2pm. €4. 848 800 288 or 06 39 96 70 501 (from abroad and mobiles). www.polomusealenapoli. beniculturali.it.
This graceful small white palace overlooks the gardens, which afford a splendid **panorama★★** and houses the **Museo Duca di Martina★**, with fine faience and porcelain.

RIONE SANITÀ★

Lodged between the National Archaeological Museum and the Royal Palace of Capodimonte, this tangle of winding streets is on both sides of Corso Amedeo di Savoia. The neighbourhood, home to three catacombs, is considered a stronghold of the Camorra but during the day is relatively safe.

"La Paranza", a group from Rione Sanità, offers guided tours. *Via Tondo di Capodimonte 13. 081 744 37 14. www.catacombedinapoli.it.*

Madre-Museo d'Arte Contemporanea Donnaregina

Via Settembrini 79. Open Wed–Mon 10am–7.30pm. €7. 081 193 13 016. www.madrenapoli.it.

Transformed into a contemporary art museum by the Portuguese architect Alvaro Siza. The ground floor houses temporary exhibitions while the upper floors hold a collection of work from local and international artists, including Horn, Rauschenberg, Warhol, Klein and Koons.

Catacombe di San Gennaro★★

North of the city. Via Tondo di Capodimonte 13. Guided tours only (40min), Mon–Sat every hour from 10am–5pm, Sun and hols 2pm. €8. 081 744 37 14. www.catacombedinapoli.it.

The catacombs are dug into volcanic rock and extend over two floors. The tomb of St Januarius, transferred here in the 6C, is decorated with frescoes of the saint (3C–10C). The upper section and the *atrium* vault is adorned with early Christian work and portraits on family tombs.

Cimitero delle Fontanelle★★

Via Fontanelle 154. Open daily 10am–5pm. 081 19 70 31 97.

The cemetery periodically closes for a variety of reasons. At the end of Via Fontanelle, the old Greco-Roman quarry houses the bones of victims (perhaps 300 000) from the deadliest century in Naples' history:

in the 1600s some three-quarters of the population died. Made famous by the Rossellini film *Italian Journey* (1953), the vast cellar has three long aisles lined with skulls, with other bones in the ground, up to 70m/230ft deep. The faithful "adopted" a skull of unknown dead, to regularly visit and pray for.

Museo Archeologico Nazionale★★★

Piazza Museo Nazionale 19. Wed–Mon 9am–7.30pm. Closed hols. €12. 848 800 288 or 06 39 96 70 501 (from mobiles). www.coopculture.it.

One of the world's richest museums for Greco-Roman Antiquities, the National Archaeological Museum collections include that of the Farnese family and treasures discovered at Pompeii and Herculaneum.

Palazzo and Galleria Nazionale di Capodimonte★★

Via Miano 2. Open Thu–Tue 8.30am–7.30pm. €10. 848 800 288 or 06 39 96 70 501 (from mobile). www.coopculture.it.

This former **royal estate★** includes a palace, a park, the remains of the 18C porcelain factory and an exceptional art gallery.

Decumanus Maximus★★

The main axis of old Naples, formed by Via S. Benedetto Croce, Via S. Biagio dei Librai and Via Vicaria Vecchia is nicknamed "Spaccanapoli" ("Split Naples"), because it cleaves the city. Once a main road through ancient Naples, the **Decumanus Maximus** now traces the Via Tribunali.

BAY OF NAPLES★★★

The Bay of Naples, from Cumae to Sorrento, is one of the most beautiful bays in Italy. Tranquil archaeological sites, the bare slopes of Vesuvius, the Sibyl's Cave or Lake Averno, contrast with nearby traffic. Industrial sprawl mars the beauty in patches. However, its islands and mountains are as lovely as they were 2 000 years ago.

CAMPI FLEGREI★★

The volcanic Phlegrean Fields extend along the Gulf of Pozzuoli. Hot springs, steam-jets and sulphurous gases rise from the ground and sea. Lakes occupy volcanic craters.

Posillipo★

This promontory separates the Bay of Naples from the Gulf of Pozzuoli. Posillipo, dotted with villas, lovely gardens and modern buildings, has splendid bay views.

Parco Virgiliano★

The park has splendid **views★★** over the Bay of Naples: Cape Miseno, the Sorrento Peninsula, and the islands of Procida, Ischia and Capri.

Pozzuoli★

Pozzuoli, of Greek origin was an active Roman trading port. Centre of the volcanic Phlegrean Fields, its ground level shifts frequently. Highlights: **Antifeatro Flavio★★**, **Tempio di Serapide★** and **Tempio di Augusto★**.

Solfatara★★

This extinct crater still has active jets of steam charged with sulphurous fumes, fumaroles that spit hot mud and bubbling jets of sand. Used for medicinal purposes since Roman times. Children enjoy the thrill of mild volcanic activity.

Baia★

This Greek colony was in Roman times a fashionable beach resort and famous thermal spa. Roman emperors and patricians had immense villas, later entombed

Practical Information

Getting Around

Location: The main access roads are the A 1, the A 3 and the A 16.
Ticket UnicoCostiera – *www.unicocampania.it.* Three days of public transport (€18).
Campi Flegrei – *89 20 21. www.trenitalia.com.* From Naples, the Metro Line 2 goes to Pozzuoli. Train lines and Cumana Circumflegrea serve other stations.

Tickets

Campania>Artecard – Valid for 3 (€32) or 7 days (€34); museums, archaeological sites, castles and other attractions, including public transport. *800 600 601 or 06 39 96 76 50. www.campaniartecard.it.*
Combination Tickets – Five site tickets (€20), three days, for Pompeii, Herculaneum, Boscoreale, Stabia and Oplontis. *www.pompeiisites.org.*

under the sea; ruins are visible in an underwater **archaeological park**★.

Cuma★

Cumae, one of the oldest Greek colonies (8C BC) dominated the Phlegrean area including Naples. The ruins include the acropolis; the lower town has remains of an amphitheatre and a temple to Jupiter, Juno and Minerva.

Lago d'Averno★

This lake within a crater is dark, still and silent, shrouded in mystery, regarded as the entrance to the Underworld. Agrippa developed a naval base and linked it with Lake Lucrino. An underground gallery 1km/0.6mi **Grotta di Cocceio** connected *Avernus* with *Cumae*; it was used by chariots.

VESUVIUS★★★

The outline of Vesuvius, one of the few still-active volcanoes in Europe, can also be observed from the rim above. It has two summits: to the north **Monte Somma** (1 132m/3 714ft) and to the south Vesuvius proper (1 277m/ 4 190ft). Fertile volcanic soil on the lower slopes help orchards of vines to produce *Lacryma Christi* wine.

TO THE PENISOLA SORRENTINA★★

Castellammare di Stabia✝

This ancient Roman spa town was destroyed by the AD 79 eruption of Vesuvius. Highlights include the **antiquarium**★ and **roman villas**.

Monte Faito★★

Monte Faito, part of the **Lattari Range**, has splendid **panoramas**★★★ of the Bay of Naples from Belvedere dei Capi and from **Cappella San Michele**.

Vico Equense★

This picturesque rocky site in the historic **centre**★ has a rare Gothic church, an Angevin castle with a beautiful garden, and lovely beaches at **Marina di Equa**★ or the Spiaggia della Tartaruga (Turtle Beach).

Sorrento★★

This important resort, known for its beautiful gardens, overlooks the bay. Orange and lemon groves perfume the countryside. Highlights include the **historic centre**★ and the **Museo Correale di Terranova**★, with its Neapolitan paintings and local intarsia work.

Penisola Sorrentina★★

This winding road skirts the Sorrento Peninsula and affords fine views of hillsides covered with olive groves, orange and lemon trees, and vines. The bends on this road afford spectacular views of enchanting landscapes, fantastically shaped rocks plunging vertically into a crystal-clear sea, deep gorges spanned by dizzy bridges and Saracen towers perched on rocks. The Amalfi Coast has a wild and rugged landscape. Charming fishing villages popular with artists are set below luxuriant Mediterranean vegetation. The cuisine is famous for abundant seafood and the local mozzarella cheese, washed down with local wines.

HERCULANEUM★★

Herculaneum is a UNESCO World Heritage Site at the foot of Vesuvius that was founded, according to tradition, by Hercules. Rich patricians came to Herculaneum for its beautiful setting above the Bay of Naples. After the AD 79 eruption of Vesuvius, much of the Roman town was buried under a mudslide preserving some wood structures. Many inhabitants died as they tried to flee. The most valuable finds, from here and from Pompeii, are in the Naples Archaeological Museum.

HIGHLIGHTS

Off the A 3, at Corso Resina.
Open Apr–Oct 8.30am–7.30pm;
Nov–Mar 5pm. €11; €20 combined
Pompeii, Herculaneum, Oplontis,
Stabiae, Boscoreale (3 days).
081 73 24 315 or 199 75 75 17.
www.pompeiisites.org.
Casa dell'Atrio a Mosaico★★ mosaic atrium; Casa a Graticcio★★ for its wooden framework; Casa del Tramezzo carbonizzato★; Casa Sannitica★★ typical of the Samnites; the frescoes and mosaics in the baths★★★; the charred bed in Casa del Mobilio carbonizzato★; the shop★ and mosaics of Neptune and Amphitrite at Casa del Mosaico di Nettuno e Anfitrite★★; the unique Casa del Bel Cortile★ courtyard, staircase and balcony; Casa del Bicentenario★ frescoes; the Pistrinum★★ (bakery); Casa dei Cervi★★ and its sculpture group of stags *(cervi)* attacked by dogs; the baths at Terme suburbane★; the theatre, teatro★; and the patrician Villa dei Papiri *(Visits by appointment, 081 73 24 315)*, where some 1 000 Greek papyrus manuscripts were discovered.

POMPEII★★★

Pompeii, a port city, was buried in AD 79 in one of the most disastrous volcanic eruptions in history. The extensive and varied ruins of the dead city, in its attractive setting, movingly evoke the ancient way of Roman city life. Pompeii is on UNESCO's World Heritage List.

Practical Information

Getting There
Pompeii is positioned off the A3.

A BIT OF HISTORY
Pompeii was founded in the 8C BC by the Oscans. By the 6C BC Greeks prevailed; By end of the 5C BC, under Samnite rule, the city prospered. In the year 80 BC, the town fell under the Romans. When the eruption of Vesuvius struck, Pompeii was a booming town of about 25 000 people. Shops and workshops have been uncovered and wide streets show deep ruts made by chariot wheels. In AD 62, an earthquake extensively damaged the town; before it could be put to rights, Vesuvius erupted (August AD 79), also destroying Herculaneum and Stabiae. In two days Pompeii was buried under a layer of ash 6m–7m/20ft–23ft deep. In the 18C systematic excavations began.

🏛 HIGHLIGHTS

Access from Porta Marina or from Piazza Anfiteatro and from Piazza Esedra. Open daily Apr–Oct 9am–7.30pm (Sat and Sun 8.30); Nov–Mar –5pm. €11; €20 combined ticket (see Herculaneum pag 140). 199 75 75 17. www.pompeiisites.org.

The **Foro★★★** (forum) was the centre for religious ceremonies, trade and justice and is adorned with statues of emperors. The **basilica★★**, the largest building in Pompeii, was for the judiciary. The **Tempio di Apollo★★** pre-dates the Romans. **Tempio di Giove★★**, dedicated to the Capitoline Triad (Jupiter, Juno and Minerva), was flanked by two triumphal arches. The **Casa dei Mosaici** and the **Comitium** reopen in 2016. The **Foro Triangolare★** has Ionic columns; vestiges of its **Doric temple** date to the 6C BC. **Teatro Grande★**, the Great Theatre built in the 5C BC, was remodelled in 2C BC, and by the Romans in the 1C AD; it held 5 000 spectators. Nearby is the **Caserma dei Gladiatori**, the Gladiators' Barracks. The **Odeon★★** (covered theatre) held concerts, oratory and ballets for up to 800 spectators. The **Tempio d'Iside★** was a temple to the Egyptian goddess Isis. Its *purgatorium*, for purification rites, held water from the Nile. The **Casa di Menandro★★** is a large patrician villa richly decorated with paintings and mosaics. The atrium has a shrine to the household gods. Evocative **Via dell'Abbondanza★★**, had shops and houses. The **Fullonica Stephani★** was a home converted for the clothing industry. Fabrics were cleaned by trampling them in vats filled with water and soda or urine. The **Termopolio di Asellina** bar sold pre-cooked dishes; jars embedded in the counter proffered food. **Termopolio Grande★** had a painted *lararium*. **Casa di Loreius Tiburtinus★** is a dwelling **decorated** in fine fourth Pompeiian style with a splendid **garden★**. **Villa di Giulia Felice★** is a dwelling with baths, an inn and shops; the garden has a fine **portico★**. The **Anfiteatro★** is the oldest known Roman amphitheatre (80 BC). In the **Necropoli Fuori Porta Nocera★**, tombs line the roadside leading out of town through the Nocera Gate. The oldest (2C BC) baths in Pompeii are the **Terme Stabiane★★★**. The official brothel of Pompeii, the **Lupanare★★** is decorated with licentious subject matter, illustrating the "specialities" of the prostitutes. Wall graffiti provides customers' opinions. **Casa dei Vettii★★★** is Pompeii's most lavishly decorated villa. **Casa degli Amorini Dorati★** is decorated with cupids *(amorini)* in a deteriorated house. **Casa dell'Ara Massima** has well-preserved **paintings★**. **Casa del Fauno★★** is a luxurious house with two atriums, two peristyles and dining rooms for all seasons. The bronze faun and mosaics (in Naples Museum) were found here. **Casa della Fontana Grande** is named after its large **fountain★**. **Torre di Mercurio★** is a tower on the town wall. The **Casa del Poeta Tragico★** features the infamous inscription *Cave Canem* (Beware of the Dog). **Via delle Tombe★★** is a melancholy street lined with monumental tombs and cypresses. **Villa dei Misteri★★★** is a Patrician villa famous for its dining room **frescoes★★★**.

POMPEII

ISOLA DI ISCHIA★★★

Ischia, known as the Emerald Island because of its luxuriant vegetation, is the largest island in the Bay of Naples. Unlike Capri, Ischia has thermal spas and shows more evidence of work-a-day life. Sparkling light plays over a coast covered with pinewoods, indented with bays and villages with colourful houses. Slopes are covered with olive trees and vineyards and an occasional crumbling tower.

Practical Information

Getting There

Ischia and Procida can be reached by ferry from Naples, Capri and Pozzuoli.

Caremar *081 18 96 66, 081 984818 (Ischia) and 081 55 13 882 (Naples); www.caremar.it.*

Alilauro Volaviamare *081 49 72 252; www.alilauro.it.*

Medmar *081 33 34 411; www. medmargroup.it.*

SNAV *081 42 85 555; www.snav.it.*

A BIT OF HISTORY

The soil is volcanic and the hot springs are touted for medicinal properties. Celebrities from Michelangelo to Elizabeth Taylor, Ibsen and Garibaldi have taken refuge here. Gods and mythological heroes, too: Ulysses visited Castiglione Hill, Aphrodite soaked in the thermal waters, and Aeneas beached in Lacco Ameno.

ISCHIA★

The capital is divided into **Ischia Porto** and **Ischia Ponte**. The Corso Vittoria Colonna, lined with caffès and smart shops, links the port, in a former crater, and Ischia Ponte. The **Castello Aragonese★★** (*open daily 9am–dusk; €10; 081 99 28 34; www.castelloaragoneseischia.com*) is a beautiful castle. The bar nearby has an enchanting **view★★**. Woods and sandy beach nearby.

Highlights

Monte Epomeo★★★

1hr 30min on foot round trip.

The dramatic landscape was the cinematic backdrop for *The Talented Mr Ripley*. Cliffs swoop down to sandy beaches, with Mount Epomeo towering above. Tourists may rent a mule in Fontana. The summit of offers a vast panorama of the island and the Bay of Naples.

Sant'Angelo★

This peaceful fishing village clusters around a small harbour. The *Roja* – the *Isolotto di Sant'Angelo* – is a volcanic cone, capped with the remains of a tower and Benedictine monastery. The Maronti Beach *fumarole* (steam plume) and the ancient Roman baths at Cava Scura are popular destinations (*access by footpaths*). Only pedestrians, mules and mopeds are allowed inside the village.

Spiaggia di Citara★

This fine beach is sheltered by Punta Imperatore.

PROCIDA★

Procida is a 15/30min boat ride from Ischia.

Procida remains the wildest island in the Bay of Naples. The fishermen, gardeners and winegrowers live in a setting of colourful houses with domes, arcades and terraces.

ISOLA DI CAPRI★★★

This island's enchantment owes much to Capri's ideal position off the Sorrento Peninsula; a beautiful rugged landscape, mild climate and luxuriant vegetation; a playground for emperors Augustus and Tiberius and for D.H. Lawrence, George Bernard Shaw, Lenin, the modern jet set and to hoards of daytrippers.

Practical Information

Getting There

By ferry to Capri from Naples, Sorrento and Amalfi Coast towns. **Marina Grande★** is the main port. A funicular connects Marina Grande to Capri; bus to Anacapri.

CAPRI★★★

Capri is like a stage-setting with its small squares, little white houses, citrus trees, and Moorish alleyways. It is also expensive; expect big-city prices, especially in outdoor bars.

Piazza Umberto I★ – This famous *piazzetta* is the centre.
Belvedere Cannone★★ – The **Via Madre Serafina★** promenade presents the mysterious Capri with winding stepped alleys.
Belvedere di Tragara★★ – Splendid view of the *Faraglioni*.
Marina Piccola★ – At the foot of Monte Solaro, a fishing harbour and beautiful small beaches.
Villa Jovis★★ – *Steep walk along Via Botteghe and Via Tiberio, 30–40min. Open May 10am–6pm (Jun–Aug 7pm, Sep–Oct 5pm, Nov–Dec 4pm). €2. www.capri.it*. Tiberius's villa, with servants' quarters, cisterns and apartments. The **panorama★★** spans the whole island. **Tiberius' Leap★** is where his victims were allegedly thrown.
Arco Naturale★ – 25min walk from Capri, along Via Sopramonte and Via Croce. Erosion created this gigantic natural rock arch.

ANACAPRI★★★

Via Roma leads to Anacapri, a delightful village with shady streets and fewer crowds than Capri.
Villa San Michele★★ – *Near Piazza della Vittoria. Daily 9am–1hr before dusk. €7. 081 83 71 401. www.san michele.org*. Built late 19C for Axel Munthe, the villa has 17–18C furniture and Roman sculptures. The **garden** has a splendid **panorama★★★** of Capri, Marina Grande, Mount Tiberius and Faraglioni.
Monte Solaro★★★ – *Via Caposcuro 10. Chairlift Mar–Apr 9.30am–4pm, Nov–Feb 3.30pm, May–Oct 5pm. €8, €11 return. 081 83 70 420. www.capriseggiovia.it*. The chairlift rises to an unforgettable **panorama★★★** of the Bay of Naples as far as the island of Ponza and the Calabria.
Belvedere di Migliara★ – *1hr on foot round trip, on Via Caposcuro*. A remarkable **view★** of the lighthouse on Punta Carena.

BOAT TRIPS

The Blue Grotto, the most famous of Capri's caves. Light enters by refraction through the water, giving it a beautiful blue colour.
Grotta Azzurra★★ – *Boats from Marina Grande. Daily (except at high tide and rough seas). 1hr. Entrance to the Grotta Azzurra costs an extra; €13*. **Laser Capri** *(081 83 75 208; www.lasercapri.com. 9am–4pm, €14);* **Motoscafisti** *(081 83 77 714; www.motoscafisticapri.com. €15).*

AMALFI COAST★★★

With its charming fishing villages and luxuriant vegetation – a mixture of orange, lemon, olive and almond trees, as well as vines and bougainvillea – the Amalfi Coast has long been popular with travellers and artists. The wild and rugged landscape contrasts with its glamorous reputation. The international jet set of the 1950s and 60s came aboard fabulous yachts in search of La Dolce Vita. Now the "Costiera" attracts tourists from all walks of life, but remains a hot-spot for the rich and famous.

POSITANO★★

Via Regina Giovanna 13.
089 87 50 67.
www.aziendaturismopositano.it.
The white cubic houses of this old fishing village reveal a strong Moorish influence; lush gardens dotted on terraced slopes go down to the sea. Positano is "the only place in the world designed on a vertical axis" (Paul Klee). Much loved and frequented in the past by artists and intellectuals (Picasso, Cocteau and Steinbeck) and by the trend setters of *La Dolce Vita* who used to meet up at the *Buca di Bacco* nightclub, today Positano is one of the most popular resorts of the Amalfi Coast. "Positano fashion" was born here in the 1950s, with its brightly coloured materials, paisley, and famous sandals.

VETTICA MAGGIORE

Houses are scattered over the slopes. From the esplanade there is a fine **view**★★ of the coast and sea.

PRAIANO

This Moorish-looking town has houses that are sprinkled along the slopes of Monte Sant'Angelo and features the lovely **Marina di Praia**★, an attractive hidden beach. It can be accessed at the marina by a path that passes by the **Asciola Torre** (*free*), built during the Saracen invasions. The painter and ceramicist Paolo Sandulli lived here, devoted to capturing local village life.

VALLONE DI FURORE★★

The Furore Valley, between two road tunnels, is the most impressive section of the coast owing to the dark depths of its steep, rocky walls and, in stormy weather, the thunder of wild, rough seas. A fishermen's village has been built where a small torrent gushes into the sea. The houses cling to the slopes and vividly coloured boats are drawn up on the shore. A foot path goes along one side of the gorge. Note the **"Art walls"** (*Muri d'autore*), contemporary paintings and sculptures.

GROTTA DELLO SMERALDO★★

Access to cave by lift from street 9.30am–4pm. €5. Or by boat from Molo Pennello, €10 round trip (admission not included). 089 87 11 07.
www.amalfitouristoffice.it.
The exceptionally clear water of this marine cave is illuminated indirectly by rays of light that give it a beautiful emerald (*smeraldo*) colour. The bottom looks quite close, though the water is 10m/33ft deep. Fine stalactites add interest. The cave became

Positano

submerged as a result of variations in ground level caused by the volcanic activity.

AMALFI★★

Set in a steep valley, Amalfi is centred on the beach. The main street, Via Genova, leads to a wild gorge with mill-ruins. 089 87 11 07. www.amalfitouristoffice.it.

Amalfi is a Spanish-looking little town with tall white houses built on slopes facing the sea in a wonderful **setting★★★**. Amalfi enjoys a mild climate, making it a popular holiday resort. Piazza Duomo, Via Genova (Via Capuano) and **Via dei Mercanti** make up the **historic centre★** and business heart of the city with its picturesque façades, flowering balconies and niches. The Islamic-looking layout of the town is characterised by winding alleyways, staircases and vaulted passages. Famous for its lemons, Amalfi produces a liqueur, *limoncello*.

Duomo di Sant'Andrea★

Chiostro del Paradiso and Museo Diocesano: Open Mar–Jun and Oct 9am–6.45pm; Jul–Sept 7.45pm; rest of the year 10am–1pm and 2.30–4.30pm.€3. 089 87 13 24. www.amalfitouristoffice.it

Founded in the 9C, the cathedral is an example of the Oriental splendour favoured by maritime cities. The façade, rebuilt in the 19C, is the focal point, with striking geometrical designs in multicoloured stone. The campanile is all that remains of the original church. A beautiful 11C bronze **door★**, cast in Constantinople, opens onto the vast *atrium* that precedes the church and into the 1268 **Cloisters of Paradise★★** (Chiostro del Paradiso), blending Romanesque austerity and Arab fantasy. The Museo Diocesano is housed in the **Basilica del Crocefisso**; its crypt holds the relics of St Andrew the Apostle, brought from Constantinople in 1206.

ATRANI★

This pleasant fishermen's village at the mouth of the Dragon Valley (Valle del Dragone) has two old churches: Santa Maria Maddalena and San Salvatore, founded in the 10C with a fine bronze door similar to that in Amalfi Cathedral. The road winds up the narrow valley, planted with vines and olive groves, to Ravello.

RAVELLO★★★

Most attractions cluster around the Piazza Vescovado. 089 85 70 96. www.ravellotime.it.

Ravello's stairways and roofed passages cling to the steep slopes of the Dragon Hill. The site★★★, suspended between sea and sky, is unforgettable. The town's aristocratic restraint has, over the centuries, beguiled artists, musicians and writers such as Virginia and Leonard Woolf, D.H. Lawrence, Graham Greene, Gore Vidal, Hans Escher and Joan Miró.

Villa Rufolo★★★

Piazza Vescovado, next to the Duomo. Open daily 9am–8pm (in winter dusk). 5€. 089 85 76 21. www.villarufolo.it

The villa built in the 13C by the rich Rufolo family of Ravello (cited in Boccaccio's *Decameron*) was the residence of several popes, Charles of Anjou and more recently, in 1880, of **Richard Wagner**; the villa's splendid garden inspired his *Parsifal*. A well-shaded avenue leads to a Gothic entrance tower. A Moorish-style courtyard has sharply pointed arches in the Sicilian-Norman style.
The terraces offer a splendid panorama★★★ of the jagged peaks as far as Cape Orso, the Bay of Maiori and the Gulf of Salerno. Summer **concerts** *(Società dei Concerti di Ravello; 089 85 81 49; www.ravelloarts.org)* in the gardens are held against a backdrop of trees, flowers and sea.

Villa Cimbrone★★

Via Santa Chiara 26. Open daily 9am–8pm (in winter dusk). €7. 089 85 74 59. www.ravellotime.it.

A charming **alley**★ leads from Piazza Vescovado to the 19C villa, passing through the Gothic porch of the convent of St Francis. The Villa Cimbrone garden for the **Bloomsbury Group** embodied the ideal aesthetic of clarity, order and harmony. The belvedere, adorned with marble busts, has an immense **panorama**★★★ over the terraced hillsides, Maiori, Cape Orso and the Gulf of Salerno.

MAIORI

This village conceals the cave church of **Santa Maria Olearia**★, an ancient medieval abbey that was built in the 10C. Note inside the remains of beautiful Byzantine frescoes dating from the 11C. Three haloed figures cover the crypt and in the main chapel, several scenes from the life of Jesus (*The Annunciation*, *The Visitation* and the *Adoration of the Magi*). *Wed 2.30–6.30pm, Sat and Sun 9am–1pm. 089 87 74 52.*

CAPO D'ORSO★

The cape with its jagged rocks affords an interesting view of **Maiori Bay**★.

CETARA

A little fishing village loved by windsurfers. The **Marina de Cetara** beach is peaceful.

VIETRI SUL MARE

At the eastern end of this stretch of coastline, Vietre sul Mare is a pretty town, known for its ceramic ware. It affords magnificent **views★★** of the Amalfi Coast.

Abbazia della Santissima Trinità★

5km/3mi N of Vietri sul Mare. Open 8.30am–12pm. €3; free entry to the church. 347 19 46 957. www.badiadicava.it.

This Benedictine abbey was founded in the 11C and was one of the most powerful in southern Italy during the Middle Ages. The church, rebuilt in the 18C, has a fine pulpit and paschal candelabra. The tour includes the halls of the monastery, the cloister, cemetery and museum.

CAVA DEI TIRRENI

This pleasant city is nestled in a valley and is marked at its entrance by a medieval bridge with six arches. Corso Vittorio Emanuele is a beautiful street lined with arcades and stucco facades.

SALERNO★

The medieval quarter starts at Corso Vittorio Emanuele and stretches along Via dei Mercanti. The largest car park is on Via Alvarez. Lungomare Trieste 7/9. 089 23 14 32. www.aziendaturismo.sa.it.

Salerno, lying along the graceful curve of its gulf, has a passenger port. Its medieval quarter is on the slopes of a hill crowned by a castle. From the Lungomare Trieste, planted with palm trees and tamarinds, there is a wide view of the Gulf of Salerno. The picturesque Via dei Mercanti, which crosses the old town, is lined with shops, old houses and oratories. At its west end stands an 8C Lombard arch, Arco di Arechi. On the way to the Duomo is a medieval medical herb garden.

Duomo★★

Mon–Sat 9.30am–6pm, Sun 4–6pm. www.cattedraledisalerno.it.

The cathedral, consecrated by Pope Gregory VII in 1085, is dedicated to St Matthew the Evangelist, who is buried in the crypt. The Norman-style building was remodelled in the 18C and was damaged in the 1980 earthquake. The church is preceded by an *atrium* of multicoloured stone with ancient columns. The square tower to the right is from the 12C. The central doorway has 11C **bronze doors★**. The interior contains two **ambos★★** encrusted with decorative mosaics and on columns with carved capitals, along with the paschal candelabrum and the elegant iconostasis. The Crusaders' Chapel at the end of the south aisle is where the Crusaders had their arms blessed. Under the altar is the tomb of Pope Gregory VII, who died in exile at Salerno (1085).

Museo Archeologico

Via San Benedetto 28. Open Tue–Sun 9am–7.30pm. 089 23 11 35. €4. www.museoarcheologicosalerno.it.

Housed in the attractive St Benedict monastery complex, the museum has artefacts dating from prehistory to the late Imperial era. Of particular note is the **bronze Head of Apollo★** (1C BC) and a fine collection of pre-Roman amber.

PAESTUM★★★

One of Italy's most important archaeological sites, Paestum was an ancient Greek colony founded around 600 BC as *Poseidonia* by colonists from Sybaris. Around the year 400 BC the city fell to the Lucanians. It became Roman in the year 273 BC, but began to decline towards the end of the Empire. The yellow limestone temples stand amid the ruins of dwellings, sheltered by cypresses and oleanders.

Practical Information

Getting There

Paestum is on the coast, close to the S 18, 48km/29.8mi south of Salerno.

VISIT

The suggested itinerary (2hrs) proceeds from south to north. The museum is north. Open daily 8.30am–7.30pm. €7. Ticket Unico – museum, Paestum and Velia – €10 for 3 days. 0828 81 10 16. www.infopaestum.it.
Take the Porta della Giustizia through the 5km/3mi-long city wall, **Cinta Muraria★**, and follow the **Via Sacra**, the principal street of the ancient city.

Basilica★★

This mid-6C BC temple, the oldest in the city, was dedicated to Hera, sister and bride of Zeus. The porch (*pronaos*) leads into the central chamber divided into two aisles, indicating that two cults were practised here.

Tempio di Nettuno★★★

This well-preserved Doric temple was thought to have been dedicated to Neptune/Poseidon, but has been identified as dedicated to Hera. Dating from the mid-5C BC, the convexity of the horizontal line makes the numerous columns look straight.
The **forum**, surrounded by a portico and shops, is overlooked by the **curia**,

the adjacent *macellum* (covered market) and the *comitium* (3C BC), where magistrates were elected. To the left of the *comitium* stands the **Temple of Peace** (2C–1C BC). The **amphitheatre**, constructed between the Republican and Imperial ages is divided by the main road.

Tempio di Cerere★★

Originally erected in the late-6C BC in honour of Athena, the Temple of Ceres combines an interesting mix of styles. On the east side is the sacrificial altar, the **ara**.

Museo★★

Via Magna Grecia. Open daily 8.30am–7.30pm (1st and 3rd Mon of the month 1.40pm). €9 including archaeological site. 0828 81 10 23. www.infopaestum.it.
The masterpieces in this museum include the famous **metopes★★**, 6C BC low reliefs in the Doric style that adorned both the *Thesauròs*, or temple of Hera (scenes from the life of Heracles and the Trojan Wars), and the High Temple (Dancing Girls) of the Sanctuary of Hera at Sele (*10km/6.2mi N near the mouth of the River Sele*), as well as the Tomb of the Diver, the **Tomba del Tuffatore★★**, a rare example of Greek funerary painting with banquet scenes and the dive, symbol of passage from life to death. The museum houses **vases★** (6C BC), a bronze sculpture, the painted Lucanian tombs (4C BC) and representations of Hera Argiva.

REGGIA DI CASERTA★★

Charles III of Bourbon chose Caserta, far from the vulnerable Neapolitan Coast, to host a magnificent edifice that could compete with other European courts. The Royal Palace of Caserta is a UNESCO's World Heritage Site.

Practical Information

Getting There

Off the A 1 (exit Caserta Nord), about 20km/12mi from Naples.

PALAZZO

Vanvitelli's masterpiece staircase. Open Wed–Mon 8.30am–dusk. Apartments, Grand Staircase, Vaulted ceiling and park and gardens €12; apartm. €9. 0823 44 80 84. www. reggiadicaserta.beniculturali.it.

In 1752 Charles III of Bourbon commissioned the architect **Luigi Vanvitelli** to erect a palace (*reggia*). Caserta has a geometric layout, its purity of line seems to anticipate the Neoclassical style, but the theatrical interior is Rococo. The vast building (249m/273yds long and 190m/208yds wide) contains four internal courtyards and magnificent **entrance hall★**. The grand staircase★★ (*scalone d'onore*) leads to the Palatine Chapel and to the royal apartments decorated in the Neoclassical style.

The **Eighteenth Century Apartment** (*Appartamento Settecentesco*) has vaulted frescoed ceilings depicting the seasons and ports by J.P. Hackert.

The **Queen's Apartment** (*Appartamento della Regina*) has some curious pieces including a chandelier adorned with little tomatoes and a cage with a clock and a stuffed bird. Sala Ellittica has an 18C Neapolitan **crib★** (*presepe*).

Park

The ideal grand Baroque garden seems infinite, arranged around a central canal that spans five mountains and three valleys with a total length of 40km/25mi. Mythological sculptures include the *Diana and Actaeon* group at the foot of the great **cascade★★** (78m/256ft high). The picturesque **English garden★★** *(giardino inglese)* was created for Maria-Carolina of Austria.

EXCURSIONS

Basilica di Sant'Angelo in Formis★★

15km/9.3mi NW of Caserta Vecchia (take the SS 87 to S. Iorio). Open daily 9.30am–12.30pm and 3.30–6.30pm. If it is closed, call 0823 96 08 17. One of the most beautiful medieval buildings in Campania. Erected in the 11C, the interior is covered in **frescoes**; local production but with a strong Byzantine influence.

Capua

6km/3.7mi SW of S. Angelo in Formis. www.comunedicapua.it. **Museo Campano★** – *At the corner of Via Duomo and Via Roma. €6. 0823 62 00 76. www.museocampano.it.* The archaeological section has an astonishing collection of 6C–1C BC **Matres Matutae**, Italic earth goddesses. Nearby, Santa Maria Capua in Vetere has the second-largest amphitheatre after Rome's Colosseum.

SARDINIA

Sardinia offers an almost primeval landscape of rocks sculpted by the wind and sea, forests of holm and cork oaks, oleander, aromatic plants and shrubs, the clear blue waters of the Mediterranean and the silence of an earlier age broken only by the sounds of nature.

SARDINIA TODAY

Sardinia, the Mediterranean's second-largest island, owes its modern role as a tourism hot-spot to two foreign entities. After World War II, the Rockefeller Foundation helped the island eliminate mosquitoes. With malaria gone, Sardinia was ripe for development. In 1961 Aga Khan IV invested in a tourist complex on the northeastern coast.

This development, the *Costa Smeralda* (**Emerald Coast**), is today a playground of the jet set. Tourism to Sardinia's beaches, as well as its wild interior, is a major component of the island's economy. The military industrial complex also contributes to Sardinia's coffers.

Although Sardinia has undergone a long period of "Italianisation", it is by definition one of the autonomous regions of Italy, which is evident in the island's culture and language. People of the island still speak a variety of dialects, including **Catalàn**, a result of Spanish influence, and Gallurese, a language akin to Corsican. Sardinia is also known among Italians for its rebellious streak. The phenomenon of banditry still exists, particularly in the mountainous **Barbagia** region. In **Orgosolo**, a collection of political murals depict the struggles the natives have endured at the hands of the Italian government and fellow islanders.

EARLIEST INHABITANTS

Sardinia has traces of human settlement dating back to prehistoric times – *domus de janas* (fairies' houses) with their disturbing human-like features, dolmens standing alone in the middle of fields and ancient **nuraghi**.

The Nuraghic civilisation lasted from 1800 to 500 BC; its golden

Isola di Spargi, Arcipelago di La Maddalena

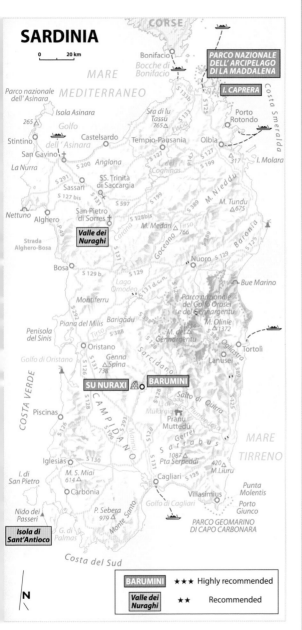

SARDINIA

0 — 20 km

CORSE

MARE MEDITERRANEO

Parco nazionale dell' Asinara

Isola Asinara
265 △

Golfo dell' Asinara

Stintino
San Gavino
La Nurra

Nettuno

Alghero

Strada Alghero-Bosa

Bosa

Bonifacio
Bocche di Bonifacio

PARCO NAZIONALE DELL' ARCIPELAGO DI LA MADDALENA

I. CAPRERA

Costa Smeralda

Sra di lu Tassu
765 △

Porto Rotondo

Castelsardo

Anglona

Tempio-Pausania

S 200

L. del Coghinas

Olbia

317 △

I. Molara

SS. Trinità di Saccargia

Sassari
S 127 bis

San Pietro di Sorres †

M. Medari △ 766

M. Nieddu

M. Tundu △ 675

Baronia

Valle dei Nuraghi

Goceano

Tirso

Nuoro   S 129

Bue Marino

Lago Omodeo

Montiferru

Barigadu

Piana del Milis

Penisola del Sinis

Oristano

Golfo di Oristano

COSTA VERDE

Piscinas

Iglesias

I. di San Pietro

Carbonia

Nido dei Passeri

Isola di Sant'Antioco

Parco nazionale del Golfo Orosei e del Gennargentu

M. Olinie △ 1372

1834 △
M. del Gennargentu

Genna Spina 738

Lanusei

Tortolì

SU NURAXI   **BARUMINI**

Salto di Quirra

Pranu Muttedu

Gerrei

Pta Serpeddì
1087 △

M. Liuru
420 △

CAMPIDANO

Cagliari

Villasimius

Punta Molentis

Porto Giunco

Golfo di Cagliari

PARCO GEOMARINO DI CAPO CARBONARA

P. Sebera 979 △

Monte Santo

G. di Palmas

Costa del Sud

MARE TIRRENO

N

BARUMINI	★★★	Highly recommended
Valle dei Nuraghi	★★	Recommended

Practical Information

Getting There
Ferries arrive in the ports of Cagliari, Golfo Aranci, Olbia, Porto Torres and Arbatax. Book in advance for summer crossings. By air, **Sardinia's airports** are in Alghero, Cagliari, Olbia and Sassari.

Sightseeing
Sardinia offers rugged scenery, views of the sea and megalithic remains. Allow at least a week to see the island fully. The east side of the island has few petrol stations, so fill the tank before your journey.

Shopping
Sardinia's cottage industries produce goldwork, ceramics, leather, wood and cork, tapestries and basketware.

What to eat and drink
Traditional Sardinian cuisine is simple but tasty, made with the island's aromatic plants and herbs. Bread includes the thin crunchy *carasau*, known as *carta da musica*. *Malloreddus,* called *gnocchetti sardi*, is Sardinia's classic shell-shaped pasta, often served with a ragù (meat sauce) of sausage and tomato. Cheeses include *fiore* and *pecorino*. Meat favorites are roast suckling pig *(porchetto da latte)* and lamb. Sweets include *papassinos made* with flour, raisins and various condiments, and *sebadas*, honey-covered doughnuts. Local wines include the white *Vermentino di Gallura* and red *Cannonau*; *mirto* is the local juniper berry liqueur.

age is considered to have been from 1200 to 900 BC.

The island has over 7 000 nuraghi, or fortified tower-houses, structures in the form of a truncated covered cone. The name comes from the root *nur*, which means both "mass" and "cavity". The *nuraghi* were built of huge blocks of stone without any mortar, possibly using an inclined plane along which they would have been pushed or rolled. They were used as dwellings, as watchtowers and, when built together as a group, as fortresses. Other structures remain from this prehistoric period, including dolmens and Giants' Tombs (*see Emerald Coast*).

As water was a rare commodity on the island, it played an important part in the Nuraghic religion. The god who lived in the wells and rivers and who had the power to overcome periods of drought was represented by the bull, often pictured throughout the island.

A BIT OF HISTORY
Sardinia has been invaded several times throughout history. The Phoenicians arrived in the 8C BC, followed by the Romans in 238 BC, the Vandals in AD 455 and the Byzantines in AD 534. The Saracens arrived in the 7C. After the year 1000 the island was fought over by the Pisans and Genovese. It then fell to the Spanish in 1295 and to the Austrian Empire in 1713. The Kingdom of Sardinia was created in 1718. The island was annexed to the new united Italy in 1861 and was made an autonomous region in 1948.

EMERALD COAST★★

This wild and undulating region is a succession of pink-granite headlands, covered with maquis scrub overlooking a clear emerald green sea. Groves of cork trees bent by the wind form dramatic shapes in the interior. This region of farmers and shepherds was discovered in 1962 by the jet set. The Emerald Coast was developed by a consortium presided over by the Aga Khan. The tourist facilities on the peninsula of the Gallura region include windsurfing, sailing, golf and tennis. The main beach resorts are Porto Cervo⌂⌂⌂, Cala di Volpe and Baia Sardinia⌂.

Practical Information

Getting There

The Costa Smeralda lies towards the northeast of the island. Arzachena is on the S 125.

ARCIPELAGO DI LA MADDALENA★★

www.lamaddalenapark.it.
The Maddalena Archipelago islands on the northern tip are Maddalena, Caprera, Santo Stefano, Spargi, Budelli, Razzoli, Santa Maria and other islets in the **Straits of Bonifacio**.
These isolated islands, occasionally frequented by Corsican shepherds, were annexed to the Kingdom of Sardinia in 1767. Maddalena then became a military base.
The archipelago was made a **national park** in 1996.

Maddalena★★

A lovely scenic route *(20km/12.4mi)* follows this small island's coastline.

Caprera★

This island was once the home of Garibaldi and is connected to Maddalena by the Passo della Moneta causeway. It now houses a sailing centre.

Casa Museo di Garibaldi★

Open Tue–Sun 9am–8pm. 6€. 0789 72 71 62. www.compendio garibaldino.it
The tree planted by Garibaldi (1807–82) on the birth of his daughter Clelia (1867) can be seen in the garden of his one-time home, where he is also buried.

INLAND

Arzachena

Once an agricultural market town, Arzachena owes its fame to its position in the heart of the Costa Smeralda hinterland at the foot of a mushroom-shaped rock (Fungo).

Megalithic Stones
The remains of a **Giants' Tomb** (*Tomba dei Giganti di Li Muri*) and a necropolis can be seen from near town, on the Arzachena–Luogosanto road. Popular tradition gave the name Giants' Tomb to these tombs dating from the Nuraghic period. The funeral chambers, lined and roofed with megalithic slabs (like a dolmen) were preceded by an arc forming the *exedra*, its area of ritual. The front of the structure is formed by a central stela with fascia in relief, which leads to the corridor of stones. This "false door" may have symbolised the connection with the afterlife.

BARUMINI★★

The town of Barumini is surrounded by numerous traces of the earliest period of Sardinian history. Nuraghi, the defensive structures specific to Sardinia, exist nowhere else in the world. The circular defensive towers in the shape of truncated cones have corbel-vaulted interior chambers and some date back to 2000 BC.

Practical Information

Getting There

Barumini is in the heartland of Sardinia, 10km/6.2mi N of Villanovaforru, off the S 197.

NURAGHI SU NURAXI★★

2km/1.2mi W, on the left-hand side of the Tuili road. Open daily 9am–1hr before dusk. Guided tours only. 10€ (ruins, Casa Zapata and Giovanni Lilliu). 070 93 68 128. www.fondazionebarumini.it.
A UNESCO World Heritage site considered the pre-eminent example of Nuraghi. The oldest part of Su Nuraxi dates from the 15C BC. The fortress was consolidated due to the threat posed by the Phoenician invaders between the 8C and 7C BC and was taken by the Carthaginians between the 5C and 4C BC and abandoned in the 3C with the arrival of the Romans.

SANTA VITTORIA DI SERRI★

38km/23.6mi E by the Nuoro road and a road to the right in Nurallao.
The town takes its name from the Romanesque church built within a prehistoric settlement of Nuraghi, excavated in the early 19C. The sight was important not only for defense, but marked the convergence of the Marmilla and Campidano plains with the mountainous Barbagia area.
The road passes through the crafts village of **Isili**, which has the Museo per l'Arte del Rame e del Tessuto (*www.marate.it*), a museum dedicated to the art of copper and hand-loomed textiles.

Nuraghi Su Nuraxi

ISOLA DI SANT'ANTIOCO★★

This volcanic island is the largest of the Sulcis Archipelago. It has a hilly terrain with high cliffs on the west coast. The chief town, also called Sant'Antioco, is linked to the mainland by a road. Catacombs, some of which have been transformed from Punic *hypogea*, can be seen under the Sant'Antioco church. They date from the 6–7C.

Practical Information

Getting There

Sant' Antioco lies off Sardinia's southwest coast. The main access road is the S 126.

VESTIGIA DI SULCIS★

Open daily 9am–7pm. 13€. Combined ticket: Museo Archeologico, Tophet, Museo Etnografico, Villaggio Ipogeo, Forte Sabaudo). 0781 80 05 96. www.archeotur.it.

Named after the ancient town of *Sulci*, founded by the Phoenicians in the 8C BC, the archaeological area comprises the Phoenician-Punic *topheta*, once believed to be where the first-born male child was sacrificed, but now understood to be a cemetery for children who died in infancy.

The archaeological museum includes a fine collection of **stelae★**.

EXCURSION

Monte Sirai

19km/11.8mi from Sant'Antioco.
Remains of a Phoenician-Punic settlement can be found on a hill near Carbonia. The area was excavated after a local youth discovered a female statue in 1962; a statue of the goddess Astarte (now in Cagliari) later came to light. Inhabited since Neolithic times, Phoenicians arrived here in 750 BC. A 6C Ipogea remains from the period when the city was destroyed in 520 BC by the Carthaginians, who built a new fortress, in turn destroyed by the Romans in 238 BC.

Vestigia di Sulcis

SICILY

An island of mythic epics and cultural crossroads, the sun-scorched summer land of Sicily turns a brilliant green after the spring rains. Its mountainous terrain climaxes with Europe's largest active volcano. Greek temples grace glorious coastlines and inland hills. Roman mosaics splash energy and colour. Some of Italy's best cuisine originates here. Sicily dishes out culture and pleasure for sybarites alike.

SICILY TODAY

The long period of foreign domination in Sicily has left its imprint not only on the art, culture and literature of the island, but also on its economy. Geographically and economically Sicily can be divided into three regions. The first region comprises the provinces of Catania, Siracusa and the southern part of Messina, which have high-quality agriculture. Palermo, Trapani and the north of Messina have a highly developed services sector and building industry. The interior is the poorest area, in the provinces of Agrigento, Caltanissetta and Enna.

Fishing is still of prime importance to local economy, however the traditional tuna catch is rapidly depleting, threatening both the ancient **mattanza** ritual and the fishing economy.

Italy's development fund for the South, created in 1950, has failed to realise projects due to corrupt officials, mismanagement, and organised crime perpetrated by the **Cosa Nostra** mafia.

A BIT OF HISTORY

Sicily's strategic location has made it a pawn for marauding forces in the Mediterranean. Phoenecians were followed by Greeks in the 8C BC, who pushed the Carthaginians to the west until the siege of Motya in 397 BC. The 5C BC was the apogee of Greek rule (*Magna Graecia*). By 241 BC, Sicily had been conquered by the Romans, who coveted its rich soil. In 535 Sicily passed to the Byzantines and in the 9C the Muslims, who were later expelled by the Normans (11C). Roger II (1095–1154) established his court

Island of Vulcano seen from Lipari, Isole Eolie

Mosaics in Cappella Palatina

at Palermo, a prosperous period of political power and cultural influence. Emperor Frederick II dominated the reign of the Swabian dynasty.

The house of Anjou followed in 1266; however, Charles of Anjou was expelled following the Palermo revolt of 1282. Power passed to the Aragon dynasty; Alfonso V reunited Naples and Sicily becoming King of the Two Sicilies (1442).

The island passed to the Bourbons of Naples by marriage until they were overthrown by Garibaldi's forces (1860). World War II also left its mark, where in 1943 the Anglo-American landings forced the Germans to abandon.

Each period has left its mark on the island's heritage. The Greeks built admirable Doric temples and splendid theatres. Romans left mosaics and villas. The Norman prosperity brought construction that blended Moorish and Byzantine styles, seen at Palermo, Monreale, Cefalù and Messina. The

Castello di Venere, Erice

© M. Pizzotti /age fotostock

INTRODUCTION

157

Renaissance left little architecture, but outstanding paintings by **Antonello da Messina**. The 18C Spanish Baroque style appears notably in Noto, Ragusa, Catania and Palermo.

LITERATURE

In the 19C Giovanni Verga created a new form of Italian novel, and Luigi Pirandello began writing. Noteworthy among the 20C writers are Elio Vittorini, Leonardo

LERMO	★ ★ ★	Highly recommended
atania	★ ★	Recommended
tagirone	★	Interesting
Messina		Other sight described in this guide

Sciascia. Gesualdo Bufalino, Salvatore Quasimodo and Giuseppe Tomasi di Lampedusa, whose epic *The Leopard* set in Sicily during the Risorgimento, became a film.

Practical Information

Getting Around

♦ **By Boat** – The main connections to Sicily are from Cagliari, Genoa, Livorno, Naples, Salerno, Reggio Calabria and Villa San Giovanni.

♦ **By Air** – Palermo and Catania are the main airports, with others at Trapani, Pantelleria and Lampedusa.

♦ **By Car** – Car ferries serve the island. Roads are well marked. You could just about get around the island in a week. (Train is not advised: only one track serves both directions, connections are poor.)

Shopping

Ceramics are produced around Caltagirone, Santo Stefano di Camastra and Sciacca. Trapani has **necklaces** and other objects made from coral, and Erice has a rug-making tradition. **Natural sponges** are on Pantelleria, and in Syracuse the papyrus may be of interest. A wide range of food products are produced, with sweets and products made from almonds and pistachios. Eastern and western Sicily both produce excellent wines, from famous reds like Nero d'Avola, Nerello and Etna Rosso to whites including Insolia, Carricante, Cataratto, Grecanico, Grillo, Malvasia and Moscato.

INTRODUCTION

159

PALERMO★★★

Palermo, the capital and chief seaport of Sicily, is built at the head of a wide bay enclosed to the north by Monte Pellegrino and to the south by Capo Zafferano. Nicknamed the "Conca d'Oro" (Golden Basin), where lemon and orange groves flourish, Palermo is an ideal city to experience Sicily's melting pot of civilisations and cultures.

A BIT OF HISTORY

Palermo was founded by the Phoenicians, conquered by the Romans and later came under Byzantine rule. From 831 to 1072 it was under the sway of the Saracens, who gave the city its special atmosphere suggested today by the luxuriance of its gardens and the shape of the domes on some buildings. Conquered by the Normans in 1072, Palermo became the capital under Roger II, who took the title of King of Sicily. This great builder succeeded in blending Norman architectural styles with the decorative traditions of the Saracens and Byzantines: his reign was the golden age of art in Palermo. Later the Hohenstaufen and Angevin kings introduced the Gothic style (13C). After three centuries of Spanish rule, the Bourbons gave Palermo its Baroque finery.

The Sicilian Vespers

Since 1266 the brother of Louis IX of France, Charles I of Anjou, supported by the Pope, had held the town. But his rule was unpopular. The Sicilians had nicknamed the French, who spoke Italian badly, the *tartaglioni* or "stammerers". On the Monday or

Practical Information

Getting There

Situated on the northwestern coast. The main road is the A 19.
The easiest and quickest way to get to Palermo is by **air**. The city airport, Falcone-Borsellino (*www.gesap.it*) (formerly known as Punta-Raisi), is situated 30km/18.6mi north of Palermo, off the A 29 dual carriageway. It is served by various airlines including Alitalia, easyJet, Eurowings, Iberia, Lufthansa, Meridiana, MistralAir, Ryanair, Tunisair, Vueling from 5am until the arrival of the last flight of the day. Buses stop in Viale Lazio, Piazza Ruggero Settimo (in front of Politeama Hotel), and the main railway station. The journey takes 50 minutes. Palermo can also be reached by **ferry** from Genoa, Livorno, Civitacecchia, Tunisi and Naples.

Getting Around

Avoid driving in Palermo, with its traffic congestion and difficult parking. Large car parks can be found on the outskirts of the city. There is a free car park in Piazza Maggiore, 300m/328yds from the Botanical Gardens. Other parking facilities (paid) include Piazza Giulio Cesare 43, Porto; Via Guardione 81, Porto and Via Stabile 10. The best way to see the city is on public transport, in a taxi, or on foot in the old town.

Palermo Cattedrale

Tuesday after Easter 1282, as the bells were ringing for vespers, some Frenchmen insulted a young woman of Palermo in the church of Santo Spirito. Insurrection broke out, and all Frenchmen who could not pronounce the word *cicero* (chickpea) correctly were massacred.

HISTORIC QUARTER

Palazzo dei Normanni (Reale)★★ – *Piazza Indipendenza 1. Open Mon–Sat 8.30am–5.40pm, Sun and hols 8.15am–1pm. Closed during Assembly. €12. 091 62 62 833. www. fondazionefedericosecondo.org.* The centre and Pisan Tower are of the Norman period, built onto a 9C Moorish fortress.

Cappella Palatina★★★ – *First floor of Palazzo dei Normanni.* Built in 1130 for Roger II, wonderful Arab-Norman decoration is evident on walls, dome and apses covered with dazzling **mosaics★★★**, among the finest in Europe. Also note the carved stalactite ceiling, marble paving, ornate pulpit and paschal candelabrum. The old royal apartments, **Antichi Appartamenti Reali★★**, house King Roger's chamber, **Sala di Re Ruggero**.

Palazzo e parco d'Orléans – Today the offices of the Regional government, this building was inhabited from 1810-14 by Louis-Philippe of Orleans, future king of France. Admire beautiful *ficus magnolioides* with buttress roots and exotic animals in the zoo in the adjacent garden.

Chiesa di San Giovanni degli Eremiti★★ – *Via dei Benedetti 18. Open Mon–Sat 9am–7pm, Sun and hols 9am–1.30pm. €6. 091 65 15 019.* This church crowned with pink domes has 13C **cloisters★** and gardens, a green oasis built with the aid of Arab architects in 1132. The tropical gardens of **Villa Bonanno★** boast superb palm trees.

Cattedrale★ – *Corso Vittorio Emanuele. Open Cathedral: Mon–Sat 7am–7pm, Sun 8am–1pm and 4–7pm; monumental area Nov–*

Apr Mon–Sat 9am–1.30pm; rest of the year see website. €7 inc. tombs, treasures, crypt. 329 39 77 513 (mobile). www.cattedrale.palermo.it. Built 1184, the cathedral retains the Sicilian-Norman style in the east **apses**★; elsewhere it has Baroque modifications. Note the tombs of Emperor Frederick II, Henry VI, Constance of Aragon and other rulers. The **Treasury** *(Tesoro* displays the **Imperial crown**★ of Constance.

QUATTRO CANTI TO THE ALBERGHERIA

"QUATTRO CANTI"★★

The busy crossroads of Via Vittorio Emanuele and Via Maqueda is decorated with statues and fountains. The mid-17C church of **San Matteo** has an astonishingly decorative interior.

Piazza Pretoria★★ – The square has a spectacular **fountain**★★ and 16C marble statues. The **Palazzo Pretorio** *(open Mon–Sat 9am–5pm; 091 74 02 216; www.palazzodelleaquile.org)*, the town hall, occupies part of this square.

La Martorana★★ – *Piazza Bellini. Open Mon–Sat 9.30am–1pm and 3.30–5.30pm, Sun and hols 9–10.30am. €2. 345 82 88 231 (mobile).* Nicknamed for the marzipan made by the nuns, Santa Maria dell'Ammiraglio (St Mary of the Admiral) was founded in 1143 by the Admiral of the Fleet to King Roger II. Stunning Byzantine **mosaics**★★ show scenes that include *Roger II Crowned by Christ (right)*, and *Admiral George of Antioch Kneeling before the Virgin.*

San Cataldo★★ – *Piazza Bellini 3. Open daily 9.30am–12.30 and 3–6pm. Closed public hols. €2.50.*

This splendid 1160 church has three Arabic rose red domes and its original mosaic floor.

San Giuseppe ai Teatini *(Corso Vittorio Emanuele)* is an eye-catching Baroque church with a theatrical **interior**★.

Palazzo Comitini *(Via Maqueda 100. Open Mon–Fri 9am–1pm and 3–6pm; closed hols; 091 66 28 111).* Built for the Prince of Gravina in the late-18C, **Sala Martorana**★, seat of the Provincial Council, is lined with wood-panelling inlaid with mirrors.

Chiesa del Gesù – *Piazza Casa Professa. 091 33 22 13.* The plain façade contrasts with the exuberant Baroque interior in stucco and semi-precious stones. The decoration of the presbytery – a triumph of *putti* by Serpotta – is particularly beautiful.

LA KALSA AND VIA ALLORO

The Kalsa district, behind the port, was razed by Allied bombs in 1943. This fascinating district, undergoing reconstruction, stretches to Corso V. Emanuele. New squares such as **Piazza Magione**, and cultural centres join the focal point, Piazza della Kalsa, with interesting monuments.

Porta dei Greci leads to the piazza and the church of **Santa Teresa alla Kalsa**, a monumental Baroque church built 1686-1706.

Via Torremuzza has the beautiful stone-framed Noviziato dei Crociferi at number 20 and **Santa Maria della Pietà**. Throughout the Middle Ages, **Via Alloro** was the main street. Most of the elegant *palazzi* have fallen into disrepair.

Palazzo Abatellis★ – A magnificent 15C Catalan-Gothic palazzo.

Galleria Regionale della Sicilia★★ – Via Alloro 4. Open Tue–Fri 9am–6.30pm, Sat–Sun and hols 9am–1pm. €8. 091 62 30 047. This museum and gallery features medieval art and 11–18C works including the dramatic fresco of **Death Triumphant★★★**, a **bust of Eleonora of Aragon★★** by Francesco Laurana, and Antonello da Messina's **Annunciation★★**.

Santa Maria dello Spasimo★ – The 1506 church and convent became a fortress, a hospice and now hosts cultural events. The Northern-Gothic **church★** reaches up towards the open sky without a roof and ends with a lovely **apse**.

Piazza Sant'Anna – The lively ancient Lattarini market square has the church of Sant'Anna (17C–18C) and the **Galleria d'Arte Moderna** (Via Sant'Anna 21; open Tue–Sun 9.30am–6.30pm; 091 84 31 605; €7; www.galleriadartemoderna palermo.it), housed in a monastery.

Piazza della Rivoluzione – The anti-Bourbon rebellion of 1848 was ignited in this square.

San Francesco d'Assisi★ – The 13C church, destroyed during World War II, was rebuilt in the original style, keeping its **portal★**.

Oratorio di San Lorenzo★★★ – Open Mon–Sat 10am–6pm. 091 582 370. A late work and masterpiece of **Giacomo Serpotta**, its stucco is an imaginative riot of putti. The Nativity (1609) by Caravaggio was stolen from here in 1969.

Palazzo Chiaramonte★ – This fine Gothic palace (1307) was a model for many buildings in Sicily. The **Giardino Garibaldi**, have spectacular **magnolia-fig trees★★**.

Stuccowork by Giacomo Serpotta, Oratorio di San Lorenzo

©2013. Photo Scala, Florence

THE OLD HARBOUR TO THE VUCCIRIA

The old harbour, the cala, was enclosed by chains now in **Santa Maria della Catena★**, the 16C Gothic-Catalan church.

San Domenico★★★ – Piazza San Domenico. Open Mon–Sat 8–12.30am and 5–7pm (Sun 8.30; winter Mon–Fri 8am–1.30pm; Sat–Sun 8.30–1.30pm and 5–7pm). 091 58 91 72. www.domenicani-palermo.it. The 1726 stucco of this church was the work of **Giacomo Serpotta**, an important artist of the Baroque.

Santa Maria di Valverde – Piazza Cavalieri di Malta. Open Mon–Sat 9am–1.30pm. 091 33 27 79. The elegant marble portal carved by Pietro Amato (1691) leads inside to a profusion of Baroque decorations in a variety of marbles, with delicate drapery on the side altars.

Santa Cita★★★ – Nov–Mar Mon–Sat 9am–3pm; Apr–Oct Mon–Fri 9am–6pm and Sat –3pm. €6 (combined ticket oratorio del Rosario in San Domenico).

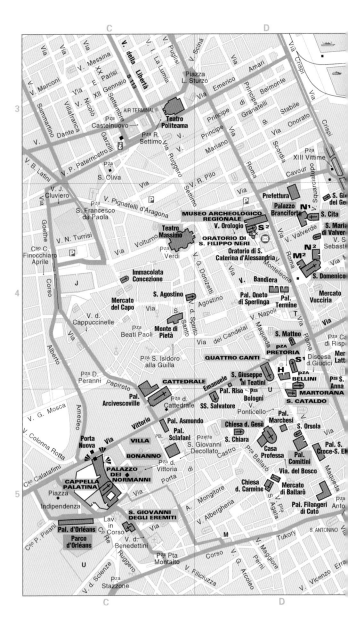

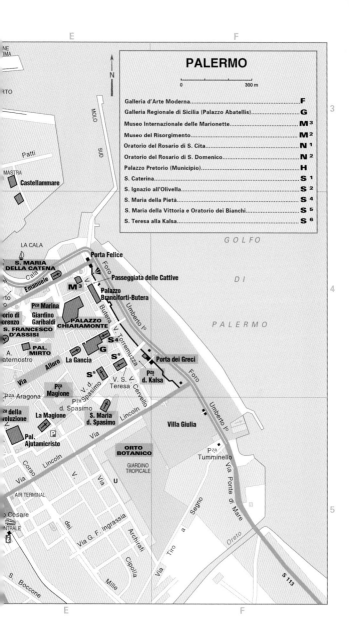

PALERMO

0 _____ 300 m

165

Teatro Massimo

091 78 53 181. This church, the masterpiece of **Giacomo Serpotta**, was sculpted between 1686 and 1718; the Battle of Lepanto, Mysteries, putti and angels adorn the walls.

Palazzo Branciforte★ – *Via Bara all'Olivella 2. Guided tours. Open Mar–Oct 9.30 am–7.30 pm (Nov.–Feb 2.30pm). €7. 091 88 87 767. www.palazzobranciforte.it.* This 16C palazzo restored by architect Gae Aulenti is a cultural centre and home to the fascinating collections of the Fondazione Sicilia. A must-see is the library, with its 50,000 volumes.

CITTÀ NUOVA

During the 19C expansion, the wealthy merchant bourgeoisie built lavishly decorated residences here.

Teatro Massimo★ – *Piazza Verdi. Guided tours. Open Tue–Sun 9.30am–5pm. 091 60 53 267. €8. www.teatromassimo.it.* This Neoclassical opera house modelled on the pronaos of an ancient temple.

Palazzo Mirto★ – *Via Merlo 2. Open daily 9am–7pm. €4.*

091 61 64 751. The main residence of the Lanza-Filangieri princes contains its original 18C and 19C furnishings. Rooms on the *piano nobile* include the **Salottino Cinese** (Chinese Room) and the **Smoking Room★**).

Museo Internazionale delle Marionette★★ – *Piazzetta Antonio Pasqualino 5 (entrance Via Butera 1). Open Mon–Sat 9am–1pm and 2.30–6.30pm. €5. 091 32 80 60. www.museo marionette palermo.it.* The celebrated *marionette* shows in Sicily featured chivalric themes; find some 3,500 works by craftsmen from around the world.

Piazza Marina – This large square is the heart of medieval Palermo and the city's night-life. The Garibaldi Garden at the centre has fine specimens of *Ficus magnolioides* with their extraordinary root system so sturdy it seems like the tree trunk itself. The square is lined by beautiful palazzi.

Museo Archeologico Regionale★ – *Piazza Olivella 24. Open Tue–Fri 9.30am–1.30pm and 2.30–5.30pm, Sun–Sat and hols mornings only. €6. 091 61 16 807.*

The archaeological museum has Phoenician sarcophagi, Egyptian and Etruscan objects, and finds from Selinus including the **metopes**★★ from the temples (6C and 5C BC). The bronzes include **Heracles with Stag**★ and the famous **Ram**★★, and marble statues, notably **Satyr**★. There are also some prehistoric works and fine 3C BC mosaics, **Orpheus with Animals** and *Mosaic of the Seasons*.

MODERN CITY

Villa Malfitano★★ – *Off the map. Via Dante 167. Open Mon–Sat 9am–3pm. €6. 091 68 20 522. www.fondazionewhitaker.it.* Known for its beautiful **gardens**★★, this Liberty-style villa has retained many Oriental furnishings.

Orto Botanico★★ – *Via Lincoln 2. Open Mon–Sun 9am–1hr before dusk. 091 23 89 12 36. €5. www. ortobotanico.unipa.it.* A garden with a fine exotic flora, including magnificent **magnolia-fig trees**★★.

BEYOND THE CITY GATES

Catacombe dei Cappuccini★★ – *Via dei Cappuccini. Open daily 9am–1pm and 3–6pm. 091 21 21 17.* These Capuchin catacombs are a macabre sight. About 8 000 17–19C mummies were preserved.

La Zisa★ – *Open daily 9am–7pm (Sun and hols 13.30pm). €6. 091 65 20 269.* This palace houses Egyptian works from the Mameluke and Ottoman periods.

Cuba Sottana★ – *Corso Calatafimi 100. Open daily 9am–1pm and 2–6.30pm (Sun 1pm). €2. 091 59 02 99.* The "Cuba Sottana" was part of the set of palaces built in the park, the Genoardo. The decorative simplicity of the building is very beautiful: a series of tall pointed arches of different width, enclosing rectangular openings.

EXCURSIONS

Monreale★★★ – *8km/5mi SW. www.monreale.net.* The 12C Benedictine **abbey** was founded by Norman King William II. The **terraces**★★★ of the **duomo**★★★ afford views over the Conca d'Oro plain. The **mosaics**★★★ inside are stunning.

Golfo di Castellammare★★★ – *25.7km/16mi W.* This gulf near soft hills is dominated by the imposing **Mount Còfano**, best seen from the promontory on **Capo San Vito**.

Rovine di Solunto★ – *19km/11.8mi E. €4. 338 78 45 140.* One of Sicily's three main Punic cities, Soluntum overlooks a headland, Capo Zafferano. Take Via Ippodamo da Mileto to the summit for a lovely **view**★★.

Marble decorations, Monreale Duomo

© Francesca Malerba

ERICE ★★★

Occupying a unique and **beautiful setting★★★**, this ancient Phoenician and Greek city presents two faces. Strategically located, it offers **splendid views★★** over the valley. In winter Erice is wreathed in mist and seems lost in time. In Antiquity Erice was famous for its temple consecrated to Astarte, then to Aphrodite and finally Venus, who was venerated by mariners of old.

Practical Information

Getting There

Erice, rising almost vertically, 750m/2 461ft above the sea, lies about 14km/9mi from Trapani.

HIGHLIGHTS

Castello di Venere – This 12C castle, built by the Normans, crowns an isolated rock on Monte Erice on the site of the Temple of Venus (Venere). From here and the nearby gardens (Giardino del Balio) there are admirable **views★★**. In clear weather you can make out Tunisia on the horizon.

Chiesa Matrice★ – This 14C church was built with stones from the Temple of Venus.

EXCURSIONS

Mozia ★★

South of Trapani on the road to Marsala along the coast are salt flats with a windmill (open to visitors) and white pyramids of sea salt that glitter in the sun. Across from the salt flats in the Stagnone Lagoon, just a few minutes by boat, is the island of Mozia (also Mothia, Motya), settled by the Phoenicians in the 8C BC. The settlement was destroyed in 397 BC by Dionysus of Syracuse. **Museo Whitaker★** – *Open 9.30am –6.30pm (winter 9am–3pm). €9 not including boat ride to island. 091 68 20 522. www.fondazione whitaker.it.* The archeological museum contains Phoenician finds from excavations on the island of Mozia (Motya); most famous of

Temple E, Selinunte

Segesta

these is the marble *Youth in Tunic*. The scrubby island makes for a pleasant stroll, where in recent years vineyards have been planted with historic grape varieties.

Selinunte★★★

Selinunte is situated on the south coast. The main access roads are the S 115 and S 115d. Open daily 9am–6pm. €6. 0924 46 277. www.selinunte.net.

Selinus was founded in the mid-7C BC by people from the east-coast city of *Megara Hyblaea* and destroyed twice, in 409 BC and 250 BC, by the Carthaginians. The huge ruins of its temples are impressive. An esplanade leads to the remains of three **temples** in varying states of restoration. **Temple G** was one of the largest in the ancient world, over 100m/330ft long; its columns were built of blocks, each weighing several tonnes. Cross the depression, Gorgo Cottone, to reach the **acropolis**. The site is dominated by the partially reconstructed (1925) columns of **Temple C** (6C BC). This, the earliest surviving temple at Selinus (initiated early-6C BC), was probably dedicated to Apollo or Heracles. Four more ruined temples stand nearby. Across the

River Modione are the remains of a sanctuary to Demeter Malophoros.

Segesta★★★

Segesta is 35km/21.7mi southeast of Trapani near the town Calatafimi. Open daily 9am–7.30pm (summer 8.30am, winter 9am–5pm). €6. A regular shuttle service operates to the theatre (€1.50). 0924 95 23 56.

The archaeological park is dominated by a fine Doric temple standing in an isolated site, splendidly situated against the hillside, its ochre colours in pleasant contrast with the vast expanse of green. Probably founded, like Erice, by the Elimi, Segesta soon became one of the main cities in the Mediterranean under Greek influence.

Tempio★★★ – The Doric temple of Segesta (430 BC) stands alone, encircled by a deep ravine, in a landscape of receding horizons. The road leading up to the theatre *(2km/1.2mi; shuttle bus available)* affords a magnificent **view★★**.

Teatro★ – This Hellenistic theatre (63m/207ft in diameter) is built into the rocky hillside. The tiers of seats are oriented towards the hills, behind which, to the right, is the Gulf of Castellammare.

AGRIGENTO AND LA VALLE DEI TEMPLI★★★

Agrigento, the Greek city of Akragas, is attractively set on a hillside facing the sea. The Greek poet Pindar referred to Agrigento as "man's finest town". A medieval quarter rests on the upper slopes above the modern town. The impressive ancient ruins are strung along a ridge below, erroneously called the Valley of the Temples (a UNESCO World Heritage Site).

Practical Information

Getting There

Agrigento is linked to Palermo by the S 189 and the north coast of the island by the S 640 and A 19.

VALLE DEI TEMPLI (VALLEY OF THE TEMPLES)★★★

Open daily 8.30am–5pm (Via Sacra and Tempio di Giove until 7pm, in summer some areas to 11pm). Museo Archeologico: Open Sun–Mon 9am–1.30pm, Tue–Sat, 9am–7.30pm. €10 archaeological site; €13.50 combined ticket with the Museo Archeologico. 0922 62 16 57.
www.parcovalledeitempli.it.

The monuments in the Valley of the Temples are grouped in two areas: the first includes the actual temples, the Giardino della Kolymbetra, the antiquaria and the paleo-Christian necropoli. The second comprises the archaeological museum, the Chiesa di San Nicola, the Oratorio di Falaride and the Greco-Roman quarter. To walk from one area to the other, visitors may follow either the very busy main road or the quiet road within the park, located near to the Temple of Zeus and the archaeological museum.
Of the many temples from the late-6C to the late-5C BC, parts of nine are still visible. The destruction of the temples, once attributed to earthquakes, is now linked to the anti-pagan activities of early Christians. Only the Temple of Concord was spared when it became a church in the late-6C AD.

Tempio di Zeus Olimpio★

Had this Temple of the Olympian Zeus (Roman Jupiter) been completed, it would have been one of the largest (113m/371ft long by 56m/184ft wide) in the ancient world. Supported by 20m/66ft-tall columns, with colossal **telamones** (columns in the form of male figures) 7.5m/25ft high, one is reconstructed in the Archaeological Museum.

Tempio dei Dioscuri★★

Of the temple of Castor and Pollux, only four columns and part of the entablature remain. A **sacred area** was dedicated to Demeter and Persephone.

Giardino della Kolymbetra★

This 5ha/12-acre basin is now a fertile grove of fruit and citrus trees, also planted with olive trees, prickly pear, poplar, willow, and mulberry. A pleasant stroll.

Tempio di Eracle★★

Dating from the late-6C, the Temple of Hercules is probably the oldest of the Agrigento temples and is built in the ancient Doric style. Eight of its columns have been raised. South of the temple is the mistakenly named **Tomba di Terone**, which instead honours Roman soldiers killed during the Second Punic War. Continuing along the path, observe the cartwheel **ruts**, eroded deep into the mud by water.

Tempio della Concordia★★★

The Temple of Concord is the most massive, majestic and best preserved of the Doric temples in Sicily. It has a peristyle of 34 tufa limestone columns. The interior dates from the Christian era (5C).

Tempio di Hera Lacinia★★

This temple dedicated to Hera (Roman Juno) has retained part of its colonnade, a sacrificial altar and an ancient cistern.

From the Antiquarium di Casa Pace, a small road to the Collina di San Nicola crosses fields of prickly pears, pistachio and olive trees, leading to the Greco-Roman Quarter, an urban complex of ruined houses, some with mosaics.

Museo Archeologico Regionale★★

Contrada San Nicola 12. 0922 40 15 65. The fine museum collection of Greek vases★ includes the Dionysius Cup and the Perseus and Andromeda Cup.

VILLA ROMANA DEL CASALE★★★

This immense 3–4C Roman villa (3 500sq m/37 680sq ft) is important for its mosaics, which cover almost the entire floor space. Picturesque and colourful, the mosaics portray scenes from mythology, daily life, hunts and circus games. Attributed to African craftsmen, this is a UNESCO World Heritage Site.

VILLA MOSAICS★★★

The villa is situated near Piazza Armerina, off the S 117b. Open daily 9am–7pm (5pm winter). €10. 0935 68 00 36. www.villa romanadelcasale.it.

The most noteworthy mosaics portray **cupids★★** fishing or playing with dolphins, a hunting scene in the **Sala della Piccola Caccia★★★**, the capturing and selling of wild animals for circus use in the **Ambulacro della Grande Caccia★★★** and sports practised by young girls, popularly dubbed "bikini mosaics" for their attire, in **Sala delle Dieci Ragazze★★**.

Interesting mosaics of the **triclinium★★★** portray the **Labours of Hercules**.

EXCURSION
Piazza Armerina★

5km/3mi SW.

The **medieval centre★** of Piazza Armerina has a Baroque **cathedral** sited on pleasant green valley slopes.

SYRACUSE★★★

Syracuse is superbly situated at the head of a beautiful bay. It was one of Sicily's, if not *Magna Graecia's*, most prestigious cities and at the height of its splendour rivalled Athens.

A BIT OF HISTORY

Greek Colony – Syracuse was colonised in the mid-8C BC by Greeks from Corinth who settled on the island of Ortigia. In the 5C–4C BC the town had 300 000 inhabitants. Captured by the Romans during the Second Punic War (212 BC), it was occupied by the barbarians, Byzantines (6C), Arabs (9C) and Normans.

Tyrants and Intellectuals – In the Greek world, tyrants had unlimited power over certain cities, in particular Syracuse. In 485 BC the tyrant **Gelon** ruled Syracuse. His brother **Hiero** brought to his court **Pindar** and **Æschylus. Dionysius the Elder** (405–367 BC) was the most famous, but even he lived in constant fear; he rigged the famous sword above the head of Damocles. He rarely left the safety of his castle on Ortigia, wore a shirt of chainmail under his clothing and changed his room every night. He had Plato expelled from the city when he came to study the political habits of the people. **Archimedes**, the geometrician born at Syracuse in 287 BC, discovered his famous principle: any body immersed in water loses weight equivalent to that of the water it displaces. Archimedes also set fire to the enemy Roman fleet by focusing the Sun's rays with a system of mirrors and lenses.

ORTIGIA (ORTYGIA)★★★
Visit: 45min.
The island of Ortigia, the most ancient area, is linked to the mainland by the Ponte Nuovo. Ortigia boasts numerous medieval and Baroque palaces, the latter in **Via della Maestranza★**.
The attractive **Piazza Duomo★** is lined by palaces. The 7C **Duomo★** was built in the on the foundations of a temple to Athena, some columns reused in the church. The **Fonte Arethusa★** is the legendary cradle of the city. The nymph Arethusa, pursued by the river-god Alpheus, took refuge on the island of Ortigia, where she was changed into a spring (*fonte*) by Artemis.

PARCO ARCHEOLOGICO DELLA NEAPOLIS★★★
Viale Paradiso 14. 2hrs on foot. Open daily 9am–1hr before dusk. €10. 0931 66 206.
www.siracusaturismo.net.
The Archeological Area of the "New City" includes the Greek theatre, the Nymphaeum, Via dei Sepolcri, the area of the Sanctuary of Apollo, a Roman amphitheatre, a necropolis, and other sights.

MUSEO ARCHEOLOGICO REGIONALE PAOLO ORSI★★
Viale Teocrito 66. Open Tue–Sat 9am–6pm (Sun and hols–1pm). €8. 0931 48 95 11.www.regione.sicilia. it/beniculturali/museopaoloorsi.
The **Villa Landolina** museum features Hellenistic and Roman artefacts from Syracuse, in addition to prehistoric finds and geological history.

CATACOMBE DI SAN GIOVANNI★★

Largo San Marciano. Guided tours only. Open Tue–Sun 9.30–12.30am and 2.30–5.30pm (rest of the year 4.30pm). €8. 0931 64 694.

After the catacombs in Rome, these are the finest examples in Italy.

EXCURSIONS

Fonte Ciane★★

8km/5mi SE. Reserve boat excursions. 0931 46 42 55.

The River Ciane links with the internal area of Pantalica, a point for **boat trips★★**. The Grand Harbour of Siracusa opens, then continues through lush vegetation to a narrow gorge and emerges in a papyrus grove linked to myth: here Cyane the water nymph tried to obstruct Pluto from abducting Persephone and was transformed into a spring.

Castello Eurialo★

9km/5.6mi NW along Via Epipoli, in the Belvedere district. Open Mon–Sat 9am–1pm. €4. 0931 71 17 73.

Castello Eurialo, one of the greatest fortresses of the Greek period, was built by Dionysius the Elder. Fine **panorama★**.

ETNA★★★

At 3 340m/10 958ft (this varies with summit eruptions) Etna is the highest point on the island. An imposing sight, Etna remains snow-capped most of the year. The volcano is active and is the largest and one of the most famous in Europe. Etna dominates the Ionic coastline between Catania and Taormina. The Circumetnea road encircles Etna, through interesting villages and varied views of the volcano.

A BIT OF GEOGRAPHY

The Parco dell'Etna covers an area of 59 000ha/145 790 acres; the huge, black cone is visible from 250km/155mi. Its fertile lower slopes host citrus and olive trees, while vineyards produce delicious Etna wine. Above those are chestnut trees; higher are oak, beech, birch and pine. Above 2 100m/6 900ft is the barren zone, of secondary craters, among the clinker and volcanic rock.

ASCENT OF THE VOLCANO

South Face★★★ – *Approx. 2hr round trip. Around €55 for insurance and guide. Funivia dell'Etna, Rifugio Sapienza, Località Cantoniera, Nicolosi.* *095 91 41 41. www.funiviaetna. com. On the south side contact Gruppo Guide Alpine Etna Sud, Piazza V. Emanuele 43, Nicolosi. 095 79 14 755. www.etnaguide. com.* The ascent stops near Valle del Bove, hemmed in by massive lava walls; potholes and crevasses belch smoke.

Northeast Face – *Piazza Annunziata 5, Linguaglossa. 095 95 51 59. www.parcoetna. ct.it.* The road goes through Linguaglossa to the winter-sports resort of **Villaggio Mareneve**. The surfaced road ends at Piano Provenzana (1 800m/5 900ft), a magnificent **view★★** . The lava landscape still smokes at times.

TAORMINA★★★

Taormina stands in a **wonderful setting★★★** at an altitude of 250m/820ft and forms a balcony overlooking the sea and facing Etna. The area is renowned for its peaceful atmosphere, beautiful monuments and gardens. The seaside resort of Giardini Naxos also hosts cultural events.

Practical Information

Getting There

The main access road is the A 18.

HIGHLIGHTS

Teatro Greco★★★ – *Via del Teatro Greco 40. Open daily 9am–2hrs before dusk. €10. 0942 24 291. www.regione.sicilia.it/turismo.* The Greek theatre dates from the 3C BC but was remodelled by the Romans who used it as an arena. Classical plays are performed in summer. The upper tiers afford an admirable **view★★★** between the stage columns of the coast and Etna.

Corso Umberto★ – The main street of Taormina passes the Gothic façade of the **cathedral**, **Piazza 9 Aprile★** with a splendid **panorama★★** of the gulf, and Piazza the 15C **Palazzo Corvaja**.

Giardino di Villa Comunale★★ – Terraced public gardens offer views of the coast.

EXCURSIONS

Castello

4km/2.5mi NW by the Castelmola road. 1hr walk there and back. The medieval castle built on the acropolis on the summit of Monte Tauro (390m/ 1 280ft) remains. Splendid **views★★** of Taormina.

Castelmola★

5km/3mi NW. This tiny village enjoys a splendid **site★**. Fine **views★** of Etna.

Gole dell'Alcantara★

17km/10.6mi W. Via Nazionale 5, Motta Camastra. €13 . 0942 98 50 10. www.golealcantara.it. Volcanic gorges with waterfalls and playful light.

Greek Theatre with Etna in the background

ISOLE EOLIE★★★

The Aeolian Islands are named for Aeolus, the God of the Winds. The archipelago comprises seven main islands, Lipari, Vulcano, Stromboli, Salina, Filicudi, Alicudi and Panarea, each distinct and all of exceptional interest for their volcanic nature, beauty, light and climate. Deep, blue, warm, clear waters, ideal for underwater fishing, harbour flying fish, swordfish, turtles, seahorses and hammerhead sharks. Boat trips provide good views of the beautiful indented coastlines and hidden coves and bays. The inhabitants of the islands fish, grow vines and quarry pumice.

LIPARI★

www.comunelipari.it.

The largest island dips vertically into the sea. The islanders fish and grow cereals and capers. Two bays (Marina Lunga, with its beach, and Marina Corta) frame the town of Lipari, dominated by its old quarter encircled by 13–14C walls. The 16C castle houses the **Museo Archeologico Eoliano★★** (*Via del Castello. Open Mon–Sat 9am– 7.30pm, Sun and hols 9am–1.30pm; €6; 090 98 80 174. www.regione. sicilia.it*), which exhibits a re-creation of Bronze Age necropoli, a lovely collection of red-figure **kraters★**, **amphorae★** and terra-cotta theatrical **masks★★**. **Boat trips★★** leaving from Marina Corta tour the rugged southwest coast. The splendid **view★★** from the Puntazze Headland includes five of the island; the belvedere at Quattrocchi affords one of the finest **panoramas★★★** of the whole archipelago.

VULCANO★★★

www.isoladivulcano.com.

Vulcan, the god of fire, was believed to have his forges on this 21sq-km/8sq-mi island made up of four volcanoes. The last eruption was in 1890, but fumaroles (smoke-holes) still spout steam, while hot sulphurous mud is appreciated for its therapeutic properties.

The scenery is wild and forbidding, with rocky shores, desolate areas and soils strangely coloured by mineral deposits. Excursions to the **Great Crater★★★** (*about 2hrs on foot there and back; www. turismoeolie.com*) afford views of the crater and of the archipelago. Island boat tours (*from Porto Ponente*).

STROMBOLI★★★

Stromboli is sombre and wild, with its black sand and plume of smoke. Some soil is cultivated with vines yielding delicious Malvasia wine. The **crater★★★**, a 924m/3 032ft cone, has frequent minor eruptions and flows of lava, best seen at night. Take a guide to see the **spectacle★★★** from the crater (*about 5hrs on foot there and back; difficult climb; CAI–AGAI guides, Porto di Scari and Piazza San Vincenzo, Stromboli; www.cairagusa.org and www.stromboliguide.it*).

SALINA★

The island is formed by six extinct volcanoes. The highest crater, Monte Fossa delle Felci (962m/3 156ft), dominates the archipelago. A panoramic road encircles the island. Capers and Mavasia grapes grow on the slopes.

FOR FUN

Italy's varied landscape has something for everyone. The Alps provide footpaths and mountains suitable for all levels of athletic expertise. The Lake District, the mountain streams and rivers are ideal for fishing. Trentino-Alto Adige/Südtirol, the Riviera del Brenta, Tuscany and Umbria are among the more suitable regions for cycling. The Maremma offers a perfect landscape for horse riding. The entire coast of Italy is an Eden for those who enjoy swimming, wind-surfing and the beach: the Adriatic coast with its shallow waters and long beaches is ideal for families with children. The waters of the Gargano, the Gulf of Policastro, Sicily and Sardinia are renowned for their crystalline purity and splendid colours, notably the emerald greens of the Costa Smeralda. The Amalfi coast and the Faraglioni of Capri are perhaps the best-known Italian coastlines; Versilia, with the Apuan Alps as a backdrop, is an essential venue for habitués of the beach, and the Ligurian Riviera offers striking views and beaches that nestle between the hills that lead down to the sea.

SPAS

Abano

Terme Montegrotto, Largo Marconi 8. 049 86 66 262. www.abanomontegrotto.it. Shaded by pines, this spa town near Padua has excellent facilities and is a popular spa.

Tivoli

Tivoli, Via Tiburtina Valeria, km 22,700. 0774 408 500. www.termediroma.org. The Terme di Tivoli has been refurbished in recent years, with outdoor thermal pools and a range of treatments. Below the town, it is a good stop coming to or from Hadrian's Villa.

Saturnia

Loc. Follonata, Saturnia, Manciano. 0564 60 01 11. www.termedisaturnia.it. This, one of Tuscany's most famous spa towns, attracts the chic set. The Terme di Saturnia offers steaming pools and a wide array of treatments. An economical option is to find the pools in open fields for a soak. Other Tuscany spa towns include Casciana, Chianciano Terme and Montepulciano.

🏔 Montecatini

Stabilimento Tettuccio, viale Verdi 41. 0572 77 81. www.termemontecatini.it. This Tuscan town boasts nine spas. The grandest of them all is the Art Nouveau style Tettuccio, the "temple of European spas".

Sant'Angelo, Ischia

Via Petrelle 15, Barano d'Ischia. 081 99 92 19. www.aphroditeapollon.it. Baths cascade down a cliff to the hot sand beach at the Aphrodite Apollon. Recently restored.

Viterbo

Strada Bagni 12. 0761 35 01. www.termedeipapi.it. The grandiose Terme dei Papi –

"baths of the popes" – has a magnificent pool, grotto and hotel. Good private bus service departs Rome at Piazza Mancini.

WINTER SPORTS

Italy has some of the most enticing ski resorts in the world with slopes for beginners, intermediate skiers and experts. Contact **FISI (Federazione Italiana Sport Invernali)**, Via Piranesi 46, Milano 02 75 731, www.fisi.org.

♦ **The Dolomites** – *Ufficio Informazioni Turistiche, Corso Italia 81, Cortina d'Ampezzo, 0436 86 90 86, www.cortina.dolomiti.org.* This is a favourite chic winter destination for skiers who flock to these 1200km/746mi of slopes for near year-round winter fun. Cortina d'Ampezzo is one of the top resorts in Europe. The Dolomites have the largest cross-country skiing area in Europe, with over 1 100 km/680mi of groomed trails. Information can be found at: www.dolomitinordicski.com.

♦ **Piemonte** – *Ufficio Turistico IAT di Saluzzo, Piazza Risorgimento 1, Saluzzo, 0175 46 710. www.saluzzoturistica.it.* Travellers can ski on some of the slopes that hosted the 2006 Winter Olympics. The Val di Susa has a particularly beautiful natural landscape and Limone is one of the oldest alpine villages in the country.

♦ **Courmayeur** – *Ufficio del turismo, Piazzale Monte Bianco 15, Courmayeur, 0165 84 20 60, http://www.lovevda.it.* Courmayeur is just opposite France's Mont Blanc and is a great place to experience alpine Italy. Peaks reach more than 4 000m/13 100ft.

OUTDOOR FUN

Canoeing

Contact *Federazione Italiana Canottaggio, Viale Tiziano 74, Rome, 06 87 97 48 01, www.canottaggio.org and Federazione Italiana Canoa e Kayak, Viale Tiziano 70, Rome, www.federcanoa.it.*

Cycling

Contact *Federazione Ciclistica Italiana, Stadio Olimpico, Curva Nord, Via dei Gladiatori, Foro Italico, Rome, 06 36 851, www.federciclismo.it.*

Fishing

Contact *Federazione Italiana Pesca Sportiva e Attività Subacquee, Viale Tiziano 70, Rome, 06 87 98 00 86, www.fipsas.it.*

Golf

Contact *Federazione Italiana Golf, Viale Tiziano 74, Rome, 06 32 31 825, www.federgolf.it.*

Hunting

Contact *Federazione Italiana della Caccia, Via Salaria 298a, Rome, 06 84 40 941, www.fidc.it.*

Mountaineering and Hiking

Contact the *Club Alpino Italiano (CAI), Via Petrella 19, Milan, 02 20 57 231, www.cai.it.*

Footpaths

Italy's walks are gloriously varied: stunning coastlines, rugged mountain terrain, wild national parks and ancient pilgrim paths like Via Francigena. The traveller can choose from a wide array depending on one's stamina and fitness. The five lands of the Cinque Terre offer very popular paths. Capri and Anacapri are a hiker's dream with trails that offer views of Saracen forts, natural grottoes and the stunning Bay of Naples. An easy jaunt from Rome, the Parco Nazionale d'Abruzzo, Lazio e Molise (*0863 91 131, www.parcoabruzzo. it*) is one of the most rugged national parks in the country.

No hiker's trip to Italy would be complete without a summit to one of Italy's famous 🌋 **volcanoes**. Both Mount Etna (*www.parcoetna.it, 095 82 11 11* and *www.funiviaetna. com, 095 91 41 41*) and Mount Vesuvius (*www.vesuviopark.it, 081 86 53 911*) offer superb hiking and views.

Dolomites

The Dolomites have a dense network of footpaths. Whether you are an expert climber or simply want to take a peaceful walk, there is a vast choice of routes for those wishing to get a better look. Maps and guides listing paths, mountain huts and bivouacs are on sale just about everywhere.

Some mountain pathways include:
No 2 (Bressanone–Feltre): This path crosses the Plose, the Puez Group, the Gardenaccia, the Sella and the Marmolada massifs.
No 3 (Villabassa–Longarone): This path winds its way through Val Pusteria, the Croda Rossa, Misurina, the Cristallo, the Sorapis and the Antelao.
No 4 (San Candido–Pieve di Cadore): ⊘ *Contact the local tourist offices before departure.* This track goes through the Sesto Dolomites, the Cadini di Misurina and the Marmarole.
Gruppo Guide Alpine Scuola di Alpinismo – *Corso Italia 69a, Cortina d'Ampezzo. 0436 86 85 05. www.guidecortina.com.* Waterfalls,

lakes, caves, routes with ropes (open to everybody) – a wide variety of organised excursions on offer in summer and lots of activities in winter too.

👥 **Fanes Nature Park** – *Parco Naturale Fanes-Sennes-Braies, www. val-pusteria.net.* All the paths and trails begin at Dobbiaco, which is the departure point for walks, and will take you to altitudes of between 1 000m and 3 000m (3 280ft and 9 840ft). Certain paths are set up for winter outings. Dobbiaco is less well equipped for skiing and more family-oriented, offering numerous activities for children in summer.

Riding and Pony Trekking

Contact *Federazione Italiana di Turismo Equestre, Largo Lauro De Bosis 15, Rome, 06 32 65 02 31, www.fitetrec-ante.it.*

Verona
Horse riding, walking – The Lessinia natural park offers numerous possibilities to explore on foot, by bicycle or on horseback. For horse-riding trips: *Basalovo Trekking, Via Palazzo 4, Stallavena (VR), 045 90 75 41 or 347 76 52 884 (mobile). www.basalovo.it.*

Speleology/Caving

Contact *Società Speleologica Italiana, Via Zamboni 6 (working headquarters Via Enrico Mattei 92) Bologna. 051 53 46 57, www.ssi.speleo.it.*

Watersports
Sailing and Windsurfing
Contact *Federazione Italiana Vela, Piazza Borgo Pila 40, Corte Lambruschini, Torre A, 16th floor Genoa, 010 54 45 41, www.federvela.it.*

Waterskiing

Contact *Federazione Italiana Sci Nautico, Via G.B. Piranesi 46, Milan, 02 75 29 181, www.scinautico.com.*

Lake Garda

Garda Yachting Charter – *Lungolago Zanardelli, Maderno (L. Garda). 0365 54 83 47. www.gyc.it.* Motorboats and yachts for hire.

Venetian Lagoon

Isola di Certosa is an excellent spot from which to discover the lagoon at your own pace. Boating courses and excursions on all kinds of boats, including kayaks and sailboats, around the Lagoon. *041 52 08 588. www.ventodivenezia.it.* You can also rent houseboats: *Via Roma 1445, Sottomarina, Chioggia (VE). 041 55 10 400. www.rendez-vous-fantasia.com.*

Padua

Take a canal cruise to visit the Veneto villas of the Riviera del Brenta; or for a shorter trip, the Padua area is beautiful and relaxing. *049 80 33 069. www.padovanavigazione.it.*

THEME PARKS

The following is a list of the main theme parks in Italy. Log onto www.parksmania.it for further details, including discounts.

◆ **Liberty City Fun –** *Via Monteoliveto 48, Volla (NA). 081 77 40 186, www.libertycityfun.com.* A fun place for kids. Inflatable castles, swimming pools, roundabouts…

◆ **Leolandia** – *Via Vittorio Veneto 52, Capriate San Gervasio (BG), 02 90 90 169, www.leolandia.it.* The Wild West theme stretches from a Mississippi paddleboat to an old-time train and a covered-wagon Ferris wheel.

◆ **Fiabilandia** – *Via G. Cardano, 15, Loc. Rivazzurra di Rimini, 0541 37 20 64, www.fiabilandia.it. The A 4 motorway, exit at Rimini Sud.* Ride concepts include Peter Pan's Beach, Merlin's Castle and a gold mine.

◆ **Gardaland** – *Via Derna, 4, Castelnuovo del Garda, Loc. Ronchi, take the A 4 or A 22 to Peschiera del Garda (VR), 045 64 49 777, www.gardaland.it.* Italy's largest theme park boasts a Robot World and Sequoia Adventure.

◆ **Italia in Miniatura** – *Via Popilia 239, Viserba di Rimini (RN), A 14 – exit at Rimini Nord, 0541 73 67 36, www.italiainminiatura.com.* A canoe splash-ride and monorail enliven the "Little Italy" theme.

◆ **Parco Le Navi - Acquario** – *Piazzale delle Nazioni 1a, Cattolica (RN), take the A 14 motorway and exit at Cattolica. 0541 83 71, www.acquariodicattolica.it.* This maritime theme park is housed in old holiday camps from the 1930s.

◆ **Mirabilandia** – *Parco della Standiana, Statale Adriatica 16 km 162, Savio di Ravenna (RA), off the E 45, 0544 56 11 11, www.mirabilandia.it.* Rides include a dinosaur tour, car splash, Ferris wheel and a London bus.

◆ **Oltremare** – *Viale Ascoli Piceno 6 (near the motorway toll booths), Riccione (RN), 0541 42 71, www.oltremare.org.* This impressive and enjoyable theme park explores the conservation of the Adriatic.

SHOPPING

Shopping in Italy tends to be about quality materials, fine craftsmanship and good design, rather than bargains. Gold, jewellery, textiles, leather, ceramics, paper, glass, food and wine are but a few.

OPENING TIMES

Most shops in Italy are open from 9am–1pm and 3.30pm–7.30pm. Some shops remain open at lunchtime in the centre of large towns and cities. Credit cards are accepted in some stores, rarely in small food shops and markets. In northern Italy, shops often take a shorter midday break and close earlier. Late-night shopping is frequent in seaside resorts. Many tourist resorts have a regular open-air market.

ITALIAN CRAFTS

Every region of Italy produces its own beautiful crafts of which they are justly proud.

♦ **Alabaster and stone** – Alabaster in Volterra and marble in Carrara (Tuscany). Liguria crafts slate.

♦ **Leather accessories** – Florence.

♦ **Paper and papier mâché** – Florence, Amalfi, Syracuse, Lecce, Verona, Bassano del Grappa (Veneto).

♦ **Ceramics** – Romagna (Faenza); Umbria (Deruta, Gubbio, Orvieto, Città di Castello); Sicily (Caltagirone).

♦ **Coral** – Naples, Torre del Greco.

♦ **Filigree** – Liguria (Genoa) and Sardinia produce fine metalwork.

♦ **High fashion** – In Milan around Via Monte Napoleone, or in Rome around Via Condotti.

♦ **Wood** – Trentino-Alto Adige (Val Gardena) and Valle d'Aosta. Intarsia (inlay): Florence, Sorrento.

♦ **Lace** – Burano, the colourful Venetian island. Also, areas of Tuscany and Umbria.

♦ **Porcelain** – Capodimonte (Campania), Bassano del Grappa.

♦ **Glass** – The island of Murano in the Venetian lagoon, from beads to chandeliers; watch glass blowing in action on the island. Also try Altare in Liguria. For wine goblets, visit Empoli in Tuscany.

FOOD AND DRINK

Italian kitchens have produced some of the world's best-known dishes, yet there is no national cuisine. Rather, it is a lavish buffet of regional and local recipes. Each region, province, and even town can reveal local specialities – pasta, breads, Parmesan, Parma and San Daniele ham and Mozzarella di Bufala. Seasonal finds abound, such as Roman artichokes in winter, while olive oil and wines vary by both terrain and locally-grown varieties of olive or grape.

The Mediterranean theme is strongest in the south, while the north's hearty alpine menus can embrace French and German influences. Naples is famous for pizza, but like Sicily has more complex fare, a legacy of its rulers, traders and invaders. Tuscany and Umbria have fragrant truffles and mushrooms in their forests, Chianina beef and pork, along with game like wild boar. The capital is disparaged for its simple "peasant" fare; Romans care little for sauces and spices, relying more on the quality and freshness of produce for interest.

REGIONAL SHOPPING

Lombardy

Milan gives its name to *minestrone alla Milanese*, a vegetable soup, *risotto alla Milanese*, rice with saffron and **costoletta** *alla Milanese*, a veal cutlet. Hearty **osso buco**, is veal knuckle with the marrow-bone. **Polenta**, a cornmeal gruel, is a country staple. Mantua makes **tortelli di zucca** (pumpkin dumplings). Cheeses include creamy **Gorgonzola** and **Taleggio**. Sweets: **Panettone**, Christmas cake with dried fruit; **torrone** (nougat) from Cremona. Franciacorta, slowly fermented in bottles, is Italy's reply to Champagne.

Milan

City life focuses around Piazza del Duomo and the adjacent shopping areas. Corso Vittorio Emanuele II and Golden Quad around Via Monte Napoleone is the realm of top designers. Trendy independent shops are on Corso di Porta Ticinese.

Bergamo

Gastronomia Mangili – *Via Colleoni 7. Closed Mon afternoons.* A high-class food shop, tempting array of jars, cured meats, wines.

Venice and the Veneto

Veneto fare: **polenta**, **bigoli** (tube pasta), **risi e bisi** (rice and peas), **risotto** and **fegato alla Veneziana** (calf's liver fried with onions). Excellent sea catch: shellfish, eels, lagoon crabs, dried cod (*baccalà*) and **sardelle in saor** (sweet-sour sardines). Black pasta made with squid ink. Veneto cheeses: hard **Grana Padano** and **Asiago**. **Pandoro** is Verona's star-shaped Christmas cake. Verona produces excellent wines: red **Amarone**, **Valpolicella**, **Bardolino**, and white **Soave**. White bubbly **Prosecco**, a favoured aperitivo, is from Valdobbiadene.

Verona Wine

Amarone and **Valpolicella**– *Via Valpolicella 57, San Pietro in Cariano (VR). 045 77 03 194. www.consorziovalpolicella.it.* This consortium of wine-makers in the Verona province have excellent wineries that produce Amarone, some in grand historic villas like Quaranta (Tommasi), Novare (Bertani). Some good wineries: Antolini, Accordini, Buglioni, Trabucchi, Cubi, Grassi, Latium. Some offer dining or accommodation.

Soave – *Foro Boario 1, Soave (VR). 045 76 81 407. www.stradadelvino soave.it.* Crisp white wine made near Verona. Visits and tastings at wineries.

Vicenza

Near Verona, Vicenza is know for its goldsmiths.

Alps and Dolomites

Sophisticated French-Swiss influences are in the west. The region has excellent meats and cheeses. Its prized wine is Barolo; other good reds are Dolcetto, Nebbiolo, Barbaresco, and white Gavi. The Alto Adige and Trentino reflect Germanic influences. Aromatic white wines, with some reds like Lagrein. Good grappa distilleries in Valle dei Mòcheni.

Turin

There are 18km/11.2mi of arcades in the historic centre. On **Via Roma**, which the architect Piacentini modernised in the 1930s, there are luxurious shops and the elegant San Federico gallery.

Art and antique lovers should head for the nearby **Via Cavour**, **Via Maria Vittoria** and **Via San Tommaso**. Most antiquarian bookshops are concentrated around **Via Po**, **Via Accademia Albertina** and **Piazza San Carlo**, while **Via Lagrange** is a gourmet's paradise. Turin specialities include *agnolotti* pasta, *bagna cauda*, grissini breadsticks and chocolate. Also seek out the grand Piemontese red wines, especially Barolo. Also, Vermouth was created in Turin in the late-18C. Two streets lead off **Piazza Castello**: Via Po and Via Garibaldi, one of the longest pedestrian streets in Europe. Every Saturday morning and all day on the second Sunday of the month is the Balôn in Porta Palazzo, Turin's traditional flea market, in existence since 1856.

Genoa and Portofino

Genoa's famous **pesto** sauce is made with basil, olive oil, pine nuts, and cheese, served with **trenette** (pasta ribbons) or fazzoletti (pasta "handkerchiefs"). Try **cima** (stuffed meat parcels) and **pansòti** (dumplings) served with walnut sauce. Delicious seafood: *buridda* (fish soup), **cappon magro** (fish and vegetable salad) and **zuppa di datteri**, a shellfish soup from **La Spezia**. White wines include Vermentino or Pigato. Sciachetrà passito (sweet) wine is from Cinque Terre.

Genoa

Antica Drogheria Torielli – *Via San Bernardo 32r*. Prestigious historic shop for spices, chocolate and teas.

Libreria Ducale – The Palazzo Ducale bookshop specialises in books and maps of Genoa.
Romanengo – *Via Soziglia 74/76r, www.romanengo.it*. An 18C confectionery shop.
Viganotti – *Vico dei Castagna 14r, www.romeoviganotti.it*. This products of this shop represent a tradition that has existed for over 300 years: you must try the pralines.

🐖 Emilia-Romagna

Emilian meat is famous: Bologna **salami** and **mortadella**, Modena **zamponi** (pig's trotters), Parma **prosciutto** (ham). *Pasta alla Bolognese* has a meat sauce.
Parmesan cheese (*Parmigiano Reggiano*) is used extensively.
Lambrusco is a fruity red wine, often sparkling.

Parma

Parma's world-class food products have fascinating dedicated museums, such as the Musei del Cibo (*www.museidelcibo.it*).
Museo del Parmigiano Reggiano – *C/o Corte Castellazzi, Via Volta 5, Soragna (31km/19.3mi NW of Parma). 0524 59 61 29. Open Mar–8 Dec Sat– Sun and public hols 10am–1pm and 3–6pm. €5 inc. taste.*
Museo del Prosciutto – *C/o Ex Foro Boario, Via Bocchialini 7, Langhirano (23km/14.3mi S of Parma). 0521 82 11 39. Open Mar– 8 Dec Sat–Sun and hols 10am–6pm. €4; €7 inc. taste.*
Museo del Salame di Felino – *C/o Castello di Felino (17km/10.6mi SW of Parma). 0521 83 18 09. Open Mar– 8 Dec Sat–Sun and hols 10am–1pm and 3–6pm. €4.*

Tuscany

Tuscans claim they taught the French to cook: Catherine de' Medici brought her chefs to the court of Henry II. Today's fare is more humble: soups, including **ribollita**; **pappardelle**, flat noodles. Florence *alla Fiorentina* specialities: dried cod (**baccalà**) with oil, garlic and pepper; **bistecca** – grilled steak fillets with oil, salt and pepper; **fagioli all'uccelletto** (beans with quails). Wild boar, Chianina beef steaks. 🍷**Chianti** is the most popular wine but other reds are **Brunello di Montalcino** and **Nobile di Montepulciano**. White, zesty **Vernaccia** is from **San Gimignano**.Also, try the sweet **Vin Santo**.

Umbria and Le Marche

Black truffles (**tartufo nero**) and pork are popular, including **porchetta**, a whole roast suckling pig. For pasta, there is **strozzapreti** ("choke the priest" cords). Umbria's prize red wine is **Sagrantino di Montefalco**, while **Orvieto** white is its most plentiful.

Lazio

Rome's simple and supposedly "crude cooking": **spaghetti all'amatriciana** (tomato and bacon) or **alla carbonara** (egg, bacon), **gnocchi**, **saltimbocca** (veal fillet, ham, sage, Marsala), and **abbacchio al forno** (roast lamb) or lamb **alla cacciatora** (white wine sauce). The **carciofi alla Giudia**, deep-fried artichokes. **Pecorino**, **caciotta**, **ricotta** cheese.

Rome

🍷 Fashion

Many luxury stores with some of the best-known names in the Italian fashion world (Armani, Gucci, Prada, Versace and Valentino) are located in **Via Condotti** and

Piazza di Spagna, and streets that fan off those like Via Frattina, Via Borgognona (Malo, Cucinelli) and Via Bocca di Leone (Marni). Rome is full of goldsmiths, most famous being **Bulgari**, but there are many small fine workshops to explore. Quality on **Via del Corso** has dropped, but there are still a few fine boutiques. More exciting are those on small streets that radiate from the Pantheon, Piazza Navona and Campo de' Fiori.

Markets

Campo de' Fiori – *Closed Sun.* Morning fruit and vegetable market.
Castroni – *Via Cola di Rienzo 196. 06 68 74 383, www.castronicoladirienzo.com. Open daily 7.45am–8pm (Sun 9.30am–8pm).* International food specialities.
Gastronomia Franchi – *Via Cola di Rienzo 200. 06 68 74 651, www.franchi.it. Closed Sun.* Meats, cheeses and hot dishes.
Eataly – *Piazzale XII Ottobre 1492. 06 90 27 92 01, www.roma.eataly.it. Open daily 10am–midnight.* Food pavillion opened 2012. Quality Italian specialities; groceries, cafes.
Mercato di Campagna Amica – *Via San Teodoro 74. Open Sat 9am–6pm, Sun–4pm.* Products direct from Lazio farmers.
Mercato di Piazza di San Cosimato – *Open Mon–Sat 6am–1.30 pm.* Lively small morning market in Trastevere.
Mercato di Testaccio– *Via Galvani, near Monte de' Cocci. Open Mon–Sat 6am–2pm.* Large food market, good selection. Renovated market in the centre of the Testaccio district.
Porta Portese – *Via Portuense, Trastevere. Sun to 2pm.* Rome's main flea market. Beware pickpockets.
Volpetti – *Via Marmorata 47. 06 57 42 352. www.volpetti.com.*

Closed Sun. Cured meats, cheeses, savoury pies, delicacies and wines.

Naples and the Amalfi Coast

Naples is the home of spaghetti, which is often prepared with shellfish (**alle vongole**). Trattorie and pizzerie serve **costata alla pizzaiola**, a fillet steak with tomatoes, garlic and wild marjoram, **mozzarella in carrozza** (cheese savoury) and especially **pizza** and **calzone** (a folded pizza), topped with mozzarella, tomato and anchovy and flavoured with capers and wild marjoram. The local **mozzarella di bufala** (cheese) is especially delicious. Other specialities include cakes and pastries, often made with ricotta cheese and candied fruit. Wines from volcanic soil have a delicate, slightly sulphurous taste: red and white Capri, white Ischia, Lacryma Christi, Fiano di Avellino, Greco di Tufo and red Gragnano and Taurasi.

Naples

The figurines from the Nativity scenes (Via San Gregorio Armeno) make lovely souvenirs and gifts. Naples and Torre del Greco sell cameos and coral pieces.

Augustus – *Via Toledo 147. 081 55 13 540. www.augustusnapoli.it.* One of the best caterers, by the Spanish Quarter.

Ferrigno – *Via S. Gregorio Armeno 8. 081 55 23 148. www.arteferrigno.it.* A boutique shop known for its figurines.

Gay Odin – *Via Toledo 214 and 427. 081 551 34 91. www.gay-odin.it. Closed Sun and 3 weeks Aug.* Masters of Neapolitan chocolate have been delighting patrons since 1894.

Il Mercato in Via Pignasecca– *Open every morning.* Fruits, vegetables, fish, shellfish, mozzarella di bufala. Bountiful, colourful street market.

Librerie Antiquarie Luigi Regina – *Via Santa Maria di Costantinopoli 51 and 103. 081 45 99 83.* Charming bookshop founded 1881. At no. 51, are prints and watercolours.

Marinella – *Riviera di Chiaia 287. 081 76 44 214 or 081 245 11 82. www. marinellanapoli.it.* Famous tie shop, founded 1914. Also women's items.

Ospedale delle Bambole – *Via San Biagio dei Librai 81. 081 20 30 67.* A historic shop restores dolls and stuffed animals.

Island of Capri

Carthusia–I profumi di Capri– *Viale Matteotti 2d, Capri (NA). 081 83 70 368. www.carthusia.com.* Capri fragrances such as lemon, rosemary, rose and carnation.

Sardinia

Gnocchi shells, **malloreddus**, are often served with a sausage-tomato sauce. Lobster soup and pork roast on a spit. Crunchy **carasau** thin bread. Ewe's cheeses, **fiore** and **pecorino**. **Sebadas** are doughnuts covered with honey. Wines: the red **Cannonau** and white Vermentino.

Sicily

Some of Italy's best and most varied cuisine. Pasta **con le sarde** (with sardines) and **alla Norma** (aubergines, tomatoes, ricotta), fish dishes. Trapani **cuscusu** (cuscus) with fish soup. Superb pastries, ices, **cannoli** (filled with ricotta and candied fruit), almond cakes and marzipan. Wines: spicey red **Nero d'Avola**, Etna reds and whites, golden **Marsala**, Pantelleria passito.

ENTERTAINMENT

The era of La Dolce Vita may be over, but the custom of going out has been going strong since the Empire. Many Italians entertain guests out- a chance to join the stylish, lively scene. *See p12 for even more events.*

MILAN, LOMBARDY AND THE LAKES

Milan

Nightlife

The villagey Brera district with its street artists and galleries is a good spot for the evening, while Milan's canal district Navigli, is also a haven for artists. The variety of bars and restaurants is amazing - the area buzzes each evening. Milan has a very lively cultural and artistic scene. The city hosts many of musical events – classical, jazz, rock – some of the world's most famous stars come to perform. There are also a number of theatres.

Blue Note– *Via Pietro Borsieri 37, district Garibaldi-Isola. 02 69 01 58 88. www.bluenotemilano.com.* Little brother of the famous New York club hosting jazz concerts.

Music

Auditorium di Milano – *Piazza Tito Lucrezio Caro 1. 02 83 38 94 01. www.laverdi.org.* Performances of classical, jazz and other music. Literary evenings, events for children, encounters with well-known artistes.

La Scala – *Piazza Scala. 02 72 00 37 44. www.teatroallascala.org.* The top for opera, also ballet. The season launches on St Ambrose's Day (7 Dec), the city's patron.

Teatro Dal Verme – *Via San Giovanni sul Muro 5. 02 87 905 201. www.dalverme.org.* Mainly classical concerts, also some plays.

Drama

Piccolo Teatro – Three theatres, all central: *Teatro Strehler, Largo Greppi 1; Teatro Grassi, Via Rovello 2; Teatro Studio, Via Rivoli 6. 02 42 41 18 89. www.piccoloteatro.org.*

Teatro Carcano – *Corso di Porta Romana 63. 02 55 18 13 77. www.teatrocarcano.com.*

Teatro Franco Parenti – *Via Pier Lombardo 14. 02 59 99 52 06. www.teatrofrancoparenti.com.*

Teatro Manzoni – *Via Manzoni 42, district Centro Storico. 02 76 36 901 or 800 914 350. www.teatromanzoni.it.*

Bergamo

Events

Festival pianistico internazionale – *030 29 79 333 or 035 41 60 602. www.festivalpianistico.it.* Prestigious piano festival at the Donizetti Theatre. May–June, with concerts also in Brescia. The city also hosts a **Jazz festival** each March.

Mantua

Events

Each September, Mantua hosts a Festival of Literature with author presentations, conferences, performances, and workshops. *www.festivaletteratura.it.*

GENOA AND PORTOFINO EVENT

International Boat Show – Top-level show, each October, began in 1962. *www.salonenautico.com.*

ALPS AND DOLOMITES

Turin

Nightlife

The several prestigious concert halls in Turin include the **Auditorium Giovanni Agnelli del Lingotto**, *Via Nizza 280, 011 63 13 721, www.lingottomusica.it* (classical music) and the **Conservatorio Giuseppe Verdi**, *Via Mazzini 11, 011 88 84 70 or 011 81 78 458, www.conservatoriotorino.eu*. Also, the **Teatro Regio**, *Piazza Castello 215, 011 88 15 557, www.teatroregio.torino.it*.

Murazzi – Along the River Po and around Piazza Vittorio, here the fashionable night-time crowd hang out.

Parco del Valentino – Numerous riverside discos.

Quadrilatère romain – *Between Via Sant'Agostino and Via delle Orfane.* The streets of this area are teeming with restaurants, literary caffès and wine bars.

Contemporary Art

The Piemontese capital is a real mecca for fans of contemporary art. There are many exhibition spaces and numerous events held throughout the year. For information, you can visit the website *www.torinoarte contemporanea.it*.

Events

Salone internazionale del Gusto e Terra Madre – *Lingotto Fiere. www.salonedelgusto.it. Oct.* The Taste Salon brings together farmers and artists, the world of university culture and chefs, novices and the great figures of the world of food and wine.

Salone Internazionale del Libro – *www.salonelibro.it. May.* The most important book fair in Italy.

Dolomites

Wine Bar

Enoteca Cortina – *Via Mercato 5, Cortina d'Ampezzo. 0436 86 20 40. www.enotecacortina.com. Open Mon–Sat 10.30am–1pm and 4.30–9pm, open throughout the day in high season.* A beautiful old door opens onto this lovely little wine bar with its wooden ceiling. Taste wines; local and beyond.

VENICE

🎵 Music

Music and theatre have always played an integral part of Venetian life. In its heyday La Serenissima had more than 20 theatres. Concerts are held in several venues and numerous churches, including La Pietà, I Frari and Santo Stefano. See listings in the local newspaper, the *Il Gazzettino*.

Gran Teatro La Fenice – *Campo San Fantin 1965, San Marco. 041 78 65 11. www.teatrolafenice.it.* Always ranks in the top 3 for opera in Italy.

Teatro A l'Avogaria – *Calle Avogaria 1617, Dorsoduro. 041 099 19 67. www.teatroavogaria.it.*

Teatro Goldoni – *Calle Goldoni 4650b, San Marco. 041 24 02 014. www.teatrostabileveneto.it/venezia.* A busy season of plays and concerts

Venice Jazz Club – *Behind Campo Santa Margherita (Dorsoduro 3102). 340 15 04 985. www.venicejazz club.com. Open Mon–Wed and Fri–Sat with concerts from 9pm and food available from 8–9pm only. Special events sometimes on Thu.* The resident quartet, frequently joined by special guests from the international circuit, plays traditional and contemporary tunes.

Bars

Al Volto – *Calle Cavalli, connecting Campiello de la Chiesa (S. Luca) to the Grand Canal, S. Marco 4081. 041 522 8945. Closed 24–25 Dec.* A cosy, inviting wine bar that is always packed and offers wine buffs plenty of scope for new discoveries.

Bistro de Venise – *Calle dei Fabbri, 4685, San Marco. 041 52 36 651. www.bistrotdevenise.com.* A huge variety of fine wines by the glass and good cellar, this also is a gathering spot for readings, exhibits, and tastings with wine producers.

Devil's Forest – *Calle degli Stagneri 5185, San Marco. 041 52 00 623. www.devilsforest.com. Closed Mon.* An English-style pub with a lively clientele. Televised sports events. Free Wi-Fi and webcam to say hi to the folks back home.

Paradiso Perduto – *Fondamenta della Misericordia 2540, Cannaregio. 041 72 05 81. Closed Tue, Wed, Dec 20–27 and Jan 7–early carnival.* Live music, art shows and good food served up in a friendly and stimulating environment.

The Irish Pub – *Corte dei Pali, Cannaregio 3847. 041 09 90 196. www.theirishpubvenezia.com. Open daily 11am–2am.* Formerly The Fiddler's Elbow, this lively bar stays open late with live music and good beer. Sports also shown.

Events
Around early September, the Lido hosts the world-famous **Venice Film Festival**: Mostra del Cinema di Venezia. Every other

year, the four-month long **Biennale** art exhibition is held in the Arsenal and Giardini districts. Both events both award the Golden Lion as their top prize.

Verona

Events
From June to the end of August, the opera season at the ancient Arena attracts music lovers from all over the world.
Fondazione Arena di Verona – *045 800 51 51. www.arena.it.* Other annual summer music festivals in Verona include the **Verona Jazz Festival** and the *Concerti Scaligeri* (world music). *www.geticket.it.*

TUSCANY AND UMBRIA

Florence

Nightlife
Antico Caffè del Moro "Café des artistes" – *Via del Moro 4r. 055 28 76 61. Closed Sun and three weeks Aug.* Artists in the 1950s would often pay for their drinks with paintings which now decorate the walls of this cheerful bar.

GranCaffè Giubbe Rosse – *Piazza della Repubblica 13/14r. 055 21 22 80. www.giubberosse.it. Open daily 8.30am–1pm.* The waiters wear their red jackets with great pride – this caffè has long been popular with writers and artists, celebrated for the early Italian Futurist movement. Indoor and outdoor tables, newspapers.

Il Rifrullo – *Via San Niccolo 55r. 055 23 42 621. www.ilrifrullo.com.* Off the beaten track near Porta San Miniato, this bar is popular with Florence's late-night revellers into the early hours while sipping house cocktails. Terrace, and fireplace.

Jazz Club – *Via Nuova dei Caccini 3.
339 498 07 52 (mobile). Open
Tue–Sun 10pm–3am. Closed Mon,
Jun–Aug.* A jazz club since 1979,
this showcases primarily Italian
musicians. Membership charge 6€.

Concerts and theatre

La Nazione and *Firenze Spettacolo*
have listings. **Box Office** – *Via delle
Vecchie Carceri 1. 055 21 08 04.
www.boxofficetoscana.it.* Sells
tickets for various theatres.
Opera di Firenze-Teatro Comunale
– *Piazzale Vittorio Gui, 1. 055 27 79
309. www.operadifirenze.it.*
Teatro della Pergola –*Via della
Pergola 12/32. 055 07 63 333.
www.teatrodellapergola.com.*
Cinema Odeon, *Piazza Strozzi.*
Beautifully restored cinema
with stained glass ceiling, plush
seats, big screen, films in original
language. A venue for film festivals.

Lucca
Events
13 September candlelight
procession, **Luminara di Santa
Croce**, illuminates Lucca.

Siena
Events
Twice a year, on 2 July and
16 August, Siena becomes a
hotbed of feverish anticipation,
excitement and vociferous rivalry
when the famous bareback horse
race, the **Palio delle Contrade**,
takes place; www.ilpalio.org.

Perugia
Events
Perugia has been the backdrop
for summer's **Umbria Jazz Festival**
since 1973, then added Orvieto
for a late December festival. *www.*

umbriajazz.com. In September,
wine enthusiasts enjoy tasting
the Sagrantino and the Rosso
di Montefalco at Montefalco's
Settimana Enologica.

Orvieto
Events
Late December, Orvieto hosts
the winter session of the **Umbria
Jazz Festival** (*see above*), with five
days of music, culture and events
culminating in New Year's Eve.

EMILIA-ROMAGNA

Bologna
Nightlife
Enoteca des Arts – *Via San Felice
9a. 051 23 64 22. Open Mon–Sat
5pm–3am.* An informal wine
bar with vaulted ceilings and a
collection of old bottles.
Il Circolo Pickwick – *Via San Felice
77a. 051 55 51 04.* Set in an old
pharmacy, this place serves a mix
of Italian wines, English beer and
Cuban cocktails.
Le Stanze – *Via Borgo San Pietro 1.
051 22 87 67. www.lestanzecafe.it.
Open Mon–Thur and Sun 6pm–2am
(Fri–Sat 3am).* A unique location
for an evening to remember. This
former chapel close to the lively
university area, features original
17C frescoes and contemporary
design elements. Events are held
frequently.

ROME
Nightlife in Rome is mainly
concentrated in four areas.
The districts around **Campo
de' Fiori**, **Piazza Navona** and
Trastevere have a wide choice
of pubs and bars, drawing a mix
of young students, foreign

ourists and the theatre crowd. lightclubs are concentrated in he **Testaccio** district.

AMALFI COAST

Naples

Nightlife
Bourbon Street Club – *Via Bellini 2/53. 338 82 53 756 (mobile). www. bourbonstreetjazzclub.com. Open Tue–Sun from 8pm.* Near Piazza Dante, this is a great meeting-place for jazz lovers. Soft lighting and comfortable booths.

Intra Moenia – *Piazza Bellini 70. 081 45 16 52. www.intramoenia.it.* This bar/bookshop is also the head quarters of apublishing house.

66 Fusion Bar – *Via Bisignano 58. 081 41 50 24. www.66napoli.it. Open Mon–Thur 6pm–2.30am (Fri–Sat .30am, Sun 6.30pm–3.30am)* The place for Neapolitan students and thirtysomethings. From 6pm, the cheerful and noisy customers spill out into the street, beer in hand.

Teatro San Carlo – *Via San Carlo 98. 081 79 72 331. www. teatrosancarlo.it. Box office: Mon– Sun 9am–6pm. 848 002 008.* With its permanent opera company, the San Carlo is one of the best opera houses in the world.

Events and Festivals
With all their ceremonial trimmings, there are a number of well-known religious festivals in Naples including Madonna di Piedigrotta (Sept), Santa Maria del Carmine (16 Jul) and especially the Feast of the Miracle of St Januarius (1st Sun in May and 9 Sept). During the Christmas period churches are decorated with Nativity scenes.

SARDINIA
Cagliari celebrates its patron, Sant'Efisio on May 1 with a four-day procession to the sea. UNESCO has declared Sardinia's songs to be an Intangible Cultural Heritage, including Canto a Tenore and Canto della Sibilla, Gregorian chant in Catalan.

SICILY

Palermo
Events
Festa di Santa Rosalia – The festival of the patron saint of Palermo, St Rosalia is celebrated on 15 July with a religious procession, a tradition since 1625, near the harbour and fireworks. Other events get underway early July.

Siracusa
Events
Festa di Santa Lucia – The festival of the patron saint of Siracusa, St Lucy, is celebrated on 13 December.

Taormina
Events
Festa del costume e del carretto Siciliani – In April and May, this festival celebrates the Sicilian cart and local costume.

Taormina Film Festival – www. taorminafilmfest.net. The June festival launches new films and attracts international celebrities.

BARS AND CAFFÈS

One of the great pleasures in Italy is sitting in a caffè watching the world go by, admiring the stylish parade, sipping one of Italy's excellent wines or coffees. Prices at table are higher than bar prices.

MILAN, LOBARDY AND THE LAKES

Milan

Gelateria Marghera – *Via Marghera 33. 02 46 86 41. Open 10am–12.30pm.* Right by the National Theatre and the exhibition centre. Deliciously creamy ice creams.

Il Massimo del Gelato – *Via Castelvetro 18. ilmassimodelgelato.it. Open noon–midnight. Closed Mon.* This ice-cream parlour in the Sempione district has a good range of inventive flavours.

Luini Panzerotti – *Via Santa Radegonda 16. www.luini.it. Open Mon 10am–3pm, Tue–Sat 10am–8pm. Closed Sun.* A local institution among hungry Milanese serving *panzerotti* – a speciality filled dough-based snack.

Panarello – *Via Speronari 3. www.panarello.com. Open 8.30am–7.30pm.* These two Milanese stalwarts have been open since 1930.

Rigoletto – *Via San Siro 2. 02 49 81 820. www.gelateriarigoletto.it.* The flavours at this little ice-cream parlour not far from the Teatro Nazionale are excellent, particularly the fruit-based choices.

Riva Reno – *Viale Col di Lana 8. 02 89 40 84 59. www.rivareno.com. Open 1pm– midnight.* A *gelateria* with branches in the Ticinese district and in Brera, serving delicious and imaginative flavours.

Shockolat Maggi – *Via G. Boccaccio 9. 02 48 10 05 97. www. chocolatmilano.it.* A contemporary ice-cream parlour close to Santa Maria delle Grazie specialising in chocolate flavours.

Bar Basso – *Via Plinio 39, district Stazione Centrale. 02 29 40 05 80. www.barbasso.com. Open 9–1.30am. Closed Tue.* This is where the "wrong" Negroni cocktail was invented, using champagne instead of gin.

Bar della Crocetta – *Corso di Porta Romana 67. 02 54 50 228. www.crocetta.com. Open 8am–midnight.* Fantastic panini at all hours of the day.

Bar Jamaica – *Via Brera 32. 02 87 67 23. www.jamaicabar.it. Open 9–2am.* The Jamaica is one of those bars with a story to tell. Opened in June 1921, between World War II and the 1960s it became a hang-out for an extraordinary generation of artists, writers and photographers, such as Piero Manzoni and Lucio Fontana, many of whose work can be seen in the Museo del Novecento.

Bar Magenta – *Via Carducci 13, district Sant'Ambrogio. 02 80 53 808. barmagenta.it. Open Sun–Thu 7.30–2.30am, Fri–Sat 7.30–4.30am.* This well-known bar has a wide-ranging clientele and serves a varied array of drinks to match. Lunches and snacks also available.

Café Trussardi – *Piazza della Scala 5. 02 80 68 8201. www.cafetrussardi.it. Open Mon–Fri 7.30am–11pm, Sat noon–11pm. Closed Sun.* Part of the modern Palazzo Trussardi, by the restigious opera house. Refined nd very busy at *aperitivo* time. **ova** – *Via Monte Napoleone 8. 2 76 00 55 99. www.pasticceria ova.it. Open Mon–Sat 7.45am– .30pm, Sun 10am–7pm.* This istoric caffè in the heart of Milan s the perfect place to stop for a offee. Cakes that look like works f art.

ataly – *See Eataly p. 188.*

Gattullo – *Piazzale Porta Lodovica 2. 2 58 31 04 97. www.gattullo.it. Open 7am–9pm. Closed Mon.* For rioches still warm from the oven nd a good cappuccino.

Hôtel Bulgari – *Via Fratelli Gabba b. www.bulgarihotels.com.* A yper-trendy atmosphere in the rera-Montenapoleone district.

a Hora Feliz – *Via San Vito 5, ehind the Basilica of San Lorenzo. 2 83 76 587. Open 6pm–2am. Closed Mon.* A little corner of Cuba n Milan, with a wide choice of ocktails and a generous selection f bar snacks.

Radetzky Café – *Corso Garibaldi 05. 02 65 72 645. www.radetzky.it. Open daily 8–1.30am.* A Milan lassic in the Mittel Europa style. Quite informal and makes a ractical choice for a snack or for runch.

Bergamo

Caffè della Funicolare – *Via Porta Dipinta 1. 035 21 00 91. www. affedellafunicolare.it. Open daily –2am.* This bar at the funicular top is ideal for a drink or snack. antastic views from the terrace.

Mantua

Caffè Modì – *Via San Giorgio 4/6.* Designer caffè behind the Ducal alace. An ideal spot for a glass of vine with a plate of cured meats

or cheeses. Music and cultural events are held.

The Lakes

Caffè Retro – *Piazza del Popolo 24, Arona (L. Maggiore). 0322 46 640. Open daily 8–2am.* From one of the loveliest outdoor terraces in Arona you get a view of this traffic-free piazza, a small church and the blue lake. Try one of the fruity cocktails.

Gardesana – *Piazza Calderini 5, Torri del Benaco (L. Garda). 045 72 25 411. www.gardesana.eu.* This elegant hotel with restaurant and terrace caffè has a lovely location beside the tower and overlooking the port.

Gelateria Cremeria Fantasy – *Via Principessa Margherita 38, Stresa (L. Maggiore). 0323 33 227.* Delicious homemade ice creams in a variety of mouth-watering flavours ideal for cooling off in the heat of summer.

GENOA AND PORTOFINO

Genoa

F. lli Klainguti – *Piazza di Soziglia 98. 010 86 02 628.* Founded 1828, this bar-*pasticceria* has period interiors and tasty specialities.

Gelateria Box Cream – *Via degli Orefici 59r. 010 24 72 992 Open daily 7am–8pm.* Making mouth-watering creations since the 1960s. **Mangini** – *Piazza Corvetto 3r. 010 56 40 13.* A famous 19C caffè where politicians meet.

Panificio Grissineria Claretta – *Via della Posta Vecchia 12r. 010 24 77 032.* Try the focaccia at this historic bakery.

BARS AND CAFFÈS

ALPS AND DOLOMITES
TURIN

Al Bicerin – *Piazza della Consolata 5. 011 43 69 325. www.bicerin.it. Open 8.30am–7.30pm. Closed Wed and Aug.* This caffè was founded in 1763, where Cavour came to forget about the tribulations of politics.

Baratti & Milano – *Piazza Castello 29. 011 44 07 138. www.barattiemilano.it. Open Tue–Sun 8am–8pm.* Founded in 1875, this was originally a sweet shop. With its Art Nouveau rooms the caffè was a favourite with Turin's high society.

Caffè San Carlo – *Piazza San Carlo 156. 011 53 25 86.* An opulent caffè that first opened in 1822 and was one of the patriot strongholds during the Risorgimento, later becoming the meeting-place for the city's artists.

Caffè Torino – *Piazza San Carlo 204. 011 54 51 18. www.caffe-torino.it. Open 7.30am–midnight.* Another of Turin's many historic caffès, this one was frequented by actors such as James Stewart, Ava Gardner and Brigitte Bardot.

Eataly – *Via Nizza 230. 011 19 50 680. www.eatalytorino.it.* This giant, contemporary space located in the former Carpano vermouth factory, brings together the cream of Italian gastronomy: wines, cheeses, specialities… You can do your shopping, go to tastings or take courses. This is a showcase for the pleasures of the table, with maturing cellars, spice sacks, meat slicers, wine cellars, etc. Other Eataly addresses: Piazza XXV Aprile, 10 Milan; Piazzale XII Ottobre 1492, Rome; Via De' Martelli 22 R, Florence; Edificio Millo Porto Antico Calata Cattaneo 15, Genoa; Via Degli Orefici 19, Bologna.

Fiorio – *Via Po 8. 011 81 73 225. www.fioriocaffegelateria.com. Ope daily 8am–1am.* Founded in 1780 this was the place for aristocrats and intellectuals to meet. Great ice cream!

Grom – *Piazza Paleocapa 1d; Via Accademia delle Scienze 4; Via Garibaldi, 11; Piazza Santa Rita 6 (Corso Orbassano). www.grom.it.* A chain of ice-cream parlours that originated in Turin in 2003, before opening outposts all over the world. The quality of the ingredients has helped to build its reputation.

Mulassano – *Piazza Castello 15. 011 54 79 90. www.caffemulassano.com.* An intimate, charming caffè founded in 1907, with lavish decoration in marble, bronze, wood and leather. It was once frequented by members of the House of Savoy and performers from the nearby Teatro Regio.

Platti – *Corso Vittorio Emanuele II 72. 011 50 69 056. www.platti.it.* This liqueur merchant's shop became a caffè over the years, frequented mainly by intellectuals and writers, including Cesare Pavese. It now contains a restaurant.

Stratta – *Piazza San Carlo 191. 011 54 79 20. www.stratta1836.it. Open Tue–Sat 9am–7pm, Sun and hols 9.30am–7pm.* This *pasticceria* dates to 1836. It is famous for its multicoloured sweets.

VENICE

Ai Nomboli – *Calle Goldoni 2717, San Polo. 041 523 09 95.* A snack bar with a huge array of *tramezzin*

– the sliced-bread sandwiches which are highly popular in Venice.

Ai Rusteghi – *Campo San Bartolomeo 5513, San Marco.* ℘*338 760 6034. www.airusteghi.com.* A wide choice of panini, accompanied by good wine.

Bistrot de Venise – *Calle dei Fabbri, 4685, San Marco. 041 52 36 651. www.bistrotdevenise.com.* The bar and lounge offer an excellent wine selection. Dining options outside or in, enjoy an historic 14–18C menu or contemporary Venetian lagoon and sea cuisine.

Caffè Florian – *Piazza San Marco 55. 041 52 05 641. www.caffe florian.com.* Dating from 1720, this world-famous caffè is almost a museum piece. The antique interiors, which exude a timeless atmosphere, are evocative of times gone by when the world's literati used to gather here. The open-air terrace, on the other hand, is an ideal spot for taking in the beauty of St Mark's while enjoying the orchestra's music and sipping a (costly) cup of coffee.

Caffè Quadri – *Piazza San Marco 121. 041 52 22 105. www.alajmo.it. Closed Mon.* You will need a break from all that sightseeing so why not treat yourself to a top-quality cup of coffee? In the 1830s, this was one of the first caffès in Venice to serve Turkish coffee.

Gran Caffè Lavena – *Piazza San Marco 133–134. 041 52 24 070. www.lavena.it.* In the same spirit as the two previous places, this little caffè with its age-yellowed mirrors also dates from the mid-18C.

Harry's Bar – *Calle Vallaresso 1323, San Marco. 041 52 85 777. www.cipriani.com.* Not far from Piazza San Marco is the legendary Harry's Bar, declared a national heritage site. Inaugurated in 1931 by Giuseppe Cipriani, who first created the Bellini – a cocktail made with sparkling white Prosecco and the juice of white peaches – the drink is still a firm favourite among guests. It's possible to come just for a drink but excellent food is also served; the menu is varied and contains a variety of dishes, both local and international specialities.

Il Caffè (Caffè Rosso) – *Campo Santa Margherita 2963, Dorsoduro. 041 5 28 7998. www.cafferosso.it. Closed Sun.* This long-standing caffè with a reggae vibe serves as a meeting-point and gets busy at *aperitivo* time and after dinner.

Marchini Time – *Campo San Luca 4589, San Marco. 041 24 13 087.* Smart *pasticceria* and caffè with cakes and pastries made on the premises.

Pasticceria Italo Didovich – *Campo di Santa Marina 5909, Castello. 041 52 30 017.* Sweet treats to put a smile on your face are sold at this well-known cake shop and bar.

Rosa Salva – *Calle Fiubera 950, San Marco. 041 52 10 544. www. rosasalva.it. Closed Sun.* Quality cakes tempt passers-by from windows throughout Venice – come here for guaranteed quality. Delicious cappuccino too.

TUSCANY AND UMBRIA

Florence

Caffè Ricchi e Ristorante – *Piazza Santo Spirito 8/9r. 055 28 08 30. Open 7.30am–11pm. Closed Sun, last two weeks Feb and Aug.* Stop by for gelato or drinks in this Altr'Arno caffè with lovely outdoor summer terrace. Busy on market days.

Gelateria Grom – *Via del Campanile. 055 21 61 58. Open daily 10.30am–midnight.* Florence's best *gelateria* is a Turin import, steps from the Duomo.

Teatro del Sale – *Via de' Macci 111r. 055 20 01 492. edizioniteatrodelsale cibreofirenze.it. Closed Mon.* This private Cibrèo club (low-cost membership) is a theatre, shop, restaurant open for three meals a day, and reading room – a quirky Florentine salon that the chef-owner frequents himself, with delicious food and wines.

Gelateria Vivoli – *Via Isola delle Stinche 7r. 055 29 23 34. www. vivoli.it. Closed Mon, hols and week of 15 Aug.* Florence's historic 1930 *gelateria* has slipped in quality, but it is handy for *gelato* or coffee near Santa Croce.

Lucca

Gelateria De' Coltelli – *Via San Paolino 10. 345 48 11 903. Mon–Thu and Sun noon–8.30pm, Fri and Sat noon–9.30pm.* Excellent homemade ice-cream with unusual flavours that vary in accordance with the fresh ingredients available.

Gelateria Sergio Santini – *Piazza Cittadella 1. 0583 55 295. Open summer daily 9am–midnight; rest of the year Tue–Sun 9am–9pm. Closed 20 days in Nov. www. gelateriasantini.it.* Lucca's historic *gelateria* also makes *paciugo* and *panettone gelato*.

Pisa

Caffè dell'Ussero – *Lungarno Pacinotti 27. 050 58 11. Closed Sat.* Grand 18C *caffè* that overlooks the Arno River.

Siena

Nannini – *Via Banchi di Sopra 22/24. 0577 23 60 09. www.pasticcerie nannini.it. Open Mon–Thu 7am–9.30pm (Fri 10.30 pm and Sun11.30pm).* Probably the most famous *caffè* in town, with over 100 Sienese specialities like *panforte*, *panpepato* and *cantucci* (biscuits).

Pasticceria Bini – *Via Stalloreggi 91/93. 0577 28 02 07. Open Tue–Sun 7am–1.30pm and 3.30–8pm.* Founded in 1944, this *pasticceria* makes *panforte margherita* (cake with honey, almonds and candied citrus fruit), *panforte oro* (with candied melon), *copate* (small white wafer biscuits) and *cannoli* (pastries with ricotta and fruit).

Piazza del Campo – *Il Campo, 46-49. 0577 28 20 55.* It is difficult to choose from the large number of *caffès* that surround this wonderful square. Look for the most comfortable chairs and get a table in the sun!

Enoteca Italiana – *Fortezza Medicea, Piazza Libertà 1. 0577 22 88 11. www.enoteca-italiana.it. Open Tue–Sat noon–8pm.* Set up in the castle ramparts with the aid of state funding, this wine cellar/bar promotes Italian and especially Tuscan wines. Organises tastings and hosts lectures for the larger wine growers.

EMILIA-ROMAGNA

Bologna

Gelateria Gianni – *Via Montegrappa 11. 051 23 30 08. www.gelateriagianni.com.* A must for lovers of quality ice cream with a wide range of classic and imaginative flavours.

Enoteca Regionale Emilia-Romagna – *Piazza Rocca Sforzesca, Dozza, 29km/18mi SE of Bologna. 0542 67 80 89. www.enotecaemiliaromagna.it.* This statuesque medieval castle is set in picturesque hilltop Dozza. The castle cellars house all the best-quality wines produced in the region. They have to be approved each year and are sold here at honest prices. Well worth the trip!

Paolo Atti & Figli – *Via Caprarie 7. 051 22 04 25. www.paoloatti.com. Open Mon–Thu 7.30am–7.15pm (Fri–Sat 7.30pm and Sun 10.30am–1.30pm) .* This well-known bakery and delicatessen, founded in 1880 and frequented by Giosuè Carducci and the painter Morandi, among others, still has original interiors. Specialities include tortellini and Bologna's rich *certosino* cake traditionally made for Christmas.

ROME

Antico Caffè della Pace – *Via della Pace 3/7, Piazza Navona district. 06 68 61 216. www.caffe dellapace.it. Closed Mon morning.* Victorian décor, but patrons more bohemian than prim.

Antico Caffè Greco – *Via dei Condotti 86, Piazza di Spagna district. 06 67 91 700. www. anticocaffegreco.eu. Open daily 9am–9pm.* Founded in 1760, it's still lovely and evocative.

Caffè Capitolino – *Piazzale Caffarelli 4, Campidoglio district. 06 66 51 05 70. www.terrazzacaffarelli.it. Open daily 9.30am–7pm.* The terrace caffè of Palazzo Caffarelli has an exceptional view over the rooftops of Rome.

Caffè Rosati – *Piazza del Popolo 4. 06 32 27 378. www.barrosati.com. Open daily 7.30am–midnight.* A pavement caffè set on the piazza.

I Dolci di Nonna Vincenza – *Via Arco del Monte 98. 06 92 59 43 22. www.dolcinonnavincenza.it. Open daily 7.30am–9pm (Fri and Sat 8am–9pm).* This authentic Sicilian pastry shop has excellent sweets. Especially good pistachio or almond granita, perfect with a brioche for breakfast.

Stravinskij Bar-Hotel de Russie – *Via del Babuino 9, Piazza del Popolo district. 06 32 88 81.* The terrace and bar lure fashionable Romans and entertainers, for caffè or cocktail.

La Casa del Caffè Tazza d'Oro – *Via degli Orfani 84. 06 67 92 768. www.tazzadorocoffeeshop.com. Open Mon–Sat 7am–8pm (Sun 10.30am–7.30pm).* A rival bar for best coffee. In summer, *granita di café*: coffee ice with whipped cream.

Pasticceria Boccione (no sign) – *Via Portico d'Ottavia, 1 Ghetto. 06 68 78 637. Closed Sat.* Not-to-miss Jewish sweets, like *torta di ricotta* (cheesecake).

Sant'Eustachio Il Caffè – *Piazza S. Eustachio 82, Pantheon district. 06 68 80 20 48. santeustachioilcaffe.it. Open Sun– Thu 8.30–1am (Fri 1.30am and Sat 2am).* Many Romans swear here is the city's best coffee.

Ice cream

Corona– *Largo Arenula 27. 06 68 80 80 54.* Excellent gelato and ices near Largo Argentina, both classic and creative flavour combinations.

Fassi Palazzo del Freddo – *Via Principe Eugenio 65. 06 44 64 740. www.gelateriafassi.com. Open*

Mon–Thu noon–midnight, Fri–Sat noon–12.30am and Sun 10am–midnight (winter Mon–Thu noon–11pm, Fri–Sat noon–11.30pm, Sun 10am–11pm). Ice in Rome since 1880, still good quality.

Fata Morgana – *Via Roma Libera 11. 06 58 03 615. www. gelateriafatamorgana.com.* Best gelato in Trastevere, also unusual flavours like basil or celery.

Il Gelato di S. Crispino – *Via della Panetteria 42 (Trevi). 06 67 93 924. www.ilgelatodisancrispino.com. Open daily 11am–0.30am.* Good Rome *gelateria*. Also at Piazza della Maddalena.

Gelateria del Teatro – *Via dei Coronari, 65. 06 45 47 48 80. www. gelateriadelteatro.it.* Fine artisanal ice cream.

Sora Mirella – *Corner of Lungotevere degli Anguillara and Ponte Cestio.* Hand-shaved ice, mixed with syrup or fresh fruit, a Roman tradition.

NAPLES AND THE AMALFI COAST

Naples

Caffè Mexico – *Piazza Dante 86. 081 41 75 82.* A Naples institution. Coffee is served sweet.

🍧 **Gran Caffè Gambrinus** – *Via Chiaia 1/2. 081 41 75 82. Open daily 7–1am (Fri and Sat 2am). www.grancaffegambrinus.com.* Near the Royal Palace and opera house, the most famous of Neapolitan caffès. Sumptuously decorated rooms have witnessed 150 years of Neapolitan history.

Gay-Odin – *Via Toledo 214 and 427; Via Benedetto Croce 61. www.gay-odin.it.* Superb quality chocolate. The Croce shop sells gelato, too.

Island of Capri

Pasticceria rosticceria Buonocore – *Via Vittorio Emanuele 35, Capri. 081 83 77 826.* This is a good place to taste the sweet specialities of the region, like torta caprese made with dark chocolate and almonds.

SICILY

Taormina

Bar San Giorgio – *Piazza Sant'Antonio 1, Castelmola, 5km/3mi from Taormina. 0942 28 228. www.barsangiorgio.com.* Established in the early 20C, this traditional caffè enjoys a wonderful location in the quiet Piazza Sant'Antonio. Try the local *vino alla mandorla* (almond liqueur).

RESTAURANTS

Traditional cuisine in Italy follows the seasons. Peruse the markets to see what is fresh and local. House wines are not always reliable; most owners will be glad to offer a taste, then let you choose a bottle if you prefer. Chic hotels can be a good source of creative cuisine.

MICHELIN GUIDE

We've selected a few restaurants from the Michelin red guide. Look for red entries in the listings:

🐷 – Best-value

❀ | ❀❀ | ❀❀❀ – Michelin-starred

✗ | ✗✗ | ✗✗✗ | ✗✗✗✗ | ✗✗✗✗✗ – Charming

WHERE TO EAT
PRICES AND HOURS

	Provinces	Cities
🍽	<€16	<€25€
🍽🍽	€16–30	€25–50
🍽🍽🍽	€30–45	€50–70
🍽🍽🍽🍽	>€45	>€70

Restaurant opening times vary from region to region (in the centre and south of Italy they tend to open and close later). Generally lunch is from 12.30pm to 2.30pm and dinner from 7.30pm to 11pm. Service is usually included, but tip if you like (a few euros at most, unless the establishment is elite). Restaurants where service is not included are marked; an appropriate percentage for a tip is suggested after the meal's price. By law, the bread and the cover charge should be included, but in some *trattorie* and especially in *pizzerie* they are calculated separately.

RESTAURANTS
Trattorie and Osterie

The distinction is no longer clear, but traditionally a *ristorante* offers fine cuisine and service while a trattoria or *osteria* is a family-run establishment serving homemade fare in a relaxed setting.

In a trattoria, the waiter explains the dishes (ask about pricing; seafood, in particular, is sold by weight and expenses mount quickly). Be wary of tourist menus. *Trattorie* used to exclusively serve house wine by the carafe, but now many have wine lists. In the mid- to upper-price range, locals dress smartly.

Pizzerie

Pizza in Italy is served *tondo* – round individual serving – or *al taglio* by the slice in a *pizzeria* or a *forno*. The best dough is made with *lievito madre* natural yeast, topped with a fresh sauce or fragrant olive oil and quality ingrediets, then baked in a wood-burning oven. Beware frozen pizza or canned toppings in touristy city centres or beaches.

Wine bars

Wine bars (*enoteche*) are increasingly popular in Italy. Like *osterie* they often have a kitchen and serve daily specials and light starters, as well as a selection of wines served by the glass or bottle.

MILAN, LOMBARDY AND THE LAKES

Milan

Local specialities include *cotoletta alla milanese* (fillet of veal fried in breadcrumbs with cheese), *ossobuco* (a knuckle of veal with the marrowbone) and *risotto alla*

197

milanese (saffron risotto). Wines to try are sparkling Franciacorta, also Valtellina and Oltrepò Pavese.

☺☺ **Be Bop** – *Viale Col di Lana 4. 02 83 76 972. www.bebo pristorante.it.* Restaurant and pizzeria with gluten-free and soya options.

☺☺ **Bottiglieria da Pino** – *Via Cerva 14. 02 76 00 05 32. Closed evening, Sun, first week Jan, Aug and last week Dec.* A down-to-earth trattoria with home cooking and decent prices. Lunch only.

☺☺ **Charleston** – *Piazza Liberty 8. 02 79 86 31. www.ristorante charleston.it.* Popular with shoppers thanks to its central location.

☺☺ **Da Giannino L'Angolo d'Abruzzo** ☺ ✕ – *Via Rosolino Pilo 20. 02 29 40 65 26. www. dagianninolangolodabruzzo.it. Booking advised.* A family trattoria serving hearty specialities from Abruzzo.

☺☺ **Dongiò** ☺ ✕ – *Via B. Corio 3. 02 55 11 372. www.ristorante-dongio.it. Closed Sat lunch, Sun, Easter, 25 Dec, 1 Jan, 2 weeks Aug. Booking advised.* Simple and authentic place serving tasty Calabrian specialities.

☺☺ **Dulcis in Fundo** – *Via Zuretti 55. 02 66 71 25 03. www. dulcisinfundo.it. Open Tue–Fri lunch, Thu all day and Sat brunch.* Post-Modern meets 1970s in an old industrial building. A vast selection of sweet and savoury snacks and a few unusual mains.

☺☺ **Giulio Pane e Ojo** ☺ ✕ – *Via L. Muratori 10. 02 54 56 189. www. giuliopaneojo.com.* A friendly place specialising in Roman cuisine.

☺☺ **Lady Bù** – *Via Buonarroti 11. 02 39 40 14 87. www.ladybu.com. Booking advised.* The restaurant houses a boutique selling excellent cheeses, as well as a bistro serving a small selection of dishes made from top quality ingredients. These include, Piennolo vine tomatoes, Matera bread, vegetables, cereals and, of course, buffalo cheeses.

☺☺ **La Vecchia Latteria** – *Via dell'Unione 6. 02 87 44 01. Open lunch. Closed Sun.* Good vegetarian food and shared tables at this busy lunch place in central Milan.

☺☺ **Masuelli San Marco** – *Viale Umbria 80. 02 55 18 41 38. www.masuellitrattoria.com. Closed Sun, Mon evenings, last week Aug, first week Sept and 26–30 Dec. Booking advised.* This historic family-run restaurant dates from 1921. Seasonal local dishes vary by the day of the week.

☺☺ **Obikà** – *Via Mercato 28. 02 86 45 05 68. www.obika.com.* A chain that features mozzarella di bufala. Also on the top floor of La Rinascente store in Piazza del Duomo.

☺☺ **Paper Moon** – *Via Bagutta 1. 02 76 02 22 97. www.papermoon milano.com. Closed Sun.* A traditional, elegant choice in Milan's fashion district.

☺☺ **Peck** – *Via Spadari 7/9. 02 80 23 161. www.peck.it. Open lunch and Sun brunch. Closed Mon.* A fine foods store with a coffee and snack bar.

☺☺ **Pizza OK 2** – *Via San Siro 9. 02 48 01 71 32. Closed Mon.* A wide variety of huge, tasty, thin-crust pizzas, a busy place.

☺☺ **Premiata Pizzeria** – *Via De Amicis 22. 02 84 34 32 27. www. premiatapizzeriamilano.it.* Great pizzas and attractive surroundings at this busy place in the Navigli district.

☺☺ **Sant'Eustorgio** – *Piazza Sant'Eustorgio 6. 02 58 10 13 96.*

www.sant-eustorgio.it. Traditional and pleasant with a menu of Italian classics.

⊝⊜ **Spontini** – *Via Gaspare Spontini 4. 02 20 47 444. www. pizzeriaspontini.it.* One of the eight restaurants of this chain to taste the best pizza by the slice in town.

⊝⊜ **Trattoria Madonnina** – *Via Gentilino 6. 02 89 40 90 89. Closed Sun.* A characteristic, informal trattoria with checked tablecloths.

⊝⊜⊜ **Alice-Eataly Smeraldo** ⋇⋇ ✿ – *Piazza XXV Aprile 10. 02 49 49 73 40. www.aliceristorante.it. Closed Sun.* In 2014, the famous Teatro Smeraldo in Milan became the setting for a large Eataly complex, in which the Alice restaurant is certainly one of the highlights. The attractive designer-style decor makes the perfect backdrop for the imaginative cuisine that includes a number of fish dishes. Using top quality ingredients, dishes with distinct flavours are carefully prepared to a consistently high standard.

⊝⊜⊜ **La Brisa** – *Via Brisa 15. 02 86 45 05 21. www.ristorante labrisa.it. Booking advised.* Opposite an archaeological site dating from Roman times, this trattoria serves modern, regional cuisine. Summer dining on the veranda overlooking the garden.

⊝⊜⊜ **Cantina della Vetra** – *Via Pio IV, 3 corner of Piazza Vetra. 02 89 40 38 43. www.cantinadell avetra.it. Closed lunch Mon and Tue.* A large veranda with a view onto the Basilica of San Lorenzo is the place to try typical and special Italian dishes.

⊝⊜⊜ **Timé** – *Via San Marco 5. 02 29 06 10 51. www.ristorantetime.it.* A spacious, classical style dining hall with a touch of unconventional modernity. The staff is efficient and helpful in the choice of appropriate menus.

⊝⊜⊜ **Trattoria del Nuovo Macello** – *Via Cesare Lombroso 20. 02 59 90 21 22. www.trattoria delnuovomacello.it. Closed Sat lunch, Sun and 3 weeks Aug. Booking advised.* Welcoming trattoria with creative cuisine based on local produce.

Bergamo

⊝⊜ **Al Donizetti** – *Via Gombito 17a. 035 24 26 61. www.donizetti.it. Closed 25 Dec, 31 Dec and 1 Jan.* Quality food, good service and hanging hams. Pleasant terrace and a rustic interior.

⊝⊜ **Albergo Il Sole** – *Via Bartolomeo Colleoni 1. 035 21 82 38. www.ilsolebergamo.com.* Pizzeria in the centre of the upper town with eclectic décor and a small garden.

⊝⊜ **Baretto di San Vigilio** – *Via Castello 1. 035 25 31 91. www.baretto.it.* A stylish restaurant serving local and creative dishes. Sit outside in summer for wonderful views over the town.

⊝⊜ **Enoteca Boschini** – *Via T. Tasso 96. 035 22 21 81. Closed Sun evening and Mon*. Large windows and a courtyard garden; great food and wines.

⊝⊜ **Osteria D'Ambrosio** – *Via Broseta 58a. 035 40 29 26. Closed Sat lunch and Sun. Reservation advised.* An authentic, rustic *osteria*. Come for a warm welcome and genuine local dishes.

⊝⊜⊜ **Ol Giopì e la Margì** – *Via Borgo Palazzo 27. 035 24 23 66. www.giopimargi.eu.* The name of this restaurant refers to the traditional masks of Bergamo. The cuisine and the waiters' costumes also pay tribute to the town and region. End your meal with some excellent cheese or something sweet from the dessert trolley.

⊜⊜🛏 **Sarmassa** – *Vicolo Bancalegno 1h. 035 21 92 57. www. sarmassa.com.* Meat, fish, sliced hams and cheeses are all on the menu in this delightful restaurant with vaulted ceilings and 200 year-old arches. The restaurant is named after the famous Barolo della Val Sarmassa vineyard.

Mantua

⊜ **Caffè Modì** – *Via San Giorgio 4.* Designer caffè behind the Ducal Palace. An ideal spot for a glass of wine with a plate of cured meats or cheeses. Music and cultural events are held.

⊜⊜ **Antica Osteria ai Ranari** – *Via Trieste 11. 0376 32 84 31. www.ranari.it. Closed Mon.* An unpretentious trattoria with a good reputation. Traditional menu.

⊜⊜ **Cento Rampini** – *Piazza delle Erbe 11. 0376 36 63 49. ristorantecentorampini.com. Closed Mon.* One of the city's oldest restaurants, located right in the centre. Tasty local specialities.

⊜⊜ **L'Ochina Bianca** – *via Finzi 2. 0376 32 37 00. www.ochinabianca.it.* Small, bistro-style restaurant. These are the backdrops for the food, clearly inspired by Mantuan cuisine with a few fish dishes. The fried seafood and vegetables is one of the house specialities. Fresh ingredients, capably prepared: simply a good meal.

The Lakes

⊜ **Aurora** ✗ – *Via Ciucani 1, Soiano del Lago (L. di Garda). 10km/6.2mi N of Desenzano on the S 572. 0365 67 41 01. Closed Wed.* Good

food at decent prices - a rarity for a restaurant specialising in fish dishes. A good choice.

⊜ **Italia** – *Via Ugo Ara 58, Isola dei Pescatori (L. Maggiore). 0323 30 456. www.ristoranteitalia-isola pescatori.it. Closed Dec–Feb.* A simple trattoria and bar with a wisteria-canopied terrace over the lake. The restaurant boat will ferry you to or from Stresa. Lake fish.

⊜ **Ristoro Antico** – *Via Bottelli 46, Arona (L. Maggiore). 0322 46 482. Closed Tue and 2 weeks in Aug. Booking advised.* Family-run with genuine and tasty home cooking.

⊜ **Agriturismo Il Monterosso** – *Loc. Cima Monterosso, Verbania Pallanza (L. Maggiore), 6km/3.7mi from Pallanza. 0323 55 65 10. www.ilmonterosso.it. 15 rooms.* Farmhouse atop Colle Monterosso; stunning setting surrounded by chestnut, pine and beech woods; breathtaking views over the lakes and Monte Rosa.

⊜⊜ **Osteria Antico Brolo** – *Via Carere 10, Gardone Riviera (L. di Garda). 036 52 14 21. www. ristoranteanticobrolo.it. Closed Nov. and Jan–mid Feb.* Occupying an old 18C residence, this restaurant offers several small rooms in which to enjoy carefully prepared regional dishes. The table on the small balcony is a real delight.

⊜⊜ **Gatto Nero** – *Via Monte Santo 69, Rovenna (L. di Como), N of Cernobbio. 031 51 20 42. Open every evening, Sat, Sun and hols lunch. Booking advised.* Stylish yet cosy with welcoming atmosphere. Fantastic views from the summer terrace.

⊜⊜🛏 **Amélie** – *Via I Maggio 17, Baveno (L. Maggiore). 0323 92 44 96 or 339 87 52 621 (mobile). www. ristoranteamelie.it. Closed Mon.*

booking advised. Few tables, smart interior and excellent cuisine.

😊😊😊😊 **Mistral** XXX ⚙ – *Via Roma 1, Bellagio (L. Como). 031 95 64 35. www.ristorante-mistral. com. Dinner only.* A superb terrace with stunning views of the lake provides the perfect location to enjoy inventive molecular dishes, alongside more traditional cuisine.

ALPS AND DOLOMITES

Turin

😊😊 **Consorzio** – *Via Monte di Pietà 23. 011 27 67 661. www. ristoranteconsorzio.it. Closed Sat lunch and Sun.* Assortment of Piedmontese specialities: simple and informal, a wide range of traditional regional dishes, wines and cheeses.

😊😊 **Porto di Savona** – *Piazza Vittorio Veneto 2. 011 81 73 500. www.foodandcompany.com.* Historic 1863 trattoria. Good selection of traditional, regional dishes such as *agnolotti* filled pasta).

😊😊 **Sfashion Cafè** – *Via Cesare Battisti 13. 011 51 60 085. www.foodandcompany.com.* Bar, traditional restaurant and pizzeria with unusual décor.

😊😊 **Tre Galli** – *Via Sant'Agostino 25. 011 52 16 027. www.3galli.com. Closed Sun.* A pleasant wine bar in the fashionable nightlife district. Good wines, cured meats and cheese. Terrace in summertime.

😊😊 **Tre Galline** XX – *Via Bellezia 37. 011 43 66 553. www.3galline.it. Closed Sun.* Traditional Piemontese dishes. Don't miss out on the *bolliti* (stewed meat) in season.

😊😊😊😊 **Casa Vicina** XXX ⚙ – *Via Nizza 224. 011 19 50 68 40. www.casavicina.it. Closed Sun*

evening and Mon. Creative, very tasty dishes in a minimalist setting.

😊😊😊😊 **Del Cambio** XXXX – *Piazza Carignano 2. 011 54 66 90. www.delcambio.it. Closed Sun evening. Reservation advised.* Dating from 1757 this extremely classy restaurant has a Baroque interior and excellent cuisine.

Dolomites *See Must Stay*

GENOA, PORTOFINO AND LIGURIAN RIVIERA

Genoa

Friggitorie

Fry-shops for quick, economical fried fish, veg and polenta. Try local specialities such as *farinata* (chick pea flour focaccia).

Antica Sciamadda – *Via S. Giorgio 14r. 010 24 68 516. Closed Sun.*
Carega – *Via Sottoripa 113r. 010 24 70 617.*
La Farinata dei Teatri – *Piazza Marsala 5r (N of Piazza Corvetto).*

😊😊 **Antica Osteria di Vico Palla** X 😊 – *Vico Palla 15r. 010 24 66 575. osteriadivicopalla.com. Closed Mon.* Rustic place serves delicious Ligurian specialities.

😊😊 **Cantine Squarciafico** – *Piazza Invrea 3r. 010 24 70 823. www.cantinesquarciafico.it. Closed Sun lunch.* Charming 16C palazzo. Authentic local cuisine.

😊😊 **Pintori** – *Via San Bernardo 68r. 010 27 57 507. www.pintori.net. Closed Sun–Mon.* Sardinian cuisine. Well-established and family-run

😊😊 **Sà Pesta** – *Via Giustiniani 16. 010 24 68 336. www.sapesta.it. Open Mon–Sat lunch. Thu–Sat evening with booking.* Authentic Ligurian cuisine, informal service.

RESTAURANTS

🍷🍽 **I Tre Merli** – *Calata Cattaneo 17. 010 24 64 416. www. itremerli.it.* Smart and refined setting for local traditional food.

Portofino
🍷🍽 **Da Paolo** – *Via San Fortunato 14. 0185 77 35 95. www. ristorantedapaolocamogli.com. Closed Mon.* Rustic little family-run restaurant, located in the old village not far from the small port; seafood cuisine according to the daily availability of produce in the market.

🍷🍽 **La Cucina di Nonna Nina** ✕ – *Via Molfino 126, San Rocco (6km/3.7mi from Camogli). 0185 77 38 35 or 347 15 46 624. www. nonnanina.it. Closed Wed, 3 weeks in Nov and 2 in Jan.* Appealing décor, delicious traditional cuisine. Lovely terrace.

Ligurian riviera
🍷 **Ristorante Ines** – *Via Vignolo 1, Noli, 019 74 80 86, www.ristorante ines.com.* Good seafood.

🍷🍽 **Enoteca internazionale** – *Via Roma 62, Monterosso, 0187 81 72 78. www.enotecainternazionale.com.* A wellestablished wine shop and wine bar also serving snacks.

🍷🍽 **Maggiorino** – *Via Roma 183, Sanremo, 0184 50 43 38. Closed Sun.* An ideal place to sample a farinata, a vegetable tart or a focaccia.

VENICE AND AROUND

Venice
Grand Canal
🍷🍽 **Ai Promessi Sposi** – *Calle dell'Oca 4367, Cannaregio. 041 24 12 747. Closed Mon and Wed lunch.* This *bacaro* near Campo Sant'Apostoli has a pleasant garden; fish specialities.

🍷🍽 **Cà d'Oro Alla Vedova** – *Calle del Pistor 3912 (following on from the Ca' d'Oro vaporetto pier, beyond the Strada Nuova), Cannaregio. 041 52 85 324. Closed Thu and Sun lunch.* This *bacaro* is often packed, so best to book; retro ambience and tasty local cuisine. Ask for recommendations.

🍷🍽 **Antica Carbonera** – *Calle Bembo 4648 (first left after the Goldoni Theatre), San Marco. 041 52 25 479. www.anticacarbonera.it Closed Tue.* Decorated with furnishings from Archduke Rudolph's yacht. Classic Venetian cuisine, seafood or meat.

🍷🍽 **Leon Bianco** – *Salizada San Luca 4153, San Marco. 041 52 21 180. www.osterialeonbianco.com.* Quick snacks at the bar or hot meals in the restaurant.

🍷🍽 **Vini da Gigio** – *Fondamenta San Felice 3628a, Cannaregio. 041 52 85 140. www.vinidagigio.com. Closed Mon–Tue, Dec 25–26–31 and Jan 1.* Rustic and informal *osteria* popular with locals. Fish a variety of ways, including marinated and grilled. Also meat dishes and a good wine list.

🍷🍽 **Alle Testiere** ✕ – *Calle del Mondo Novo 5801, Castello. 041 52 27 220. www.osterialletestiere.it. Closed Sun and Mon and 22 Dec– 10 Jan. Reservation advised.* This little restaurant is renowned for its seafood and its bold flavour combinations: from John Dory with citrus fruit to *capesante* (scallops) with liqueur or *canestrelli* with lemon and mint. For less adventurous tastes, there is also a selection of grilled fish.

Piazza San Marco
🍷🍽 **Enoiteca Mascareta** – *Calle Longa di S. Maria Formosa,*

Castello 5183. 041 52 30 744.
www.ostemaurolorenzon.com.
A wine bar serving up plates of
cichèti (marinated fish, ham and
cheese, platter of Italian cheeses) or
hot dishes (allow €35 for a full meal)
n an inviting atmosphere.

⊝⊝⊜ **Bistrot de Venise** – *Calle
dei Fabbri, S. Marco 4685. 041 523
5651. www.bistrotdevenise.com.*
A chic bistro-style lounge with an
elegant zinc bar, dining room, and
sidewalk seating. Sergio's passion
for Venetian culinary history has
put a few historic dishes on the
menu, such as bisato de vale,
roast eel flavoured with oranges
n wine, cinnamon and bay. Most
of the menu explores traditional
and contemporary cuisine. Some
500 wines are available here by the
glass, more by the bottle.

Schiavoni–Arsenale

⊝⊜ **Rivetta** – *Salizada San
Provolo 4625, Castello, between
Piazza San Marco and Campo San
Zaccaria. 041 52 87 302. Closed
Mon.* A wide choice of cicheti right
by San Zaccaria.

⊝⊝⊜⊜ **Met** XXXX – *Riva degli
Schiavoni 4149, Castello. 041 520
5044. www.hotelmetropole.com.*
Creative cuisine, attentive
service, and plush pampering
surroundings for an elegant,
memorable evening.

Rialto-Frari–San Rocco

⊝⊜ **Al Ponte del Megio** – *Ponte
del Megio 1666 (corner of Calle
Larga leading to Campo San
Giacomo dell'Orio), Santa Croce.
041 71 97 77. Closed Sat evening
and Sun.* At the "millet bridge",
this trattoria serves excellent fish
specialities.

⊝⊜ **La Patatina** – *Calle Saoneri
2741a, San Polo. 041 52 37 238.
www.lapatatina.it. Reservation
advised.* A friendly popular rustic
trattoria. Good food, with plenty
of fish.

⊝⊜ **All'Arco** – *Calle dell'Occhialer
436 (from Ruga San Giovanni
take Sottoportego dei Do Mori),
San Polo. 041 52 05 666. Closed
Sun.* Tiny and packed during peak
market hours for cicheti and an
excellent choice of wines.

⊝⊜ **Antico Dolo** – *Ruga Rialto
778, San Polo. 041 52 26 546.
www.anticodolo.it.* Small osteria
with red wood walls. Tripe, crostini,
polenta and baccalà mantecato, plus
a tasting menu. Wine and cicheti
are served throughout the day.

⊝⊜ **Da Ignazio** – *Calle dei
Saoneri 2749. 041 523 48 52. www.
trattoriadaignazio.com. Closed Sat,
2 weeks in Aug and 2 weeks in Jan.*
A quiet trattoria where you dine
beneath a pergola. The cooking
celebrates Venetian tradition with
products from the sea and gardens
of the Venetian islands. Excellent
desserts.

⊝⊜ **Dona Onesta** – *Ponte de la
Dona Onesta 3922 (not far from
Ca' Foscari), Dorsoduro. 041 71
05 86. www.donaonesta.com.* An
excellent trattoria: the sarde in
saor with raisins and pine nuts are
exemplary .Remarkable grilled fish.
Diligent, friendly service.

⊝⊜ **La Zucca** – *Ramo del Megio
1762, Santa Croce. 041 52 41 570.
www.lazucca.it. Closed Sun.
Reservation advised.* Varied and
slightly exotic dishes, lightly
prepared. A simple trattoria, with a
good selection of vegetable dishes.

⊝⊜ **Vecio Fritolin** X – *Calle
della Regina 2262 (behind Campo
San Cassiano), Santa Croce. 041*

52 22 881. *www.veciofritolin.it.*
Closed Mon and Tue lunch. This
little place has a good reputation.
Market produce (try the swordfish
tartare with olives and lemon) and
delicious pasta.

Accademia–Salute

⊜⊜ **Antica Locanda Montin**
– *Fondamenta di Borgo 1147,
Dorsoduro. 041 52 27 151.
www.locandamontin.com.*
Famous trattoria by a peaceful
canal with a shady courtyard.
Accommodation, too.

⊜⊜ **Linea d'Ombra** – *Dorsoduro
(Punta della Dogana) 19, La Salute.
041 24 11 881. www.ristorante
lineadombra.com. Closed Tue and
Dec–Feb. In summer open daily.*
Contemporary interior and creative
cuisine, stemming from local
traditions. A treat for all the senses.
At Punta della Dogana, terrace
tables overlook action on the
waterways.

⊜⊜⊜ **La Calcina** – *Zattere ai
Gesuati, Dorsoduro 782. 041 520
6466. www.lacalcina.com.* The
wood terrace hangs right at the
Zattere's edge, perfect for ship- and
boat-watching. The ample menu
selection offers fish, meat, and
good vegetarian dishes, plus pasta,
salads, and the Zattere's best gelato,
handmade the traditional way.

Cannaregio–Ghetto

⊜⊜ **Algiubagiò** – *Fondamenta
Nuove 5039, Cannaregio. 041 52 36
084. www.algiubagio.net.* Stylish
restaurant with lagoon view, near
the vaporetto stop to the islands.

⊜⊜ **Alla Fontana** – *Fondamenta
Cannaregio 1102, Cannaregio. 041
71 50 77. Closed Mon.* Local wine
bar with small restaurant serving
tasty food. Tables on the canalside.

⊜⊜ **All'Antica Mola** –
*Fondamenta Ormesini, 2800
Cannaregio. 041 71 74 92. Closed
Wed, 7–22 Jan and 1–15 Ago.* Set
beside a small canal, a stone's throw
from the Ghetto. Unpretentious but
very tasty Venetian cuisine.

⊜⊜ **Anice Stellato** ✗ ☺ –
*Fondamenta de la Sensa 3272,
Cannaregio. 041 72 07 44. www.
osterianicestellato.com. Open Tue
evening Apr –Sep. Closed Mon and
Tue, Nov–Dec 2 weeks and Aug 16–
30.* Simple, modern, with a good
choice of fish at decent prices.

⊜⊜ **Da A'Marisa** – *Ponte dei Tre
Archi 652b, Cannaregio. 041 72 02
11. Closed Sun–Tue evening.* One of
few that specialise in meat, run by
a family of butchers. Excellent food,
generous portions.

⊜⊜ **Gam Gam** – *Ghetto Vecchio
1122. 366 25 4505. www.gamgam
kosher.com. Closed Fri evening, Sat
and Jewish holidays. Reservation
advised.* Popular kosher restaurant
in the historic Ghetto.

⊜⊜ **La Perla** – *Rio Terà dei
Franceschi 4615, Cannaregio. 041
52 85 175. Closed Wed, Aug and
24–26 Dec.* Simple pizzeria with
many options, some unusual.

Sant'Elena–San Pietro

⊜⊜ **Dal Pampo** – *Calle Generale
A. Chinotto 24, Island of Sant'Elena.
041 52 08 419. Closed Tue.* Trattoria
serving traditional cuisine, also
outside tables. A favourite of
Biennale artists and exhibitors.

⊜⊜ **Dai Tosi Grandi** – *Secco
Marina 985, Castello. 041 24 12
299. www.trattoriadaitosigrandi.it.
Closed Tue.* Near the Biennale. Wide
choice of pizzas, incomparable
pasta.

Certosa-Mazzorbo

Il Certosino – *Polo Nautico Vento di Venezia, Island of Certosa. 041 52 00 35. www.ristorante ilcertosino.com. Closed Wed (only Feb–Apr and Oct–Nov) and Dec–Jan.* Delightful restaurant next to the boatyard serves creative Veneto cuisine.

Venissa – *Fondamenta Santa Caterina 3, Island of Mazzorbo. 041 527 2281. www.venissa.it. Closed Tue and Nov–Apr 13.* Set by the restored vineyard, select wines and creative cuisine.

Venetian Lagoon

Ristorante Da Franco – *Strada Romea 364/a, 30015 Sant'Anna di Chioggia, 8km/5mi S of Chioggia on the S 309 Romea. 041 49 50 301.* Welcoming (mostly) fish restaurant. Good list of wines and whiskeys.

La Colombara – *Via S. Zilli 34, Aquileia, 2km/1.2mi NW of Aquileia. 0431 91 513. www.lacolombara.it. Sun and Mon evenings only in winter.* Carefully prepared fish dishes; rustic décor and outside dining.

Padua

Antica Trattoria Bertolini – *Via Altichiero 162, Altichiero, 5km/3mi N of Padua. 049 60 03 57. www.bertolini1849.it. Closed Sat, Sun evening, 2 weeks in Aug and 26 Dec–5 Jan. 14 rooms.* Just outside Padua, this long-standing restaurant serves good traditional dishes. Close to the motorway, it's also a good place to stay for travellers.

Belle Parti – *Via Belle Parti 11. 049 87 51 822. www.ristorantebelle parti.it. Closed Sun.* A very elegant setting for a seasonal menu of tasty meat and fish dishes.

Da Giovanni – *Via P. Maroncelli 22. 049 77 26 20. www. ristorantedagiovannipd.it. Closed Sat lunch, Sun and Aug.* An historic restaurant to enjoy good home-made pasta and tasty stews.

Osteria dal Capo – *Via degli Obizzi 2. 049 66 31 05. www.osteriadalcapo.it. Closed Mon lunch and Sun and 7–28 Ago.* A traditional trattoria near the cathedral. Specialities from Padua and the Veneto.

Osteria L'Anfora – *Via dei Soncino 13. 049 65 66 29. Closed Sun.* Good for just a drink or a meal in an attractive, informal setting at the heart of the Ghetto.

Trattoria San Pietro – *Via San Pietro 95. 049 87 60 330. Closed Sun and public hols.* A renowned trattoria in the historic centre, elegant décor. Tables are limited, so reservations are essential.

Belle Parti – *Via Belle Parti 11, Altichiero, 5km/3mi N of Padova. 049 875 1822. www. ristorantebelleparti.it. Closed Sat.* An elegant atmosphere with paintings on the walls, mirrors and woodwork; the menu offers seasonal specialties, including a delicious selection of meat and fish.

Vicenza

Al Pestello ✕ – *Contrà Santo Stefano 3. 0444 32 37 21. www. ristorantealpestello.it. Closed Thu and Jan.* Local cusine, its menu is in dialect. There is also a lovely outdoor area.

Antica Osteria da Penacio ✕✕ – *Via Soghe 22, Arcugnano, 10km/ 6.2mi S of Vicenza on the S 247. 0444 27 30 81. www.penacio.it. Closed Wed , Thu lunchs and 10 days in Feb and 10 in Nov.* Creative tasty cuisine with local ingredients and lovely presentations. Family-run for several generations; warm, welcoming atmosphere.

Verona

⊖ **Kulmbacher Bier-Haus** – *Via Marconi 72. 045 59 75 17. www.kbh.it. Closed Sat lunch.* Bavarian tavern offers generous servings of tasty food in a convivial atmosphere.

⊖⊖ **Al Bersagliere** ✕ 😊 – *Via Dietro Pallone 1. 045 80 04 824. www.trattoriaalbersagliere.it. Closed Sun, Mon and Aug 10–31.* A typical little trattoria with dining in the cellar or at tables outside.

⊖⊖⊖ **San Basilio alla Pergola** ✕ 😊 – *Via A. Pisano 9. 045 52 04 75. www.trattoriasan basilio.it. Closed Sun and Jan the first week.* Rustic dining rooms and splendid wooden floorsa pleasant, country feel. Traditional but imaginative cooking.

EMILIA-ROMAGNA

Bologna

⊖ **Bottega del Vino Olindo Faccioli** – *Via Altabella 15b. 051 22 31 71. www.enotecastoricafaccioli.it. Closed (Apr–Sep) Sun, (Jul) Sat, 1 week in Jan and 3 weeks in Aug.* A family *enoteca* since 1924, over 500 Italian wines. Atmosphere and a concise menu of quality bites.

⊖ **Tamburini** – *Via Caprarie 1. 051 23 47 26. www.tamburini.com.* A historic delicatessen famous for its tortellini. Tasty lunch at the self-service section.

⊖⊖ **Cantina Bentivoglio** – *Via Mascarella 4b. 051 26 5416. www.cantinabentivoglio.it. Closed Sun only Jun–Aug.* Live jazz nightly, featuring international musicians.

Great menu and wonderful wines. Come for an evening to remember.

⊖⊖ **Gigina** – *Via Stendhal 1. 051 32 23 00. www.trattoriagigina.it.* Just outside the centre, this cosy family-run trattoria has a good reputation for traditional Bolognese specialities.

⊖⊖ **Osteria dell'Orsa** – *Via Mentana 1. 051 23 15 76. www.osteriadellorsa.com. Closed 25 Dec and 1 Jan.* An institution among staff and students from the university. Serves authentic local dishes, open late.

⊖⊖ **Teresina** – *Via Oberdan 4. 051 22 89 85. www.ristorante teresinabologna.it. Closed Sun. Reservation advised.* A busy trattoria close to the main sights of the centre, with local food plus dishes of the day.

⊖⊖ **Trattoria del Rosso** – *Via A. Righi 30. 051 23 67 30. www.trattoriadelrosso.com.* Good traditional food and low prices make this centrally located informal trattoria a popular place!

⊖⊖ **Trebbi** – *Via Solferino 40b. 051 58 37 13. www.trattoria-trebbi.com. Closed (Jun–Aug) Tue, Sat lunch in winter. Reservation advised.* Since 1946, simple trattoria near the law courts. Interesting menu, good food, vegetable buffet.

Ferrara

⊖ **Tassi** ✕✕ 😊 – *Viale Repubblica 23, Bondeno, 20km/12.4mi NW of Ferrara on the S 496. 0532 89 30 30. www.ristorantetassi. Closed Sun evening and Mon.* Long established, specialising in local meat dishes. Also has rooms.

⊖⊖ **Ca' d'Frara** ✕ 😊 – *Ca' d'Frara – Via del Gambero 4. 053 22 05 057. www.ristorantecadfrara.it. Closed Tue and Wed lunch.* Don't be taken in by the modern decor, this Ferrarese house is a bastion of tradition: hung hams, *pasticcio di maccheroni*, and *salama da sugo* with mashed potato.

🍷🍽 **L'Oca Giuliva** – *Via Boccacanale di Santo Stefano 38/40. 0532 20 76 28. www. ristorantelocagiuliva.it. Closed Tue.* An elegant, refined restaurant. Local cuisine, magnificent choice of wines.

🍷🍽 **Quel fantastico giovedi** ✗✗ 😊 – *Via Castelnuovo 9. 0532 76 05 70. quelfantasticogiovedi.it. Closed Wed.* Contemporary décor. Young team serves imaginative takes on traditional dishes.

Parma

🍷🍽 **Antica Cereria** – *Borgo Rodolfo Tanzi 5. 0521 20 73 87. www.anticacereria.it. Closed Mon.* Pleasant restaurant, customers choose their wine from the cellar. Local dishes with good antipasti.

🍷🍽 **Enoteca Fontana** – *Strada Luigi Farini 24. 0521 28 60 37.* Enoteca-cum-restaurant; good wine and food.

🍷🍽 **Trattoria del Tribunale** – *Vicolo Politi 5. 0521 28 55 27. www.trattoriadeltribunale.it.* Well-known near the law court. Best of local tradition with appealing new ideas.

Ravenna

🍷 **Ca' de Vén** – *Via Corrado Ricci 24. 0544 30 163. www.cadeven.it. Closed Mon. Reservation advised.* A rustic trattoria, timeless atmosphere. Famous for its *piadina* – the local flatbread.

TUSCANY AND UMBRIA

Florence

In Florence, many bars sell sandwiches and ready-cooked food, while restaurants cater to tourists – but few are good. Best to head for the little *trattorie* which serve traditional Florentine dishes including Chianina (*prized local beef*), tripe (*trippa and lampredotto*), vegetable soup (*ribollita*), bread cooked with tomatoes (*pappa al pomodoro*), pasta dishes including *rigatoni strascicati*, steak (*bistecca alla Fiorentina*), stewed meatloaf (*polpettone in umido*), sausages with beans (*salsiccia con i fagioli all'uccelletto*). *Biscotti* with *vin santo* (crunchy biscuits with sweet wine).

🍷 **Nuova Tripperia Fiorentina** – *San Lorenzo central market, open market hours.* Legendary tripe sandwiches, the family business since the 19C.

🍷 **Palle d'Oro** – *Via Sant'Antonino 43. 055 28 83 83. www.trattoria palledorofirenze.com. Closed Sun and Aug. Reservation advised.* Near the San Lorenzo market, early-20C wine shop with Tuscan specialities, first courses, sandwiches.

🍷 **Vini e Vecchi Sapori** – *Via dei Magazzini 3r. 055 29 30 45. Closed Sun and some days in Aug. Reservation advised.* Small, pleasant and busy, behind the Palazzo Vecchio. Local specialities include vegetable soup *(ribollita)* and tripe (*lampredotto*), crostini, salami.

🍷🍽 **Accademia** – *Piazza San Marco 7r. 055 21 73 43. www. ristoranteaccademia.it.* Across from San Marco, art professors, bankers and locals enjoy specialities like mushroom strudel with Parmesan sauce, rabbit roll stuffed with artichokes, and lasagna with lamb *ragù*. Good wines.

🍴🍷 **Cafaggi** – *Via Guelfa 35r. 055 29 49 89. www.ristorantecafaggi. com. Closed Sun and Mon.* Vintage 1960s décor in this 1922 trattoria near San Marco. Reasonable prices. Good Tuscan fare like black cabbage soup, *pappardelle* with wild boar sauce and braised veal.

🍴🍷 **Cibrèo Trattoria (il Cibrèio)** 🍴 😊 – *Via dei Macci 122r. 055 23 41 100. www.edizioni teatrodelsalecibreofirenze.it. Closed Mon, Aug and 1 week in Feb. Reservation advised.* Wine bar is informal, friendly and trendy; its lower-priced food comes from the Cibrèo kitchen. Very popular, reliable for delicious food and quality wines.

🍴🍷 **Del Fagioli** 🍴 😊 – *Corso Tintori 47r. 055 24 42 85. Closed Sat–Sun and Aug.* A perfect Chianina steakhouse. A bastion of Florentine tradition.

🍴🍷🍷 **Gucci Caffetteria Ristorante** – *Piazza della Signoria 10. 055 759 23827. Open 9am–11pm, restaurant noon–10pm.* Sleek and minimalist Gucci Museum caffè offers fresh light fare; a bar for wine or coffee.

🍴🍷 **Il Latini** 🍴 😊 – *Via dei Palchetti 6r. 055 21 09 16. www. illatini.com. www.illatini.com. Closed Mon, 1 week in Aug. Reservation advised.* Wooden tables heaving with diners, prosciutti hanging overhead, a Florentine traditional menu, and witty banter. Wines are French and Italian.

🍴🍷 **Osteria de' Benci** – *Via de' Benci 11/13r. 055 23 44 923. www. osteriadeibenci.it. Reservation advised.* Servers are university students, atmosphere is rustic, soundtrack is jazz, and dishes

range from traditional Tuscan, to creative spaghetti. Tuscan wines only.

🍴🍷 **Il Santo Bevigore** 🍴 😊 – *Via Santo Spirito 64–66r. 055 21 12 64. www.ilsantobevitore.com.Closed Mon lunch.* Tradition meets modern in minimalist decor. Excellent duck prepared two ways.

🍴🍷 **Se-Sto on Arno** – *Piazza Ognissanti 3. www.sestoonarno. com. 055 2715 1. (6th floor The Westin ExcelsiorFlorence).* The Rooftop terrace with updated 1960s decor, overlooks the Arno and Santo Spirito. Delightful, fresh cuisine, reasonable lunch specials.

🍴🍷 **Trattoria 13 Gobbi** – *Via del Porcellana 9r. 055 28 40 15. Closed 25 Dec dinner and 1 Jan lunch. Reservation advised.* Popular cheerful trattoria, authentic Tuscan cooking, rustic décor s. Summer service in the lovely little courtyard.

🍴🍷🍷 **Baccarossa** – *Via Ghibellina 46r. 055 24 06 20. www. baccarossa.it. Closed Sun, lunch by reservations.* Contemporary cuisine: carpaccio, gnocchi with seafood, pasta with fresh tuna and citrus pesto.

🍴🍷🍷 **Borgo San Jacopo** 🍴🍴🍴 – *Borgo San Jacopo 62r. 055 28 16 61. www.lungarnocollection.com. Closed lunch.* Set along the Arno, creative and traditional cuisine; good brodetto fish soup.

🍴🍷🍷 **Cibrèo** – *Via Andrea Verrocchio 8r. 055 23 41 100. www.edizioniteatrodelsale cibreo firenze.it. Closed Mon, Aug, 1 week in Feb. Reservation advised.* No pasta is served in this informal but very stylish establishment near Sant'Ambrogio market. Chef Picchi passionately researches Tuscan traditions and ingredients, then does them his way, all beautifully

MUST EAT

presented. The service is attentive and excellent-quality wines are reasonably priced.

⊖⊜⊜ **Santa Elisabetta** – *Piazza Santa Elisabetta 3. 055 27 370. www.hotelbrunelleschi.it. Dinner only, closed Mon, Sun and Aug.* Intimate, cozy, elegant restaurant set in Florence's Byzantine Pagliazza Tower. Creative cuisine and very attentive service.

Lucca

⊖⊜ **Antica Osteria** – *Via Santa Croce 55. 349 84 23 069. anticaosteria.wix.com/1650.* Correct prices for this local cooking in attractive, atmospheric rooms.

⊖⊜ **Osteria Baralla** – *Via Anfiteatro 5/7/9. 0583 44 02 40. www.osteriabaralla.it. Closed Sun.* Charming, in a medieval palazzo. One room has a vaulted ceiling, others are smaller. Daily menu features typical Tuscan dishes.

⊖⊜ **Buca di Sant'Antonio** ☼☼☼ – *Via della Cervia 3. 0583 55 881. www.bucadi santantonio.it. Closed Sun evening and Mon.* Founded in 1782, this rustic spot remains a favourite of Luccans for traditional cuisine at reasonable prices.

⊖⊜ **Giglio** – *Piazza del Giglio 2. 058 34 94 058. www.ristorante giglio.com. Closed Tue and Wed lunch.* Set in an 18C palazzo right in the city centre, offering local meat and fish dishes.

⊖⊜ **Trattoria da Leo** – *Via Tegrimi 1. 0583 49 22 36. www. trattoriadaleo.it.* ⊟. Steps from San Michele in Foro, lively with simple,abundant cuisine. Some outside tables.

⊖⊜ **Gli Orti di Via Elisa** – *Via Elisa 17. 0583 49 12 41. www.ristorante gliorti.it. Closed Wed, Thu lunch.* Traditional and creative fare, from grilled meats to huge salads to pizza (evening), to daily specials, with a bistro ambience.

⊖⊜/⊖⊜⊜ **Ristorante All'Olivo** ☼☼ – *Piazza San Quirico 1. 0583 49 62 64. www.ristorante olivo.it. Closed Wed in winter.* On a picturesque square, this small refined restaurant serves on the terrace.

⊖⊜⊜ **Puccini** – *Corte Lorenzo 1. 338 98 05 927 (mobile. www. ristorantepuccini.com. Reservation advised.* Near the Puccini house, fish arrives fresh daily from Versilia; they offer a good meat selection too.

⊖⊜⊜ **Ristorante Villa Bongi** – *Via di Cocombola 640, Montuolo. 6.5km/4mi from Lucca. 348 73 40 143 (mobile). www.villabongi.it.* Pretty rooms, splendid panoramic terrace. Traditional and modern Tuscan cuisine. Large garden.

Pisa

⊖⊜ **La Clessidra** – *Via del Castelletto 26/30. 050 54 01 60. www.www.ristorantelaclessidra. net. Open Mon–Sat (lunch only reservation). Closed Sun, 5–25 Aug and 1-8 Jan.* Simple and pleasant. Tuscan cuisine has innovative variations, in one of the smartest historic parts of town.

⊖⊜ **Hostaria Pizzeria Le Repubbliche Marinare** – *Vicolo Del Ricciardi 8. 050 22 05 06. www. repubblichemarinare.eu. Closed Mon. Jul–Aug dinner only.* A quiet oasis in Sant'Antonio with terrace, the speciality is fish.

⊖⊜ **Osteria dei Cavalieri** ☼ – *Via San Frediano 16. 050 58 08 58. Closed Sun lunch, Sat, 3 weeks Aug, 24–26 Dec, 31 Dec, 1 Jan.* A favourite of Pisans that serves traditional cuisine.

Da Bruno – *Via Luigi Bianchi 12, Porta a Lucca. 050 56 08 18. anticatrattoriadabruno.it. Closed Tue and Wed lunch.* One of the city's best restaurants. Pisan and Tuscan specialities.

Siena

Hosteria Il Carroccio – *Via Casato di Sotto 32. 0577 41 165. Closed Tue lunch, Wed evening, 15 days in Jan and Jul.* This establishment is renowned for its authentic Sienese cooking and delicious salads. A small but welcoming rustic-style trattoria which is popular with the locals. Located a few minutes' walk from the Piazza del Campo.

Osteria la Chiacchiera – *Costa di Sant'Antonio 4. 0577 28 06 31. www.osterialachiacchera.it. Closed Tue.* The wait for a table can be long, but is worth it. Summer tables set in the little street between Santa Caterina and Piazza del Campo. Traditional Tuscan cooking.

Trattoria Papei – *Piazza del Mercato 6. 0577 28 08 94. www.anticatrattoriapapei.com.* Classic Sienese trattoria, with a lively and friendly atmosphere. Simple, décor. Summer meals are served in the busy Piazza del Mercato, with the Torre del Mangia in the background. Good value.

Antica Trattoria Botteganova – *Strada statale 408, 29 / Montevarchi. 0577 28 42 30. www.anticatrattoriabotteganova.it. Closed Mon and Sun evening. Reservation advised.* One of the best restaurants in town. Elegant vaulted ceiling, rustic decor.

San Gimignano

Osteria del Carcere – *Via del Castello 13. 0577 94 19 05. Closed Thu lunch, Wed, 6 Jan and 2 weeks before Easter.* Simple, rustic eatery near Piazza della Cisterna/ Daily specials. Excellent meat.

Assisi, Foligno, Spello

Da Cecco – *Piazza San Pietro 8. 075 81 24 37. www.hotelberti.it. Closed Wed.* Rustic décor with Umbrian specialities in Hotel Berti.

Da Erminio – *Via Montecavallo 19. 075 81 25 06. www.trattoriadaerminio.it. Closed Thu.* Uphill near La Rocca, an open fire grills Umbrian dishes.

Le Mura – *Via Bolletta 19. Foligno. 0742 35 46 48. Closed Tue.* You'll find a fiery grill in the main room, fresh pastas and a convivial atmosphere in this restaurant known for its Umbrian specialties.

Piazzetta dell'Erba – *Via San Gabriele dell'Addolorata 15b. 075 81 53 52. www.osteriala piazzetta.it. Closed Mon.* Innovative cuisine, nice wines, good service.

Villa Roncalli – *Via Roma 25, Loc. Sant'Eraclio, Foligno. 0742 39 10 91. www.villaroncalli.com. Open dinner only. Closed Mon. 10 rooms.* Maria Luisa's sophisticated Umbrian cooking attracts diners from well beyond Umbria. Lovely villa hidden off a commercial area.

Redibis Ristorante – *Via Dell'Anfiteatro 3, Bevagna. 320 71 59 577. foodie.bio/ ristorante. Closed Tue.* Creative cuisine set in an ancient Roman amphitheatre foundation.

Perugia

Dal Mi'Cocco – *Corso Garibaldi 12. 075 57 32 511. Closed Mon. Reservation advised.* An alternative establishment set in former stables. A 15€ fixed-price menu features

Umbrian specialities. Home made bread and pasta.

◙◙ **Da Cesarino** – *Piazza IV Novembre 4/5. 075 57 28 974. Closed Wed.* This large room, frequented by locals, is good for crostini (mushrooms, liver, onions) or pasta with vegetables.

◙◙◙ **Antica trattoria San Lorenzo** XX – *Piazza Danti 19a. 075 57 21 956. www.anticatrattoria sanlorenzo.com. Closed Sun. Reservation advised.* By the Duomo, in an intimate vaulted room. Fresh Umbrian cuisine, refined, and bold.

Orvieto

◙◙ **La Palomba** – *Via Cipriano Manente 16. 0763 34 33 95. Closed Wed.* Good traditional Umbrian food at reasonable prices.

◙◙◙ **I Sette Consoli** XX – *Piazza Sant'Angelo 1a. 0763 34 39 11. www.isetteconsoli.it. Closed Wed, Sun evenings. Reservation advised.* Imaginative cooking. Nice rustic-style interior. Garden with a stunning view of the Duomo.

ROME

Campo de' Fiori

◙ **Forno di Campo de' Fiori** – *Campo de' Fiori 22. 06 68 80 66 62. www.fornocampodefiori.com.* The legendary bread bakery also sells pizza by the slice, breakfast rolls, some sweets and seasonal treats. No chairs or tables.

◙◙ **Ditirambo** – *Piazza della Cancelleria 74. 06 68 71 626. www. ristoranteditiramboroma.it. Closed Mon lunch.* Behind Campo de' Fiori, small tastefully furnished restaurant. Delicious dishes. Various breads and pastas are made here.

Isola Tiberina

◙◙ **Al Pompiere** – *Via S. Maria de' Calderari 38, Torre Argentina. 06 68 68 377. www.alpompiereroma.com. Closed Sun.* A range of Roman-Jewish traditional dishes served in the spacious rooms of an old palazzo. The crostata di ricotta e visciole (ricotta and sour cherry tart) is highly recommended.

◙◙ **Sora Lella** XX – *Via di Ponte Quattro Capi 16. 06 68 61 601. www.trattoriasoralella.it.* Traditional family restaurant, on Tiber Island.

Largo Argentina/ghetto

◙◙ **Esatto Ars** – *Piazza Costaguti 15. 06 68 30 94 20. www.esattoars.it. Closed Tue.* A perfect and original blend of art and cuisine, tradition and creativity.

◙◙◙ **Piperno** – *Via Monte de' Cenci 9, Ghetto. 06 68 80 66 29. www.ristorantepiperno.it. Closed Sun dinnertime, Mon and Aug.* This ghetto favourite serves Jewish-Roman fare, including carciofi alla giudia (deep-fried artichokes) and zuppa di ceci (garbanzo-bean soup). The elegant cuisine is matched by the setting, a secluded piazza engulfed by the 15C Palazzo Cenci, where a noble family self-destructed.

Montecitorio

◙ **Maccheroni** – *Piazza delle Coppelle 44. 06 68 30 78 95. www. ristorantemaccheroni.com.* Good Italian cuisine attracts nearby Parliament officials. Efficient service. Terrace and cellar seating.

◙◙ **Trattoria dal Cavalier Gino** – *Vicolo Rosini 4. 06 68 73 434. Closed Sun and Aug.* Friendly, good Roman specialities like gricia, oxtails and involtini at affordable prices. Small trattoria popular with local office workers at lunch.

Pantheon

⊜⊜ **Da Fortunato** – *Via del Pantheon 55. 06 67 92 788. Open daily.* Bastion of Roman tradition, Roman cuisine. Reliable pasta, meat and artichokes. A very few outside tables have a view of the Pantheon.

⊜⊜ **Enoteca Casa Bleve** ⅄ – *Via Teatro Valle 48/49. 06 68 65 970. Closed Sun.* Upmarket wine bar; various dishes with excellent wine selection.

⊜⊜⊜⊜ **La Rosetta** ⅄ – *Via della Rosetta 9. 06 68 61 002. larosettaristorante.it. Closed 2 weeks Aug. Reservation required.* This restaurant fluctuates wildly according to how patrons are assessed, which mandata mailmeans the sophisticated can dine sublimely while tourists may be treated to both indifferent food and service. Whether fish is marinated, smoked, raw or cooked, it can be perfection itself. The generous *antipasti* (marinated and smoked fish) offer subtle flavours.

Piazza del Popolo

⊜⊜ **La Penna d'Oca** – *Via della Penna 53. 06 32 02 898. www. lapennadoca.com. Closed Mon– Fri lunch. Reservation advised.* Charming restaurant serves traditional cuisine, innovative fish and seafood dishes. Pleasant veranda offers a glimpse of the Roman street scene.

⊜⊜ **Margutta Vegeteriano RistorArte** – *Via Margutta 118. 06 32 65 05 77. www.ilmargutta.bio.* Friendly restaurant decorated with flair. Exclusively vegetarian cuisine, with plenty of creativity and a

Neapolitan touch. Art exhibits. Good-value lunch buffet.

Piazza Navona

⊜ **Da Francesco** – *Piazza del Fico 29, Piazza Navona. 06 68 64 009. www.dafrancesco.it. Booking recommended.* The attractive *Piazza del Fico* is home to this lively trattoria which serves typical Roman dishes, including pizzas, an excellent focaccia with dry-cured ham and various types of pasta. A cheerful atmosphere.

⊜ **L'Orso 80** – *Via dell'Orso 33. 06 68 64 904. www.orso80.it. Closed Mon and Aug.* Abundant cuisine, quality regional products, affordable.

⊜ **Pizzeria Da Baffetto** – *Via del Governo Vecchio, 114. 06 68 61 617. www.pizzeriabaffetto.it.* Excellent classic thin-crust Roman pizza, brusque service. Expect to queue.

⊜⊜ **Hostaria dell'Orso** ⅄⅄⅄⅄ – *Via dei Soldati 25. NW of Piazza Navona near Ponte Umberto. 06 68 30 11 92. www.hdo.it/html/ ristorante.asp. Closed Sun and 1 Jul–31 Aug.* Superb creative Mediterranean cuisine and lovely presentations in an enchanting elegant medieval tavern.

Termini / San Lorenzo / Monti

⊜ **Da Franco Ar Vicoletto** – *Via dei Falisci 2. 06 49 57 675. Closed Sun.* Fish and seafood at prices below others'. The quality is a bit rustic, but the quantity is generous. A big friendly dining hall.

⊜⊜ **L'Asino d'Oro** – *Via del Boschetto 73. 06 48 91 382. Closed Sun and Mon.* Creative cuisine, unusual sublime combinations, prepared with top international ingredients.

⊜⊜ Pommidoro – *Piazza dei Sanniti 46. 06 44 52 692. Closed Aug.* Superb traditional Roman trattoria. Excellent pasta, game, meat and grilled fish. Frequented by politicians and artists.

Testaccio

⊜⊜ Checchino dal 1887 ⅩⅩ – *Via Monte Testaccio 30. 06 57 46 318. www.checchino-dal-1887. com. Closed Sun–Mon. Booking advised.* A Roman tradition for meats and offal, accompanied by the best wine.

Trastevere

⊜ Pizzeria Dar Poeta – *Vicolo del Bologna 45. 06 58 80 516. www.darpoeta.com.* A lively spot, rustic ambience, where pizzas are made with special dough.

⊜ Trattoria Augusto – *Piazza de' Renzi 15. 06 58 03 798.* Simple food, family run, tables face the square.

⊜⊜ Trattoria Da Enzo – *Via dei Vascellari 29. 06 58 12 260. www.daenzoal29.com. Closed Sun.* Savour generous dishes like cannelloni, and lamb.

⊜⊜ Paris in Trastevere – *Piazza San Callisto 7a. 06 58 15 378. www.ristoranteparis.it. Closed Mon lunch and Aug.* Delicious Jewish-Roman cuisine, served in a tranquil dining room or outside.

Via Veneto/Porta Pia

⊜⊜⊜ Doney – *Via Vittorio Veneto 125. 06 47 08 2783. www. restaurantdoney.com.* Freshly updated décor inside greets diners to this longstanding fixture in Via Veneto. Patrons savour juniper-flavored grilled veal *tagliata*, or selection of fish.

NAPLES AND THE AMALFI COAST

Naples

⊜ Antica Pizzeria Da Michele Ⅹ – *Via Cesare Sersale 1/3. 081 55 39 204. www.damichele.net. Closed Sun.* Popular pizzeria, simple décor. Queuing is part of the experience.

⊜ Antica Pizzeria De' Figliole– *Via Giudecca Vecchia 39. 081 28 67 21. Closed Sun.* Located at the heart of Spaccanapoli, this crowded pizzeria is a great place to try Naples' fried pizza.

⊜ Antica Pizzeria Gino Sorbillo – *Via Tribunali 32. 081 44 63 43. www.sorbillo.it. Closed Sun.* One of the best pizzerias in town. Gino is one of 21 *pizzaioli* in the family. Great ambience and fantastic pizzas.

⊜ Brandi – *Salita di S. Anna di Palazzo 1/2. 081 41 69 28. www. brandi.it. Closed Mon.* In 1889 the legendary pizza margherita, named in honour of the queen, was born here. Brandi is a bit touristy but still loved in Naples.

⊜ Campagnola – *Via Tribunali 47. 081 45 90 34. www. lacampagnolaviatribunali.it. Closed Sun in winter and Tue in summer.* A clean, simple osteria with daily specials listed on the blackboard. Nice wine cellar.

⊜ Hosteria Toledo – *Via Giardinetto 78. 081 42 12 57. www.hosteriatoledo.it. Closed Tue evening.* Located in the Spanish Quarter, this hosteria celebrates the flavours of Naples. Great attention is given to the choice of ingredients.

⊜ Pizzeria Di Matteo Ⅹ – *Via dei Tribunali 94. 081 45 52 62. www. pizzeriadimatteo.com. Closed Sun.* Many celebrities from Mastroianni to Bill Clinton have enjoyed this pizza. Unbeatable prices and service.

⊝ **Trianon da Ciro** – *Via Pietro Colletta 44/46. 081 55 39 426. www.pizzeriatrianon.it.* In 1920s style, in addition to pizza, the chef might treat you to poetry.

⊝⊜ **'A Tiella** – *Riviera di Chiaia 98/100. 081 76 18 688. Closed Wed.* Fish dishes and homemade pasta are good choices here after a walk on the beach. Sit outside, where lemon and ivy keep company with old Nepalese.

⊝⊜ **Il Garum** – *Piazza Monteoliveto 2a. 081 54 23 228.* Near Spaccanapoli, this place is always full. Professional staff serve delicious regional cuisine. Excellent fish.

⊝⊜ **La Cantina di via Sapienza** – *Via Sapienza 40/41. 081 45 90 78. www.cantinadiviasapienza.it. Closed Sun.* Trattoria frequented by students and doctors from the nearby hospital. Good value veggie-based cuisine.

⊝⊜ **L'Europeo di Mattozzi** ╳ – *Via M. Campodisola 4/6/8. 081 55 21 323.* Authentic home cooking; seasonal ingredients are super-fresh. Friendly courteous staff transmit love for food.

⊝⊜ **Mimì alla ferrovia** – *Via A. d'Aragona 21. 081 553 85 25. www. mimiallaferrovia.it. Closed Sun.* A temple of Neapolitan cooking famous for its range of entrées (40 in total), plus for the quality, freshness and preparation of its fish. The speciality is *linguine alla Mimi*, made with giant prawns, scampi and seafood.

⊝⊜ **Napoli Mia** – *Riviera di Chiaia 269. 081 55 22 266. www. ristorantenapolimia.it. Closed Mon.* Small, family-run restaurant offers authentic cuisine and local dishes. Friendly owner, nice service.

⊝⊜ **Un Sorriso Integrale** – *Vico S. Pietro a Majella 6. 081 45 50 26. www.sorrisointegrale.com.* Located in the back of a courtyard, nice vegetarian fare: Broccoli with lemon, cabbage meatballs, pancakes with ricotta and spinach, all organic products.

Bay of Naples

⊝ **Abraxas**– *Via Scalandrone 15, loc. Lucrino, Pozzuoli. 081 85 49 347. www.abraxasosteria.it. Closed Tue and Sun evening.* Restaurant/wine bar with a beautiful panorama. Delicate cuisine, wine tastings.

⊝⊜ **Cicciotto** – *Calata Ponticello a Marechiaro 32. 081 57 51 165. www.trattoriadacicciotto.it. Reservations advised.* A romantic tavern to enjoy excellent fish cuisine; authentic local dishes.

⊝⊜ **Taverna del Capitano** – *Piazza delle Sirene 10/11, Marina del Cantone, Massalubrense. 8km/5mi SW of Sant'Agata sui Due Golfi. 081 80 81 028. www. tavernadelcapitano.com. Closed Mon–Tue except in summer.* Sober and elegant, huge windows overlook the sea. Pretty restaurant with Mediterranean dishes, some raw fish.

ISLAND OF ISCHIA

⊝ **Pizzeria Il Califfo** – *Via San Montano 37, 081 98 60 68. Lacco Ameno.* Typical family pizzeria with wood-fired oven.

⊝⊜ **Gorgonia** ╳ – *Via Marina Corricella, Procida. 081 81 01 060.* An great place to taste the catch of the day. Dishes are served on the quay of the fishing port.

◖◗ **Scarabeo La Pergola** – *Via Salette 10, Loc. Ciraccio, Procida. 081 89 69 918. Closed Sept–Jun lunch.* Situated in a beautiful pergola of lemon trees, specialities are from the land and the sea.

◗ **Trattoria da Peppina di Renato** ✕ – *Via Montecorvo 42, Forio. 081 99 83 12. www.trattoria dapeppina.it.* Spectacular views of the sea from the shade of a pergola on their interesting wrought-iron sofas. Delicious home-style cooking.

◖◗/◖◗◗ **Caracalè** – *Via Marina Corricella 62, Procida. 081 89 69 192.* In a former boat-house or, in summer, outdoors, a few metres from the water. Simple but fragrant fish dishes.

ISLAND OF CAPRI

◗ **Pulalli Wine Bar** – *Piazza Umberto I, Capri. 081 83 74 108. Closed Tue, 1 Nov–13 Apr.* A pleasant wine bar near the tourist office. Tables on the terrace are popular for the good view over the piazza. Excellent wine list.

◖◗◗ **Da Paolino** ✕✕ – *Via Palazzo a Mare 11, 80073 Marina Grande. www.paolinocapri.com. 081 83 76 102. Open 14 Apr– 14 Oct. Reservations required.* A Mediterranean Garden of Eden, deliciously with the aroma of lemons. Warm, friendly ambience. Nice wrought-iron tables.

AMALFI COAST

◗ **Hostaria Il Brigante** – *Via Fratelli Linguiti 4, Salerno. 089 25 13 91. Closed Mon.* Authentic traditions served with a twist. Local specialities, just steps away from the Duomo.

◖◗ **A' Paranza** ✕– *Traversa Dragone 1, Atrani. 089 87 18 40. www.ristoranteparanza.com. Closed Tue except in summer and 7–31 Jan.* Steps from the village's main square, the authentic cuisine celebrates local flavours.

◖◗◗ **Da Memé** – *Salita Marino Sebaste 8, Amalfi. 089 83 04 549.* A trattoria-pizzeria in a former Benedictine monastery. Fresh, homemade pasta and fish soup are some of the specialities.

◖◗◗ **Giardiniello** ✕✕ – *Corso Vittorio Emanuele 17, Minori 5km/3mi NE of Amalfi on the S 163. 089 87 70 50. www. ristorantegiardiniello.com. Closed Wed except in summer.* Situated in the heart of the village with a large airy dining room. Meals, specialising in fish, served under the pergola in summer. Pizzas served in the evening.

◖◗◗ **Il Ritrovo** – *Via Montepertuso 77, loc. Montepertuso. 4km/2.5mi N of Positano. 089 81 20 05. www. ilritrovo.com. Closed Wed (only Nov –Dec) and Feb–Mar.* A few miles above Positano, traditional fish and meat dishes. Outdoor dining in summer and Cooking classes.

◖◗◗ **Saraceno d'Oro** – *Via Pasitea 254, Positano. 089 81 20 50. www. saracenodoro.it.* Traditional cuisine, pizza and good takeaway.

SARDINIA

Emerald Coast
◗ **La Terrazza** – *Via Villa Glori 6, La Maddalena. 0789 73 53 05. www.ristorantelamaddalena.com. Closed Sun in Oct–Apr.* The varied menu focuses on fish – always of the best quality – and includes regional specialities. Meals are

served on the terrace, which boasts a wonderful panoramic view.

⌖ **La Vecchia Costa** – *07021 Arzachena, 5km/3mi SW of Porto Cervo (in the direction of Arzachena). 0789 98 688. www. lavecchiacosta.it.* Good pizza made with *carasau*, peculiar to Sardinia, deliciously thin and crispy. Very reasonable prices, unusual in this area.

⌖ **Panino Giusto** – *Piazzetta Clipper, Porto Cervo. 0789 91 259. www.paninogiusto.it.* At the Porto Cervo marina, overlooking the yachting harbour, for a snack or a light meal.

⌖⌖⌖ **Gastronomia Belvedere** – *Loc. Farina, Porto Cervo. 0789 96 501 or 338 47 29 413. Closed Tue (except in summer) and Nov–mid Mar. www.ristorantegastronomia belvedere.com.* Rosticceria transformed into a restaurant without a fixed menu. Excellent fish and meat. Also gluten-free menu.

⌖⌖⌖ **Casablanca** – *Loc. Baja Sardinia. 339 29 40 837 (mobile). www.ristorante-casablanca.it. Open May–Sep.* One of Sardinia's most renowned restaurants, in a fantastic panoramic setting opposite the Maddalena archipelago. Very high quality.

OFF THE BEATEN TRACK

⌖⌖ **Terza Spiaggia** ✕✕ – *Via degli Asfodeli, Loc. Terza Spiaggia, Golfo Aranci, 44km/27.3mi SE of Arzachena. 0789 46 485. www. terzaspiaggia.com.* Relax on the beach next to the crystal-clear sea, and a wonderful view of the Golfo Aranci. Tuck into a delicious sandwich or opt for a simple fish (caught by the owners).

SICILY

SICILIAN FAST FOOD – Local specialities include snacks such as *u sfinciuni* or *sfincione* (a pizza topped with tomato, anchovies, onion and breadcrumbs), *pani ca' meusa* or *panino con la milza* (roll filled with charcoal-grilled pork offal), *panelle* (fried chickpea flour pancakes) and *babbaluci* (marinated snails sold in paper cornets), which are sold from stalls in the markets.

Palermo

⌖⌖ **Antica Focacceria San Francesco** – *Via A. Paternostro 58. 091 32 02 64. www.antica focacceria.it.* Situated opposite San Francesco Church, this historic family caffè (founded in 1834) has marble tables and serves traditional *focaccia con la milza* from an antique cast-iron stove. It offers a selection of *focaccia farcita* (flat, heavy pizza dough baked with various fillings) as well as *arancini di riso* (a Sicilian staple), and *torte salate* (Sicilian savoury "cakes").

⌖⌖ **Cafeteria Galleria d'Arte Moderna** – *Via Sant'Anna 21. www.gampalermo.it. Closed Mon.* In the new modern art museum, this pleasant cafeteria is fresh and bright, serving snacks, salads and a few hot dishes.

⌖⌖ **Enoteca Picone** – *Via G. Marconi 36. 091 33 13 00. www. enotecapicone.it. Closed Sun dinner.* One of the city's largest wine selections (over 4 000 different bottles) in this family-run *enoteca* since 1946.

⌖⌖ **Focacceria Basile** – *Via Bara all'Olivella 76, Quartiere Massimo. 091 33 56 28. Closed Sun.* Attractive trattoria-cum-*rosticceria* has akeaway pizza and *focacce*, fast-cooked meals and two somewhat plain dining rooms.

◎◎ **I Cuochini** – *Via R. Settimo 8. 091 58 11 58. www.icuochini. com. Closed Sun.* This tiny shop, for 70 years in the inner courtyard of the Palazzo del Barone di Stefano, sells an irresistible range of Sicilian specialities, such as *pizza*, *panzerotti* (fried pastries) and *arancini*. Not to be missed!

◎◎ **Pizzeria Tonnara Florio**– *Discesa Tonnara 4, Arenella/Parco della Favorita district. 392 11 88 13. www.tonnaraflorio.com. Closed Mon evening in winter.* Pretty Art Nouveau building with a pleasant garden was formerly a *tonnara* (tuna fishing centre). Now a pizzeria and nightclub.

◎◎ **Trattoria da Totò** – *Via Coltellieri 5. 333 31 57 558 (mobile).* For three generations, a fishing family has offered delicious fresh fish dishes in the Vucciria quarter.

◎◎◎ **Ai Vecchietti di Minchiapititto** – *Piazza S. Oliva 10. 091 58 56 06. www. aivecchiettidiminchiapititto.com.* This restaurant with a separate pizzeria is in a 19C building.

◎◎◎ **Al Canceletto**– *Via O. D'Aragona 34. 091 58 30 69. Closed Sun and 2 week Aug–first week Sep.* Plain family trattoria serves ultra-fresh cuisine. Buffet of *antipasti*, homemade pasta and delicious meat dishes. Quality at good prices.

◎◎◎ **Casa del Brodo** – *Corso Vittorio Emanuele 175. 091 32 16 55. www.casadelbrodo.it. Closed Sun in summer, Tue in winter and first 2 weeks Jul.* Founded in 1890, ambience is now more elegant. Copious *antipasti* buffet and excellent Sicilian cuisine, with fish specialities. Good value.

◎◎◎ **Osteria Pantelleria** – *Vicolo Pantelleria 30 (near Largo Cavalieri di Malta).091 58 65 95. Closed Wed.* At this *osteria* just behind the church of San Domenico, enjoy the wines with a generous cheese plate or specialities such as stuffed squid and spaghetti with sea urchins.

◎◎◎ **Il Mirto e la Rosa** – *Via Principe di Granatelli 30. 091 32 43 53. www.ilmirtoelarosa.com. Closed Sun.* The food focus is vegetarian, with dishes such as *caponatina di melanzane*, a sweet and sour aubergine stew, served with pistachio couscous. Very welcoming.

◎◎◎ **La Cambusa** – *Piazza Marina 16. 091 58 45 74. www. lacambusa.it. Closed Wed in winter.* Over-looking Piazza Marina, this elegant, quiet restaurant specialises in fish dishes. Excellent *antipasti* buffet.

Erice

◎◎◎ **La Pentolaccia** – *Via G. F. Guarnotti 17. 0923 86 90 99. www. ristorantelapentolaccia.it. Closed Tue and Jan–Feb.* On arrival at this 17C convent converted into a restaurant, you are greeted by an antique Sicilian cart. Upstairs, enjoy high-quality Sicilian cuisine in the two dining rooms. Wide selection of antipasti. An institution.

◎◎◎ **Monte San Giuliano** ✗✗ – *Vicolo San Rocco 7. 0923 86 95 95. www.montesangiuliano.it. Closed Mon. Booking advised.* Fine restaurant in the heart of Erice specialises in local cuisine. Wide-ranging menu, meals served in pleasant, rustic dining rooms or under a pretty arbour in a cool inner courtyard.

Siracusa

🍴 **Castello Fiorentino** – *Via del Crocifisso 6, Ortygia. 0931 21 097. Closed Mon.* One of the most popular trattoria-pizzerias with a large, slightly down-at-heel dining room, in which a squadron of waiters perform their own surrealist ball: running, turning, whirling and yelling out orders with gusto to add to the already-deafening hubbub. Succulent pizzas and well-sauced pasta.

🍴 **Sicilia in Tavola** – *Via Cavour 28, Ortygia. 392 46 10 889 (mobile phone). www.siciliaintavola.eu. Closed Mon.* The strong point of this rustic-looking little trattoria is its wide choice of fresh pasta, home-made the way it should be and cooked with love. Go for the pasta over the meat and fish dishes, which are more expensive and less exciting.

🍴🍴 **Castello Fiorentino** – *Via del Crocifisso 6, Ortigia. 0931 21 097. Closed Mon. Booking advised.* A popular trattoria-pizzeria with a large, slightly worn dining room where a squadron of waiters run, turn, whirl and yell out orders with gusto.

🍴🍴🍽 **Darsena da Jannuzzo** – *Riva Garibaldi 6, Ortigia. 0931 61 522. www.ristorantedarsena.it. Closed Mon.* Enjoy simple, delicious seafood cuisine either in the dining room or on the veranda, with its view of the canal.

Taormina

🍴 **Porta Messina** – *Largo Giove Serapide 4. 0942 23 953. www.ristoranteportamessina.it.* Enormous selection of pizzas in this friendly place, with unusual options too.

🍴🍴🍽 **La capitaneria** – *Via Nazionale 177, Loc. Spisone. 0942 62 62 47. www.pietrodagostino.it/il-ristorante. Closed Mon.* Welcoming restaurant with young owners that offers innovative regional cuisine.

🍴🍴🍽 **Al Saraceno** – *Via Madonna Rocca 16-18. 0942 63 20 15. www.alsaraceno.it.* The splendid view from the terrace extends as far as the Straits of Messina.

AEOLIAN ISLANDS

🍴🍴🍽 **Filippino** ✕✕ – *Piazza Mazzini, Lipari. 090 98 11 002. www.filippino.it. Closed Mon (only 1 Nov–30 Mar) and 20 Nov– 20 Feb. Compulsory 5/100 service charge.* This century-old restaurant is renowned throughout Sicily region for its wonderful traditional fish. Relaxed atmosphere, friendly service and a delightful view of Piazza della Rocca.

🍴🍴🍽 **Punta Lena** – *Via Marina 8, loc. Ficogrande, Stromboli. 090 98 62 04. Closed Nov–Apr.* High-quality fresh fish and delicious seafood specialities served under an arbour with magnificent sea views.

🍴🍴🍽🍽 **E Pulera** – *Via Isabella Conti, Lipari. 090 98 11 158. www.pulera.it. Closed lunch. Booking advised.* E Pulera has a garden for dining. In July and August, a menu of typical Aeolian dishes is accompanied by folk dancing.

HOTELS

Italy has the full range of accommodation, from luxurious hotels in historic castles, villas, and palaces, to thermal baths and spas, farm stays, bed and breakfasts, monasteries, hostels, and campsites. Holidays (see calendar p12) and trade fairs tend to increase prices.

MICHELIN GUIDE

We've selected a few restaurants from the Michelin red guide. Look for red entries in the listings and the following comfort ratings:

🏠 | 🏠 | 🏠 | 🏠 | 🏠

WHERE TO STAY

PRICES

	Provinces	Cities
🍷	<70€	<90€
🍷🍷	70–95€	90–120€
🍷🍷🍷	95–120€	120–160€
🍷🍷🍷🍷	>130€	>160€

Book accommodations well in advance for popular regions and cities, especially from March to October. Typically, prices are far lower – and many hotels offer discounts or special weekend deals – from November to February, less in the art cities such as Florence, Venice and Rome, as well as other historic centres. Always check prices before booking, as rates can vary depending on the time of year and availability of rooms. The best prices may be offered through websites or from the hotel directly. New municipal laws impose a new **hotel tax** for the cities of Rome, Florence, and Venice. The fee applies to all guests in any overnight accommodation; the only exceptions are in hostels and for children under the age of 18. The fees are paid at the end of each stay. The fee ranges from 2€ to 5€ per person, per night with a maximum of 10 nights (5 nights at campsites).

HOTELS AND PENSIONI

Generally, the word *pensione* describes a small, family-run hotel. Sometimes situated within residential buildings, these offer basic rooms, often with shared bathrooms. A hotel may also be labelled an *albergo* or *locanda*.

RURAL ACCOMMODATION

The rural guesthouse, *agriturismo*, was originally conceived to combine accommodation, farm life, homemade products (olive oil, wine, honey, vegetables and meat) and homecooked local specialities. Now, some guesthouses are as elegant as the best hotels, with prices to match. Catering could range from a DIY kitchenette to breakfast or a complete menu celebrating the farm's produce. The guesthouses included in the guide usually accept bookings for one night only, but in high season the majority prefer longer stays or require half or full board. Prices for the latter are only given when this formula is compulsory. Many rural guesthouses publish their rates as per person, with the assumption that two or more will share a room. Solo travellers should ask for, but not expect, a discount. Book well in advance.

Consult the following websites for further details: *www.terranostra.it (Associazione Terranostra; 06 48 99 32 09)*, *www.agriturist.it*. Information is also available from **Turismo Verde** *(Via Mariano*

Fortuny 20, Roma; 06 32 40 111, www.turismoverde.it).

BED AND BREAKFAST

Sometimes indistinguishable from a hotel, a B&B may be the hosts' home – an apartment, house or villa with rooms to rent (usually between two and four). Credit cards not necessarily accepted. Normally, a B&B offers a cosier atmosphere than a hotel. In Italy the experience is often delightful and reasonably priced. Enquire about curfews before booking, however.

Contact **Bed & Breakfast Italia**, *06 94 80 67 81, www.bbitalia.it.* Also try the following websites: *www.bedandbreakfast.it; www.primitaly.it/bb.*

SHORT-TERM RENTAL OR SWAP

For privacy and self-catering, a short-term rental is ideal. Generally cheaper than hotels, apartments also have basic cooking facilities. (*www.realrome.com, www.lifein italy.com/rent, www.airbnb.com*). Homeowners can also swap spaces. (*www.homeexchange.com, www.homelink.org*). Check references before trading places.

HOSTELS AND BUDGET ACCOMMODATIONS

Hostel accommodation is only available to members of the **Youth Hostel Association**, *www.yha. org.uk.* Join at any YHA branch for worldwide access. There is no age limit for the annual membership. Other establishments, mainly frequented by young people, offer dorms at very reasonable prices (*www.italian.hostelworld.com, www.hiusa.org*) Italian hostels

sometimes enjoy spectacular settings: villas, fortresses, palaces and old monasteries. Most are run by the **Associazione Italiana Alberghi per la Gioventù** (AIG), *Via Nicotera 1, Roma; 06 48 71 152, www.aighostels.it.* Case per ferie (holiday homes), more common in the big cities, offer decent, cheap accommodation; the only disadvantage being a curfew (typically 10.30pm). Contact the tourist offices and **CITS, Centro Italiano Turismo Sociale, Associazione dell'ospitalità religiosa**, *06 48 73 145, www. citsnet.it.* Convents run by nuns or priests also may take paying guest

CAMPSITES

Campsites offer reasonable rates close to cities, as well as in the country. Few wilderness options exist in Italy. **Club Alpino Italiano** *02 20 57 231; www.cai.it.* **Camping and Caravanning Club**, *Greenfield House, Westwood Way, Coventry CV4 8JH, 024 76 47 54 42, www.camping andcaravanningclub.co.uk.* **Federazione Italiana del Campeggio e del Caravanning**, *Via Vittorio Emanuele 11, Calenzano (FI), 055 88 23 91; www.federcampeggio.it.*

HOTELS

MILAN, LOMBARDY AND LAKES

Milan

Most hotels increase prices during the frequent trade fairs and exhibitions; budget travellers could try outside the city.

Ostello A.I.G. Piero Rotta – *Via A. Salmoiraghi 1. 02 39 26 70 95.*

ww.italian.hostelworld.com.
asic, good value. Centre
5 minutes by metro.

Hotel San Francisco 🏨 –
iale Lombardia 55. 02 23 60 302.
ww.hotel-sanfrancisco.it.
8 rooms. Simple accommodation
ear the centre. Pretty garden.

Albergo Città Studi – *Via*
, Saldini 24. 02 74 46 66. www.
otelcittastudi.it. 45 rooms. In the
usy university area. Quiet, simple,
dequate hotel.

Hotel des Etrangers 🏨
Via Sirte 9. 02 48 95 53 25. www.
oteldesetrangers.it. 94 rooms.
ear the trade fair district and
ublic transport. Comfortable
ooms.

Hotel Gala – *Viale Zara 89.*
2 66 80 08 91. www.hotelgala
ilano.it. 22 rooms. Well placed if
ou arrive by car. Easy access to the
entre. Family-run, quiet location
nd lovely garden.

Hotel Regina – *Via C.*
orrenti 13. 02 58 10 69 13.
ww.hotelregina.it. 43 rooms.
rand, elegant hotel with a glass-
overed courtyard lobby.

Hotel Cavour 🏨 –
ia Fatebenefratelli 21. 02 62 00 01.
ww.hotelcavour.it. 120 rooms.
nderstated elegance. Run by a
ilan family of hoteliers.

Hotel Dei Cavalieri
Piazza G. Missori 1. 02 88 571.
www.hoteldeicavalieri.com.
77 rooms. On lively piazza.
ontemporary décor, pleasant
tmosphere. Restaurant with
anoramic terrace.

Hotel Gran Duca di
ork 🏨 – *Via Moneta 1. 02 87 48*
3. www.ducadiyork.it. 33 rooms.
ovely rooms and atmosphere.
'egant 18C palazzo in the
istoric centre.

Bergamo

Agnello d'Oro –
Via Gombito 22. 035 24 98 83.
www.agnellodoro.it. 20 rooms.
Simple, comfortable. Restaurant
has good local cuisine.

Mantua

Hotel Paradiso – *Via Piloni*
13, Pietole (7km/4.3mi S on the
S 62). 0376 44 07 700. www.
albergohotelparadiso.it. 7 rooms.
Closed 28 Dec–1 Jan. Quiet
location, simple spacious rooms
overlooking a garden. Breakfast
outside or in conservatory.

Hotel Casa Poli 🏨 –
Corso Garibaldi 32. 0376 28 81 70.
www.hotelcasapoli.it. 27 rooms.
Minimalist design, refined comfort.

The Lakes

Agriturismo Il Bagnolo –
Loc. Bagnolo di Serniga, Salò
(L. Garda). 0365 20 290. www.
ilbagnolo.it. 12 rooms. This farm
guesthouse has a wonderful
setting and serves excellent food,
made with their own produce.

Hotel Il Chiostro – *Via F.lli*
Cervi 14, Verbania Intra
(L. Maggiore). 0323 40 40 77.
www.chiostrovb.it. 100 rooms.
Former 17C convent has a frescoed
reading room, charming cloisters,
simple rooms.

Hotel Cangrande – *Corso*
Cangrande 16, Lazise (L. Garda),
5km/3mi S of Bardolino on the
N 249. 045 64 70 410. www.
cangrandehotel.it. 18 rooms.
Closed Nov–15 Mar. Charming.
Simple, attractive rooms, one in
the medieval stone walls.

Hotel Désirée – *Via San*
Pietro in Mavino 2, Sirmione
(L. Garda). 030 99 05 244.
www.hotel-desiree.it. 34 rooms.

Unpretentious. Quiet location near the beach, thermal baths. Rooms have balconies

⊝⊝ **Hotel La Fontana** – *Strada Statale del Sempione 1, Stresa (L. Maggiore). 0323 32 707. www.lafontanahotel.com. 19 rooms.* In a 1940s villa, rooms have lake views and retro décor. Reasonable prices.

⊝⊝ **Hotel Palazzina** 🏛 – *Via Libertà 10, 25084 Gargnano (L. Garda). 0365 71 118. www. hotelpalazzina.it. ⌇. 25 rooms. Closed 11 Oct–12 Apr.* Relaxed atmosphere. Panoramic terraces and an open-air swimming pool and restaurant.

⊝⊝🛏 **Albergo Silvio** – *Via P. Carcano 10/12, 22021 Bellagio (L. Como), 2km/1.2mi SW of Bellagio. 031 95 03 22. www. bellagiosilvio.com. 20 rooms and 5 aparts.* Family run since 1919. Charming place, stunning location. Excellent restaurant with lovely terrace; fresh lake fish on the menu.

⊝⊝🛏 **Hotel Miravalle** – *Via Monte Oro 9, Riva del Garda. 0464 55 23 35. www.hotelvilla miravalle.com. ⌇. 32 rooms.* Central location, lovely garden and swimming pool simple yet stylish rooms. Restaurant and free Wi-Fi.

⊝⊝🛏 **Hotel Rigoli** – *Via Piave 48, Baveno (L. Maggiore). 0323 92 47 56. www.hotelrigoli.com. 31 rooms.* Spacious rooms. Sunny, pleasant public areas, lakeside terrace garden with lovely views over the Isole Borromee.

⊝⊝🛏 **Hotel Garni La Contrada dei Monti** – *Via Contrada dei Monti 10, Orta San Giulio (L. Orta). 0322 90 51 14. www.lacontradadei monti.it. 16 rooms. Closed Nov–Easter (except for New Year).* Charming, in a beautifully restored

palazzo; great attention to detail in the rooms.

GENOA AND PORTOFINO

Genoa

👁 *During international events, hotels tend to raise their prices.*

⊝⊝ **Albergo Cairoli** – *Via Cairoli 14/4. 010 24 61 454. www.hotel cairoligenova.com. 12 rooms and 2 aparts.* Smallish rooms, good terrace, small gym. In the historic centre.

⊝⊝ **Albergo Soana** – *Via XX Settembre 23 (int. 8 scala a). Genova. 010 56 28 14. soana. genoa-hotels.com. 15 rooms.* Centrally located no-frills hotel. Wi-Fi

⊝⊝ **Hotel Balbi** – *Via Balbi 21/3. 010 27 59 288. www.hotelbalbi genova.it. 13 rooms, 1 apart. Closed 18–26 Dec.* Spacious bedrooms with frescoed ceilings at this family-run hotel.

⊝⊝ **Hotel Galles** 🏛 – *Via Bersaglieri d'Italia 13. 010 24 62 820. www.hotelgallesgenova.com 21 rooms.* Between the station and the port, comfortable rooms, wooden floors.

⊝⊝🛏 **Hotel Cristoforo Colombo** – *Via di Porta Soprana 27. 010 25 13 643. www.hotelcolombo.it. 16 rooms.* Characterful central hotel has a curious display. Breakfast terrace.

⊝⊝🛏 **Hotel Le Nuvole Residenza d'Epoca** – *Piazza delle Vigne 6. 010 25 10 018. www. hotellenuvole.it. 12 rooms.* Just 5 minutes walk from the port, the hotel is set in a beautiful period palazzo. Elegant rooms with designer decor.

⊝⊝🛏 **Locanda di Palazzo Cicala** 🏛 – *Piazza San Lorenzo 16*

10 25 18 824. www.palazzocicala.it.
0 rooms and 3 aparts.
prestigious palazzo, historic
nd contemporary styles blend.

ortofino

Agriturismo Villa Gnocchi – *a Romana 53, San Lorenzo della osta. 3km/1.8mi W of Santa argheritaLigure. 0185 28 34 31. ww.villagnocchi.it. 12 rooms.* onderful setting, magnificent ews from lovely terrace garden. iendly and homey.

Albergo La Camogliese 🏨 *Via Garibaldi 55, Camogli. 0185 7 14 02. www.lacamogliese.it. 1 rooms.* Comfortable family-run, ear the sea. Some rooms have ea views.

igurian Riviera

Albergo Rosita – *Via Mànie 7, Finale Ligure (3km/1.8mi NE). 19 60 24 37. www.hotelrosita.it. 1 rooms. Restaurant* ⊜⊜. plendid clifftop location with sea ews. A good seafood restaurant ith terrace.

B&B Le Terrazze – *Via Fieschi 02, Corniglia. 0187 81 20 96. www. terrasse.it. 4 rooms and aparts. losed 8–28 Feb.* Old family clifftop ome is tastefully decorated.

Hotel Ca' d'Andrean – *Via A. iscovolo 101, Manarola. 0187 2 00 40. www.cadandrean.com. 0 rooms. Closed Dec–Feb.* Upper llage. Small, charming hotel. Free i-Fi. Lovely garden.

Hotel-ristorante Due emelli – *Via Litoranea 1, iomaggiore. 4.5km/2.8mi E of iomaggiore. 0187 92 06 78. www. uegemelli.it. 13 rooms.* A simple lace with splendid panoramic ews from the balconies and rrace restaurant.

⊜⊜ **Hotel Ines** – *Via Cavour 10, Varazze. 019 97 302. www.hotel inesvarazze.it. 12 rooms.* Pretty villa in the centre of Varazze, 100m/110yds from the sea. Comfortable rooms and a terrace.

⊜⊜ **Hotel Suisse** – *Via Mazzini 119, Alassio. 0182 64 01 92. www. suisse.it. 40 rooms. Closed Oct– Dec.* A central Art Nouveau hotel. Private beach, bicycles.

⊜⊜ **Hotel Villa Beatrice** – *Via Sant'Erasmo 6 (Via Aurelia), Loano. 019 66 82 44. www.panozzohotels.it.* 🏊. *30 rooms.* Near the port and old town. Luxuriant garden, pool, gym and restaurant.

⊜⊜ **Pensione Miramare** – *Via Fiascherino 22, Tellaro (4km/2.5mi from Lerici). 0187 96 75 89. www. miramaretellaro.com. 22 rooms.* Welcoming family-run guesthouse, terrace views of the Bay of Poets and restaurant.

⊜⊜⊜ **Da Ö Vittorio** – *Via Roma 160, Recco. 0185 74 029. www.dao vittorio.it. 29 rooms.* A former coaching inn; good restaurant serves local dishes.

⊜⊜⊜ **Villa Nova Agriturismo** – *Loc. Villanova, 1.5km/0.9mi E of Levanto. 0187 80 25 17. www. agriturismovillanova.it. Closed 6 Nov –1 week Mar. 9 rooms and 4 aparts.* Splendid farm property, attractive accommodation. Lovely garden.

⊜⊜⊜ **Villa Argentina** – *Via Torrente San Lorenzo 2, Moneglia. 0185 49 228. www.villa-argentina.it. 18 rooms.* An early-20C villa with bright airy rooms and garden.

⊜⊜⊜⊜ **Bel Soggiorno** – *Corso Matuzia 41, Sanremo. 0184 66 76 31, www.belsoggiorno.net. 36 rooms.* Bright, renovated rooms in an older building close to the seafront.

⊖⊖⊟⊟ **Hotel e Residenza Beau Rivage** 🏩 – *Lungomare Roma 82, Alassio. 0182 64 05 85. www.hotelbeaurivage.it. Closed 15 Oct–26 Dec.* Painter Richard West worked here 1885–1905. Pleasant rooms and apartments.

ALPS AND DOLOMITES

Turin

🕭 *During trade fairs hotels tend to put their prices up.*

⊖ **Hotel Artuà & Solferino** – *Via Brofferio 1/3. 011 51 75 301. www.hotelartuasolferino.it. 40 rooms and 5 aparts.* Pretty building in the quiet Piazza Solferino district. Plain, comfortable rooms. Prices vary according to comfort level.

⊖ **Hotel Dogana Vecchia** – *Via Corte d'Appello 4. 011 43 66 752. www.hoteldoganavecchia.com. 58 rooms.* Late-18C coaching house hosted Mozart, Napoleon and Verdi. Period or modern rooms, in city centre.

⊖ **Albergo Vinzaglio** – *Corso Vinzaglio 12. 011 56 13 793. www. albergovinzaglio.it. 14 rooms.* Small, bright hotel in an old building 20 minutes' walk from the centre. Functional well kept rooms, some without bath. Good value.

⊖⊖ **Ai Savoia B&B** – *Via del Carmine 1H. 339 12 57 711 (mobile). www.aisavoia.it. 15 rooms and 4 aparts . Closed Aug.* Elegant B&B located in Palazzo Saluzzo Paesana, in the fashionable and artistic centre, aristocratic rooms.

⊖⊖ **Hotel Alpi Resort** – *Via Bonafous, 5. 011 81 29 677. www. hotelalpiresort.it. 40 rooms and 2 aparts. Closed Aug.* Pleasant. Comfortable, well-furnished rooms near Piazza Vittorio Veneto.

⊖⊖ **Hotel Bologna** – *Corso Vittorio Emanuele II 60. 011 56 20 193. www.hotelbolognasrl.it. 44 rooms.* Late-19C building near Porta Nuova station. Carefully presented, comfortable rooms.

⊖⊖⊟ **Hotel Genio** 🏩 – *Corso Vittorio Emanuele II 47. 011 65 05 771. www.hotelgenio.it. 120 rooms.* Near Porta Nuova station. Elegant, cosy rooms. Good weekend rates.

⊖⊖⊟ **NH Lingotto Tech** – *Via Nizza 230. 011 66 42 000. www.nh-hotels.it/hotel/nh-torino-lingotto-tech. 140 rooms.* By architect Renzo Piano. Superb views. Contemporary design.

⊖⊖⊟⊟ **Hotel Santo Stefano** – *Via Porta Palatina 19. 011 52 23 311. www.nh-hotels.com. 125 rooms.* Designer hotel in excellent location between the Duomo and the Royal Palace. Natural materials and high-tech features. Turkish baths open to all

⊖⊖⊟⊟ **Hotel Victoria** 🏩 – *Via Nino Costa 4. 011 56 11 909. www.hotelvictoria-torino.com. 106 rooms.* Charming, classy. Extremely refined rooms, period furniture, and lavish drapery.

Dolomites Road

Most accommodation in the mountains is half-board or full-board with traditional and/or creative menus. Prices generally reflect half-board rates. Many close for a period in fall and/or spring.

⊖⊖⊟ **Chalet Gérard** – *Plan de Gralba 37, Selva di Val Gardena. 0471 79 52 74. www.chalet-gerard. com. 12 rooms. Closed mid Apr –May and mid Oct – Nov.* Food is traditional (polenta and local produce). Enchanting view from this chalet.

☎🖂 **Hotel Cavallino d'Oro** – *Piazza Kraus, Castelrotto, Alpe di Siusi. 26km/16.2mi NE of Bolzano. 0471 70 63 37. www.cavallino.it. 24 rooms. Closed Nov.* Romantic, typical Tyrolean: four-poster beds, elegant antiques. Dine in 17C wood-panelled *Stuben*. Wellness centre, historic wine cellar.

☎🖂🖥 **Hotel Gran Ancëi** – *Str. Prè de costa 10, San Cassiano Badia, 26.5km/16.5mi W of Cortina d'Ampezzo. 0471 84 95 40. www.granancei.com. 29 rooms.* Surrounded by woodland and located near the ski slopes. Mountain décor mostly in wood. Relaxing, peaceful. Spacious and airy, wonderful views over the Dolomites. Restaurant and Spa.

☎🖂🖥 **Hotel Colfosco-Kolfuschgerhof** – *Via Rönn 7, Colfosco di Corvara, 2km/1.2mi E of Passo Gardena on the S 244. 0471 83 61 88. www.kolfuschgerhof.com. 50 rooms. Closed Oct–Nov and May.* Near the lifts, facilities include squash courts, table-tennis, sauna, Turkish baths and massage. Typical Tyrolean, friendly atmosphere. Peaceful and quiet.

South of Cortina

☎🖂 **Rifugio Sennes** – *Loc. Alpe di Sennes 32046 – San Vito di Cadore, 9km/5.6mi S of Cortina d'Ampezzo on the S 51. 0474 50 1092 or 328 79 45 579 (mobile). www.sennes.com. 60 bads and 2 aparts. Closed Nov–Apr.* Accessible by car or a lovely, invigorating walk. Traditional mountain hut-cum-restaurant; carefully prepared local cuisine. Very good views.

Val Puseria and around

☎🖂 **Hotel Erika** – *Via Braies di Fuori 66, Braies, 5km/3mi N of Lago di Braies. 0474 74 86 84. www.hotelerika.net. 30 rooms. Closed 21 Oct–19 Dec and 21 Mar–19 May.* Friendly, enthusiastic staff. Comfortable rooms, chunky wooden furniture.

☎🖂 **Hotel Masl** – *Valles 44, Valles, 7km/4.3mi from Rio di Pusteria. 0472 54 71 87. www.hotel-masl.com. 55 rooms.* Elegant, friendly large Messner family 17C house decked with summer flowers.

☎🖂🖥 **Hotel Lavaredo** – *Via Monte Piana 11, Misurina. 0435 39 227. www.lavaredohotel.it. 28 rooms. Closed Oct–23 Dec.* Lakeside setting overlooked by the magnificent mountain peaks of the Cime di Lavaredo. Family-run, comfortable rooms, spacious public areas (lots of wood!). Tennis, table tennis, sauna and restaurant.

☎🖂🖥 **Monika Hotel** – *Via del Parco 2, Sesto. 0474 71 03 84. www.monika.it. 46 rooms.* Simple comfortable rooms. Elegant dining room. Stylish, spacious wood-panelled public areas. Well-equipped wellness centre. Gorgeous natural surroundings.

VENICE AREA

Venice

See the information on the city's hotel tax on p198; ask when booking.
The hub of daytime life is Piazza San Marco, which pulses with people – and pigeons – year round. The accommodation includes religious orders that offer

reasonably priced guest rooms; possible drawbacks are curfews and cash-only payments

Hostels, monasteries, holiday homes

⊖ **Casa Cardinal Piazza** – *Fondamenta Contarini 3539a, Cannaregio. 041 72 13 88. 24 rooms. www.casacardinalpiazza.org*

⊖ **Casa di Ospitalità Papafava** – *Ponte della Guerra 5402, Castello. 041 52 25 352. www.sangiuseppe caburlotto.com. 14 rooms. Closed 23–26 Dec.* Popular with families.

⊖ **Ostello Venezia** – *Fondamenta Zitelle 86, Giudecca. 041 877 8288. www.hostelvenice.org. 260 beds.* Youth hostel with an idyllic waterfront location on the Giudecca. Dormitory accommodation.

⊖⊖ **B&B Cà Fujiyama** – *Calle Lunga San Barnaba, 2727a, Dorsoduro. 041 72 41 042. fujiyama.life. 4 rooms.* Venice, gateway to the East... Run by a Japanese couple, this small guesthouse is impeccably clean and boasts a cosy atmosphere where you'll be warmly welcomed and enjoy Japanese furnishing. Tearoom in the afternoon.

⊖⊖ **Casa Caburlotto** – *Fondamenta Rizzi 316/318, Santa Croce. 041 71 08 77. www. sangiuseppecaburlotto.com. 52 rooms. Closed 25–26 Dec.* Simple, mid-priced.

⊖⊖ **Centro Culturale Don Orione Artigianelli** – *Zattere 909a, Dorsoduro. 041 52 24 077. www.donorione-venezia.it. 62 rooms.* Spacious and pleasant; restaurant.

⊖⊖ **Foresteria Valdese** – *Palazzo Cavagnis, at the end of Calle Lunga S. Maria Formosa 5170,* *Castello. 041 52 86 797. www. foresteriavenezia.it. 48 rooms.* Pleasant rooms, have frescoes or canal views.

⊖⊖ **Patronato Salesiano Leone XIII** – *Calle S.Domenico 1281, Castello. 041 52 30 796. www.salesianivenezia.it/alloggi. html. 33 rooms. Closed Dec and Jan.* Quiet location near Biennale Gardens.

⊖⊖⊖ **Domus Ciliota**– *Calle delle Muneghe, San Marco 2976. 041 52 04 888. www.ciliota.it. 51 rooms.* Restored former Augustinian monastery: comfortable, pleasant.

Hotels

⊖⊖ **Agriturismo Le Garzette** – *Lungomare Alberoni 32, Lido. 041 73 10 78. www.legarzette.it. 5 rooms.* Country, quiet end of Lido Island, *agriturismo* (farmstay) is ideal for families. Home cooking, own produce.

⊖⊖ **Locanda al Leon** – *Calle degli Albanesi 4270, Castello. 041 27 70 393. www.hotelalleon.com. 11 rooms.* Near St Mark's, small guesthouse furnished in Venetian style.

⊖⊖ **Locanda Ca' Foscari** – *Calle della Frescada 3887, Dorsoduro. 041 71 04 01. www. locandacafoscari.com. 12 rooms (some without bathrooms).* Simple but pleasant; light, airy rooms, family atmosphere. Extremely good value.

⊖⊖⊖ **Casa Rezzonico** 🏛 – *Fondamenta Gherardini 2813, Dorsoduro. 041 27 70 653. www.casarezzonico.it. 6 rooms.* Quiet, peaceful, near lively Campo Santa Margherita. Well-maintained interiors, canal views and a pleasant garden.

⊜⊜🅂 **Locanda Art Déco** 🏨 – *Calle delle Botteghe 2966, San Marco. 041 27 70 558. www.locandaartdeco.com. 5 rooms.* Beamed ceilings, wooden furniture, cosy rooms. Central location in a pleasant area.

⊜⊜🅂 **Locanda Ca'le Vele** 🏨 – *Calle delle Vele 3969, Cannaregio. 041 24 13 960. www.locandalevele. com. 6 rooms.* Small guesthouse, Venetian atmosphere, 16C palazzo.

⊜⊜🅂 **Locanda Casa Querini** – *Campo San Giovanni Novo 4388, Castello. 041 24 11 294. www. locandaquerini.com. 6 rooms.* Small 16C palazzo; comfortable, mid-sized rooms.

⊜⊜🅂 **Locanda Fiorita Ca'Moro** – *Campiello Novo 3457, San Marco. 041 52 34 754. www.locanda fiorita.com. 10 rooms.* Delightful, in a charming, flower-filled square. 18C furniture.

⊜⊜🅂 **Pensione La Calcina**– *Fondamenta Zattere ai Gesuati 780, Dorsoduro. 041 52 06 466. www.lacalcina.com. 26 rooms.* The old 19C guesthouse of Ruskin is a very pleasant choice. Excellent location on the Giudecca Canal, light-filled interior. Very good reasonable restaurant *(see Restaurants, Rome, Accademia-Salute, La Calcina)*.

Venetian Lagoon

⊜⊜ **Hotel Park** – *Lungomare Adriatico 74, Lido di Sottomarina, 10km/6.2mi E of Chioggia. 041 49 07 40. www.hotelparkchioggia.it. 40 rooms.* Family-run, situated opposite the beach. Restaurant, occasionally has music. Spacious, simple rooms.

⊜⊜ **Sole** 🏨 – *Via Mediterraneo 9, Sottomarina, Chioggia. 041 49 15 005. 🅂. www.hotel-sole.com.*

54 rooms and 12 aparts. Clean, comfortable rooms, private beach and pool and restaurant.

⊜⊜ **Park Spiaggia** 🏨 – *Via Mazzini 1, Grado. 0431 82 366. www.hotelparkspiaggia.it.* A simple, traditional hotel in the pedestrianised area of Grado.

Padua

⊜ **Al Cason** – *Via Frà Paolo Sarpi 40. 049 66 26 36. www.hotel alcason.com. 48 rooms.* Close to the railway station. Family run, basic facilities. Simple but high-quality cooking.

⊜ **Hotel Al Fagiano** 🏨 – *Via Locatelli 45. 049 87 50 073. www.alfagiano.com. 37 rooms.* Near Basilica di Sant'Antonio,. Pleasant. Attractive rooms.

⊜ **Ostello Città di Padova**– *Via Aleardo Aleardi 30. 049 87 52 219.* Centrally located youth hostel. Simple, suitable for all kinds of visitors, including families.

⊜⊜ **Terme Milano** 🏨 – *Viale delle Terme 169, Abano Terme, 13km/8mi SW of Padua. 049 86 69 444. www.termemilano.it. 🅂 89 rooms.Closed Jan–Feb.* Pedestrian area. Indoor and outdoor pools with thermal waters. Gym, tennis.

⊜⊜ **Villa Lussana** – *Via Chiesa 1, Teolo, 21km/13mi SW of Padua. 049 99 25 530. www.villalussana.com. 7 rooms. Closed 6 Jan– 15 Feb.* An attractive Art Nouveau villa with fine views over the Colli Euganei.

⊜⊜🅂 **Le Camp Resort** – *Via Giovanni Anghinoni 10. 049 87 62 144. www.lecampspa.it. 9 rooms.* Situated in the historic centre of Padua, it offers luxurious, designer rooms and an exclusive spa featuring a hammam and gym.

Vicenza

🛏🛏 **Hotel Victoria** 🏨 –
*Strada Padana (in the direction of
Padua) 52, 7km/4.3mi E of Vicenza
on the SS 11. 0444 91 22 99.
www.hotelvictoriavicenza.com.*
🛶. *123 rooms.* Reasonable prices,
comfortable surroundings. Good-
sized rooms and apartments.
Outdoor pool. Near motorway
and the centre.

🛏🛏🛏🛏 **G Boutique Hotel** 🏨 –
*Via Giuriolo 10. 0444 32 64 58.
www.gboutiquehotel.com.
16 rooms.* Classic exterior, super-
stylish comfortable rooms. Near
Teatro Olimpico.

Verona

Trade fairs and exhibitions increase
prices. Good accommodation at
reasonable prices outside the city.

🛏🛏 **Cavour** – *Vicolo Chiodo 4.
045 59 01 66. www.hotelcavour
verona.it. 21 rooms.* Quiet, central
location between Castelvecchio
and Piazza Bra. Simply furnished
rooms.

🛏🛏 **Hotel Torcolo** – *Vicolo
Listone 3. 045 80 07 512. www.
hoteltorcolo.it. 19 rooms.* Simple,
pleasant rooms, each in a slightly
different style.Wi-Fi.

TUSCANY AND UMBRIA

Florence

*See the information on the ciy's hotel
tax on p198; ask when booking.*
Some accommodation includes
religious orders (addresses, no
description) for reasonably priced
rooms to visitors.

🛏 **Istituto Sette Santi Fondatori**
–*Via dei Mille 11. 055 50 48 452.
www.7santi.com. 65 rooms.*

🛏🛏 **Hotel Locanda Orchidea** –
*Borgo degli Albizi 11. 055 200 14
10. www.hotelorchideaflorence.it.
7 rooms.* Little *pensione* on the
first floor of a palazzo in the
historic centre. English owner,
gracious atmosphere, reasonably
spacious rooms have high ceilings.
Cheerfully pale pink with antiques.
Shared bathrooms.

🛏 **Albergo Scoti** – *Via
Tornabuoni 7. 055 29 21 28.
www.hotelscoti.com. 10 rooms.*
Eclectic residence in a Renaissance
palazzo, richly frescoed salon.
Charming genteel aristocratic
decline. Tiny, shared bathrooms.

🛏🛏 **Casa della Madonna del
Rosario** – *Via Capo di Mondo 44.
055 67 96 21. www.madonna
delrosario.it. 31 rooms.*

🛏🛏 **Convitto Ecclesiastico della
Calza** – *Piazza della Calza 6. 055
22 22 87. www.calza.it. 36 rooms.*

🛏🛏 **Hotel Cimabue** – *Via
Bonifacio Lupi 7. 055 47 56 01.
www.hotelcimabue.it. 21 rooms.*
Art Nouveau frescoed ceilings in
some rooms, all are spacious and
tastefully furnished.

🛏🛏 **Residenza Johanna I** –
*Via Cinque Giornate 12. 055 473
377. www.johanna.it. 6 rooms.*
Pleasant, great attention to detail,
lovely antiques. Small breakfast
buffet, cosy salon. Near Piazza
San Marco.

🛏🛏🛏 **Hotel Cellai** 🏨 – *Via
XXVII Aprile 14 52/R. 055 48 92 91.
www.hotelcellai.it. 55 rooms.* Near
San Marco. Decorated with great
flair, savvy gracious hospitality,
splendid lounges and rooms,
candlelit breakfast, afternoon tea,
free bikes.

🛏🛏🛏 **Hotel La Scaletta** –
*Via Guicciardini 13. 055 28 30 28.
www.hotellascaletta.it. 14 rooms.*

Warm colours and lovely antique furniture. Cosy. Wonderful roof terrace near Palazzo Pitti overlooks the whole of the historic centre. Rooms are bright and airy. Ample breakfast and free Wi-Fi.

⊖⊜🛏 **Locanda di Firenze** – *Via Faenza 12. 055 28 43 40. www. locandadifirenze.com. 6 rooms.* Near San Lorenzo in an 18C palazzo, hospitable ex-university professor's home is comfortable with good rates. Free Wi-Fi.

⊖⊜🛏 **Marignolle Relais** 🏛 – *Via di San Quirichino 16. 055 2286910. www.marignolle.com.* 🏊. *10 rooms.* Beautifully decorated hilltop villa, 3km/1.8mi south of Porta Romana. Attentive service. Swim in the pool, take a cooking course, play night tennis, or tee off in a local golf course.

⊖⊜🛏 **Relais Uffizi** 🏛 – *Chiasso de' Baroncelli-chiasso del Buco 16. 055 26 76 239. www.relaisuffizi.it. 12 rooms.* Elegant, convivial, in a 16C Florentine palazzo. Splendid lounge; breakfast area overlook Piazza della Signoria. Furnished in Tuscan style. Pets are welcome.

⊖⊜🛏 **Antica Torre Tornabuoni 1** – *Via Tornabuoni 1. 055 26 58 161. www.tornabuoni1.com. 22 rooms.* Warm beige tones in spacious rooms are inviting. The roof terrace overlooks the Arno and Duomo, lovely for buffet breakfast, or hot drinks. A lovely place.

⊖⊜🛏🛏 **Brunelleschi** 🏛 – *Piazza Santa Elisabetta 3. 055 27 370. www.hotelbrunelleschi.it. 70 rooms.* Near Piazza della Repubblica in its own quiet piazza with Byzantinne tower, rooms are bright, spacious, modern with beautiful design elements.

Lucca

⊖🛏 **Hotel Stipino** – *Via Romana 95. 0583 49 50 77. www.hotelstipino. com. 20 rooms.* In the outskirts near the centre, a well-maintained and run small family hotel.

⊖🛏 **Lucca in Villa San Donato**– *Villa delle Tagliete Prima 49. 0583 58 28 80 or 347 55 39 099 (mobile). www.bedandbreakfast luccainvilla.it. 6 rooms.* Near the historic centre, lovely Art Nouveau villa. Kitchen facilities, bicycle rental and tours.

⊖🛏 **Ostello San Frediano** – *Via della Cavallerizza 12. 0583 48 477. www.ostellolucca.it. 140 beds.* Part of the former Real Collegio, hotel comforts at guesthouse prices. Comfortable and spacious public areas, plus a lovely garden.

⊖🛏 **Piccolo Hotel Puccini** 🏛 – *Via di Poggio 9. 0583 55 421. www. hotelpuccini.com. 14 rooms.* Near the church of San Michele in Foro, small hotel. Puccini memorabilia.

⊖⊜🛏 **Albergo San Martino** 🏛 – *Via della Dogana 9. 0583 46 91 81. www.albergosanmartino.it. 9 rooms.* Near the Duomo. Spacious, airy rooms, pleasant, modern furnishings and amenities. Tours.

⊖⊜🛏🛏 **Alla Corte degli Angeli** 🏛 – *Via degli Angeli 23. 0583 46 92 04. www.allacortedegli angeli.com. 21 rooms.* Near romantic Piazza dell'Anfiteatro. Spacious rooms, décor is inspired by flowers.

PISA

⊖🛏 **Hotel Amalfitana** – *Via Roma 44. 050 29 000. www. hotelamalfitana.it. 21 rooms.* This 15C palazzo near the university is small, comfortable, has courteous service and good rates.

⊝⊜ **Hotel Galileo** – *Via Santa Maria 12 (1st floor, no lift). 050 40 621. 6 rooms.* In the centre, simple with large windows, reasonable rates. Most baths en suite.

⊝⊜ **Royal Victoria Hotel** – *Lungarno Pacinotti 12. 050 94 01 11. www.royalvictoria.it. 48 rooms.* Along the Arno,14C palazzo. A double without bath is as low as 78€.

⊝⊜⊜ **Hotel Bologna** – *Via Mazzini 57. 050 50 21 20. www.hotelbologna.pisa.it. Shuttle to Duomo or airport. 64 rooms.* Tasteful historic residence all comforts in a lovely setting.

⊝⊜⊜ **Hotel Francesco** – *Via Santa Maria 129. 050 55 54 53. www.hotelfrancesco.com. 13 rooms.* Quiet part of town, near the Leaning Tower. Modern spacious comfortable rooms. Breakfast al fresco in summer.

⊝⊜⊜⊜ **Green Park Resort** – *Via dei Tulipani, Calambrone. 050 31 35 711. www.greenparkresort.com. 148 rooms.* Set in a pine forest on the coast, enjoy spa treatments and fine dining options.

SIENA

⊝ **Santuario Casa di Santa Caterina Alma Domus** – *Via Camporegio 37. 0577 44 177. www.hotelalmadomus.it. 28 rooms.* A few rooms with balcony overlook the Duomo. Lovely reading room.

⊝⊜ **Albergo Cannon d'Oro** – *Via Montanini 28. 0577 44 321. www.cannondoro.com. 30 rooms.* Once the home of Sapia, who appears in Dante's *Divine Comedy*. Three flights of old stairs, some ground floor rooms.

⊝⊜ **B&B Palazzo Bulgarini** – *Via Pantaneto 93. 0577 15 24 466.. www.bbpalazzobulgarini.com. 6 rooms.* In an ancient palazzo 300m/330yd from Piazza del Campo, this B&B offers comfortable, newly renovated rooms.

SAN GIMIGNANO

⊝ **A La Casa de' Potenti** – *Piazza delle Erbe 10. 327 18 33 950 (mobile) www.casadeipotenti.com. 9 rooms.* 14C palazzo, very central. Some rooms overlook the piazza and Duomo. Impressive décor and price.

⊝⊜⊜ **Agriturismo Il Casale del Cotone** – *Località Il Cotone, via Cellone 59. 2.5km/1.6mi N towards Certaldo. 0577 94 32 36. www. casaledelcotone.com. 17 rooms and 2 apts.* Elegant 18C farmhouse. Tasteful antiques and furnishings.

ASSISI AND HILL TOWNS

⊝ **Casa Santa Brigida** – *Via Moiano 1. 075 81 26 93. www. brigidine.org. 20 rooms.* Tranquil spot run by nuns, small garden. Light meals traditional cooking.

⊝ **Hotel Pallotta** – *Via San Rufino 6. 338 74 07 574 (mobile). www.pallottaassisi.it. 7 rooms.* Centrally located medieval building with comfortable rooms, very busy, restaurant (closed 1 week Feb –Mar).

⊝⊜ **Hotel Degli Affreschi** – *Corso Mameli 45, Montefalco. 0742 37 81 50. www.hoteldegliaffreschi.it. 11 rooms.* Economical, near the main piazza.

⊝⊜⊜ **Castello di Barattano** – *Via Puccini 16. Loc. Barattano, Gualdo Cattaneo. 0742 98 250. www.ilcastellodibarattano.it. 2 apts.* Medieval *borgo*, situated on a hill in Sagrantino wine country, has stone rooms with kitchenette and rustic furnishings.

🍴🛏🛏🛏 **Hotel Palazzo Bocci** 🏨 – *Via Cavour 17, Spello. 0742 30 10 21. www.palazzobocci.com. 23 rooms.* Elegantly furnished rooms, frescoes in the reading room. On Spello's main street.

🍴🛏🛏 **Hotel Palazzo Brunamonti** 🏨 – *Corso Giacomo Matteotti 79, Bevagna. 0742 36 19 32. www.brunamonti.com. 21 rooms.* Lovely frescoes in the breakfast area, friendly staff, and bicycles to ride.

🍴🛏🛏 **Residenza del Marchese** – *Via Villa del Marchese 15, Gualdo Cattaneo. 0742 91 340. www.residenzadelmarchese.it.* 🏊 *7 aparts.* Each room or apartment has a kitchenette; garden has a grill and swimming pool, and the owners make their own olive oil and wine. Dinner served weekends and by request.

🍴🛏🛏🛏 **Hotel Villa Pambuffetti** – *Viale della Vittoria 20. 0742 37 94 17. www. villapambuffetti.it.* 🏊. *18 rooms.* Genteel villa at the edge of town, good restaurant, elegant atmosphere. Pool.

🍴🛏🛏🛏 **L'Orto degli Angeli** – *Via Dante Alighieri 1, Bevagna. 0742 36 01 30. www.ortoangeli.it. 14 rooms.* Tasteful, comfortable rooms in medieval structure. Lovely sitting areas, and fireplaces in some rooms. An enchanting spot.

🍴🛏🛏🛏 **Tenuta di Saragano La Ghirlanda** – *Loc. Saragano, Gualdo Cattaneo. 0742 98 731. www.laghirlanda.it.* 🏊. *13 rooms. Closed Dec–Mar.* Classy country estate that has even hosted a Thai princess. Restaurant, bikes, horses.

🍴🛏🛏🛏 **Villa Zuccari** 🏨 – *Loc. San Luca Montefalco. 0742 39 94 02. www.villazuccari.com.* 🏊 *30 rooms and 2 aparts.* Lovely pink villa in the valley below towns.

PERUGIA

🍴🛏 **Hotel Priori** – *Via dei Priori 40. 075 57 23 378. www. hotelpriori.it. 60 rooms.* Pleasant, no-frills; splendid terrace over the old alleyways and the roofs. Simple rooms, some with a view.

🍴🛏 **Fortuna** 🏨 – *Via Bonazzi 19. 075 57 22 845. www.umbria hotels.com. 51 rooms and 2 aparts.* Near Piazza IV Novembre. Charming old-fashioned rooms, frescoes in reading room, nice roof terrace.

🍴🛏🛏 **Castello di Monterone** – *Strada Montevile 3. 075 57 24 214. www.castellomonterone.it.* 🏊. *18 rooms.* Atmospheric 13C castle Lovely rooms with handsome wrought-iron furnishings locally crafted in Spello. Fine **restaurant**❁. Wellness centre, pool.

🍴🛏🛏 **La Rosetta Hotel & Restaurant** – *Piazza Italia 19. 075 57 20 841. www.larosetta. eu. 82 rooms.* Some rooms have frescoed ceilings and gorgeous antique furnishings; others feel less elegant. In the heart of the city.

ORVIETO

🍴 **Hotel Corso** 🏨 – *Corso Cavour 343. 0763 34 20 20. www. hotelcorso.net. 16 rooms and 2 aparts.* Stone palazzo has pretty terrace. Family-run, comfortable.

🍴🛏 **Albergo Filippeschi** 🏨 – *Via Filippeschi 19. 0763 34 32 75. www.hotelfilippeschi.it. 15 rooms.* Simple, in an old family palazzo. Centre of town.

ᗒᗕᗕᗕ **Locanda Palazzone** – *Loc. Rocca Ripesena 67. 0763 39 36 14. www.locandapalazzone.com. ⌕. 7 rooms. Closed 3 Jan–20 Mar and 20–26 Dec.* Beautifully restored medieval cardinal's country house, set amid the vineyards of one of Orvieto's best wineries. Idyllic stay. Swimming pool. Restaurant open to outside guests.

EMILIA-ROMAGNA

Ferrara
ᗒᗕ **Dolcemela** – *Via della Sacca 35. 0532 76 96 24. www.dolcemela. it. 6 rooms and 1 apart.* City-centre B&B; homemade cakes and biscuits for breakfast, in summer on patio.

ᗒᗕ **Locanda Borgonuovo** – *Via Cairoli 29. 0532 21 11 00. www. borgonuovo.com. 4 rooms.* Delightful B&B in the heart of the historic centre. Free Wi-Fi; bicycles. Apartments also available.

ᗒᗕ **Locanda il Bagattino** – *Corso Porta Reno 24. 0532 24 18 87. www. ilbagattino.it. 6 rooms.* Attractive guesthouse in the old town. Comfortable, welcoming rooms.

ᗒᗕᗕᗕ **Hotel & Spa Duchessa Isabella** – *Via Palestro 70. 0532 19 14 293. www.duchessaisabella ferrara.it. 26 rooms and 1 Depend (Principessa Leonora 22 rooms).* Ferrara's most elegant hotel; fine furnishings in all the rooms. Lovely restaurant with traditional and creative cuisine is popular well-heeled locals. Bicycles.

Bologna
Many hotels raise their prices during trade fairs.

ᗒᗕ **Albergo Centrale** – *Via della Zecca 2. 051 00 63 937. www.albergocentralebologna.it.*

25 rooms. A historic building in the centre; pleasantly simple rooms.

ᗒᗕ **Albergo delle Drapperie** – *Via delle Drapperie 5. 051 22 39 55. www.albergodrapperie.com. 20 rooms.* Beautifully renovated rooms, each individually decorated. Good value.

ᗒᗕ **Hotel San Vitale** – *Via San Vitale 3949, Medicina. 051 85 61 00. www.hotelsanvitale.com. 17 rooms.* Pleasant with simple rooms, hospitable service and free Wi-Fi.

ᗒᗕ **Hotel Villa Azzurra** – *Viale Felsina 49. 051 53 54 60. www. hotelvillaazzurra.com. 15 rooms.* Peaceful attractive 19C villa with a pretty garden. Not central but handy for drivers.

ᗒᗕᗕᗕ **Hotel Orologio** – *Via IV Novembre 10. 051 74 57 411. www. bolognarthotels.it. 33 rooms and 1 apart.* Informal atmosphere and neat rooms in this hotel 5 minutes far from the Towers in the center of Bologna.

Ravenna
ᗒᗕ **Hotel Ravenna** – *Via Maroncelli 12. 0544 21 22 04. www.hotel ravenna.ra.it. 25 rooms.* Simple comfortable rooms.

ᗒᗕ **Ostello Galletti Abbiosi** – *Via di Roma 140. 0544 31 313. www.galletti.ra.it. 37 rooms and 8 aparts.* In Ravenna's old town centre; spacious and comfortable.

ᗒᗕᗕ **Cappello** – *Via IV Novembre 41. 0544 21 98 13. www.albergocappello.it. 7 rooms.* Distinguished historic palazzo, in the centre. Elegant rooms, charming atmosphere. Restaurant.

Parma
⊙ *Hotel tariffs often increase during exhibitions and trade fairs.*

🛏 **Antica Torre** – *Via Case Bussandri 197, Cangelasio, Salsomaggiore Terme (from Salsomaggiore, head towards Cangelasio for 8km/5mi, then follow the signs for "Antica Torre"). 0524 57 54 25. www.anticatorre. it. 8 rooms. Closed mid Nov–Feb.* Country farm. Pleasant rooms with simple, rustic furnishings and friendly hosts. Delicious local cuisine.

🛏🛏 **Hotel Button** – *Borgo della Salina 7. 0521 20 80 39. www.hotelbutton.it. 40 rooms.* In the heart of the historic centre, between the Teatro Regio and Piazza del Duomo, this somewhat spartan hotel is convenient.

ROME

See the information on the city hotel tax on p198; ask when booking. The city of Rome runs **www. turismoroma.it**, *06 06 08*, to assist with information and reservation of hotels, pensions, camping, etc. Accommodation in convents and monasteries appeals to pilgrims as well as the budget-minded; some have curfews or may separate men and women guests. Contact the **Peregrinatio ad Petri Sedem**, *Piazza Pio XII 4 (Vaticano–San Pietro district), 06 69 88 48 96* or *CITS (Centro Italiano Turismo Sociale), Via della Pigna 13a, 06 48 73 145 or 06 47 43 811. www.citsnet.it.*

Districts

A good selection of *pensioni* and hotels are in the **historic centre**, highly in demand for atmosphere and the high concentration of tourist sights and shops; however, many establishments have limited capacity and as a result are often full. **Trastevere**, with its lively nightlife, is also pleasant but options are limited, too. The **Vatican** and **Prati** districts are close to the centre, are quieter and more reasonably priced. Accommodation around **Via Cavour** (Monti district), between **Termini Station** and the Fori Imperiali, is also good for mid-range hotels. Many cheaper *pensioni* and smaller hotels are in the area around Termini Station. Many luxury hotels are near **Via Veneto** and **Villa Borghese**.

Aventino

🛏🛏🛏🛏 **San Anselmo** – *Piazza San Anselmo 2. 06 57 00 57. www.aventinohotels.com. 34 rooms.* In green residential Aventino, three villas, lovely gardens; rooms have antiques. Breakfast in courtyard.

Campo de' Fiori

🛏🛏🛏 **Residenza Farnese** – *Via del Mascherone 59. 06 68 21 09 80. www.residenzafarneseroma.it. 31 rooms.* On a quiet street next to Palazzo Farnese. Gracious, nicely appointed rooms (some with frescoed ceilings), billiards room, delicious breakfast buffet and roof terrace.

🛏🛏🛏🛏 **Hotel Teatro di Pompeo** – *Largo del Pallaro 8. 06 68 72 812. www.hotelsananselmo.com. 13 rooms.* Breakfast room shows Pompey's Theatre foundations. Comfortable rooms, some with views.

Colosseo

🛏🛏🛏 **Hotel Lancelot** – *Via Capo d'Africa 47. 06 70 45 06 15. www.lancelothotel.com. 60 rooms.*

Restaurant ⊝. Near the Colosseum, family-run, economical. Lovely Oriental carpets. Pleasant dinners are good value. A terrace and some rooms have Colosseum views.

Pantheon

⊝⊝ **Hotel Mimosa** – *Via Santa Chiara 61 (2nd floor, no lift) 06 68 80 17 53. www.hotelmimosa.net. 11 rooms.* Behind the Pantheon. Modest, clean, simple, somewhat worn rooms, not all with private bath.

⊝⊝ **Pantheon View B&B** – *Via del Seminario 87 (last floor). 06 69 90 294. www.pantheonview.it. 4 rooms. Closed 9 Jan–Feb. S*mall building, comfortable rooms with a view of the Pantheon.

⊝⊝⊝ **Pensione Barrett** – *Largo di Torre Argentina 47. 06 68 68 481.www.pensionebarrett.eu. 20 rooms.* Pleasant, some rooms face ancient temples on Largo Argentina. Jacuzzi, foot hydromassage.

⊝⊝⊝ **Hotel Portoghesi** – *Via dei Portoghesi 1. 06 68 64 231. www.hotelportoghesiroma.it. 28 rooms.* Facing the "Monkey Tower", pleasant rooms have antiques. Terrace views of the rooftops of old Rome.

Piazza Navona

⊝⊝⊝ **Hotel Navona** – *Via dei Sediari 8. 06 68 30 1252. www. hotelnavona.com. 18 rooms.* Delightful hotel. Cool, attractive rooms in classic style. Family run in a 16C palazzo built above the Baths of Agrippa.

⊝⊝⊝⊝ **Hotel Due Torri** – *Vicolo del Leonetto 23. 06 68 80 69 56. www.hotelduetorriroma.com. 26 rooms.* Delightful. Central, quiet, attractive street. Each room has

unique décor, quality furniture, some antiques. A favourite address in Rome.

⊝⊝⊝⊝ **Raphaël** – *Largo Febo 2. 06 68 28 31. www.raphael hotel.com. 51 rooms.* One of Rome's most romantic: ivy-covered palazzo in the quiet piazza, rooftop dining with breathtaking views. Opt for classic rooms, or modern designed by Richard Meier.

Piazza di Spagna

⊝⊝ **Eva's Rooms** – *Via dei Due Macelli 31. 06 69 19 00 78. www.evasrooms.com. 12 rooms.* Good value for this well-situated guesthouse.

⊝⊝⊝⊝ **Hotel Art** – *Via Margutta 56. 06 32 87 11. www.hotelart.it. 46 rooms.* High-tech with vibrant colours, set in an old convent.

⊝⊝⊝ **Hotel Panda** – *Via della Croce 35. 06 67 80 179. www.hotel panda.it. 28 rooms.* The 17C palazzo near the Spanish Steps has quiet, simply furnished rooms, some with shared bath. Lacks charm, but is well kept and reasonable.

⊝⊝⊝ **Hotel Pensione Suisse** – *Via Gregoriana 54 (3rd floor, lift). 06 67 83 649. www.hotelsuisse rome.com. 12 rooms.* A residential building, with a warm family welcome. Tastefully decorated, has an interior courtyard. Guests are requested to return by 2am. Breakfast served in room.

Porta Pia

⊝ **Hotel Virginia** – *Via Montebello 94. 06 49 77 48 74. www.hotel virginiaroma.com. 30 rooms.* In a residential area near the train station. Clean, comfortable rooms. Near the centre, is good value.

MUST STAY

Termini
(railway station)

🛏🛏 **M&J Place** – *Via Solferino 9. 06 44 62 802. www.mejplace hostel.com. 30 rooms. Restaurant*🛏.Comfortable dormitories or single rooms. Colourful modern style. Lively youth hostel with restaurant.

🛏🛏 **Le Petit Real** – *Via Cavour 58. 06 48 23 566. www.lepetitreal.it. 6 rooms.* This B&B has comfortable rooms; suites have Jacuzzi and hydro-massage. Cosy.

🛏🛏🛏 **Hotel Quirinale** – *Via Nazionale 7. 06 47 07 804. www.hotelquirinale.it. 210 rooms.* Pleasantly large rooms, good transportation hub near Piazza della Repubblica, and secret passageway to Teatro dell'Opera. Restaurant.

Trastevere

🛏🛏 **Hotel Cisterna** – *Viale della Cisterna 7/9. 06 58 17 212. www. hotelcisternarome.com. 20 rooms.* In a small 18C building on a narrow street. Wood-beamed ceilings. A room on the top has a terrace.

🛏🛏 **Hotel Trastevere** – *Via Luciano Manara, 24a/25. 06 58 14 713. www.hoteltrastevere.net. 9 rooms.* Modern décor and conveniences. Some rooms face Piazza San Cosimato.

Vatican/Prati

🛏🛏 **Colors Hotel** – *Via Boezio 31. 06 68 74 030. www.colorshotel. com. 21 rooms.* Magnificently renovated. 5 dormitories have varying prices. Kitchen, sitting room. Hybrid hotel-hostel.

🛏🛏🛏 **Hotel della Conciliazione** – *Borgo Pio 163/166. 06 68 75 400. www.hotelconciliazione.it.*

67 rooms. 200m/650ft from Piazza di San Pietro on historic medieval street. Elegant furnished, some antiques.

🛏🛏🛏 **Atlante Star Hotel** – *Via Vitelleschi 34. 06 68 63 86. www. atlantehotels.com/star. 73 rooms. Restaurant* 🛏🛏🛏. Choose from antique-filled rooms with whimsical retro touches, or modern style. Some with stunning view of St Peter's.

Via Veneto/Villa Borghese

🛏🛏🛏🛏 **Hotel Aldrovandi Palace** – *Via Ulisse Aldrovandi 15. 06 32 23 993. www.aldrovandi.com. 🏊. 103 rooms. Restaurant* 🛏🛏🛏. On the edge of Villa Borghese. Beautiful garden with pool. Elegant. Spacious rooms. Oliver Glowing restaurant.

🛏🛏🛏🛏 **Hotel Lord Byron** – *Via Giuseppe de Notaris 5. 06 32 20 404. www.lordbyronhotel.com. 28 rooms. Restaurant* 🛏🛏. This small, elegant hotel is in a quiet spot, and overlooks the Villa Borghese gardens. The restaurant is well-renowned for fine dining.

Outskirts

🛏 **Hotel Louis** – *Via Montegrappa 33, Ciampino. 06 79 18 095. www.hotel-louis.it. 9 rooms.* Cosy hotel next to Ciampino Airport.

Tivoli

🛏 **B&B La Panoramica** – *Viale N. Arnaldi 45. 0774 33 57 00. www. villadestetivoli.it. 3 rooms.* Pleasant early 19C villa in Tivoli near Villa d'Este has a panoramic view.

NAPLES AND THE AMALFI COAST

Naples

I Vicoletti – *Via San Domenico Soriano 46. 347 90 85 207 (mobile). www.ivicoletti.it. 3 rooms and 1 apart.* The vast terrace overlooks Castel Capuano. Spacious. Friendly staff. In historic centre, exudes a Mediterranean atmosphere. Shared bathrooms and lots of stairs.

La Locanda dell'Arte – *Via E. Pessina 66. 081 54 43 15. 10 rooms.* Simple, elegant rooms, large windows. Historic centre. Early 19C palace. By Academy of Fine Arts.

Pignatelli 🏛 – *Via San Giovanni Maggiore Pignatelli 16. 081 65 84 950. www.hotelpignatelli napoli.com. 12 rooms.* In the heart of the historic centre near Piazza San Domenico Maggiore. Aparts were the home of the Marquis Pignatelli. Spacious, bright rooms.

B&B Cappella Vecchia 11 – *Vicolo Santa Maria a Cappella Vecchia 11. 081 24 05 117. 6 rooms.* Near Piazza dei Martiri, bright and cheerful B&B. Minimalist style, great central location. Internet.

B&B Donna Regina – *Via Luigi Settembrini 80. 081 44 67 99. www.discovernaples.net. 4 rooms and apart.* B&B in a 13C monastery. Grand Bohemian salon with high walls covered with paintings. Terrace opens to the old cloister.

B&B Sansevero – *Via Foria 42. 347 56 47 117 (mobile). 5 rooms.* Three stylish 18C *palazzi*. Good-sized rooms, attractively decorated. Cheerful, sunny. Rooms with shared bathrooms are cheaper.

Chiaja Hotel de Charme 🏛 – *Via Chiaia 216 (1° floor). 081 41 55 55. www.hotelchiaia.it. 33 rooms.* The former apartment of Marquis Nicola Lecaldano Sasso La Terza, on the first floor of a 17C noble palace. Tasteful with modern comforts.

The Fresh Glamour Accommodation 🏛 – *Via Donnalbina 7. 081 02 02 255. www.the-fresh.it. 6 rooms.* Nice B&B near Via Monteoliveto. Comfortable rooms, original furniture design. Breakfast served in room. Competitive prices.

Costantinopoli 104 🏛 – *Via Santa Maria di Costantinopoli 104. 081 55 71 035. www. costantinopoli104.it. ⚓ 19 rooms.* Top floor of an old building, delights art lovers. Hearty breakfast in kitchen with majolica tiles. Spacious rooms with antiques. Private bath outside the room.

Bay of Naples

Villa Oteri 🏛 – *Via Miliscola 18, Bacoli. 081 52 34 985. www. villaoteri.it. 9 rooms.* Early-19C Campi Flegrei villa, elegant and refined. Rooms have beautiful fabrics. Ask for a room facing Lake Bacoli.

Residenza Storica Villa Avellino – *Via Carlo Maria Rosini 21/29, Pozzuoli. 081 30 36 812. www.villaavellino.it. 18 apts.* A perfect combination of contemporary design and historic architecture, the hotel has comfortable apartments.

La Ginestra – *Via Tessa 2, loc. Santa Maria del Castello. 10km/6.2mi SE of Vico Equense in the direction of Moiano. 081 80 23 211. www.laginestra.org. 7 rooms.* 17C farmhouse on Mt Faito slopes; nice terraces, playground, spacious rooms. Organic farm products.

Island of Ischia

�✉ **Agriturismo Il Vitigno**– *Via Bocca 31, Forio. 081 19 36 80 26. www.ilvitigno.com.* ⚓. *17 rooms.* Wedged between vineyards and olive groves, beautiful panoramic views. Simple tasteful rooms.

⌖✉ **Villa Antonio** – *Via S. Giuseppe della Croce 77, Ischia Ponte. 081 98 26 60. www. villantonio.it. 20 rooms.* By Castello Aragonese, run by a family of artists. Private, rocky beach.

⌖✉✉✉ **Agriturismo Pera di Basso** – *Via Pera di Basso 10, Casamicciola Terme. 081 90 01 22. www.peradibasso.it.* ⚓. *10 rooms. Closed Nov–12 Apr.* A hidden paradise near the beach with lemon trees and vineyards.

Island of Capri

⌖✉ **Da Giorgio** – *Via Roma 34, Capri. 081 83 75 777. www.da giorgio capri.com. 9 rooms.* **Restaurant** ⌖✉. Pleasant. Wonderful veranda, huge windows splendid views over Gulf of Capri.

⌖✉ **Hotel Florida** – *Via Fuorlovado 34, Capri. 081 83 70 710. 19 rooms.* Small, central. Simple1950s-style. Breakfast on garden terrace.

⌖✉✉ **La Minerva** – *Via Occhio Marino 8, Capri. 081 83 77 067. www.laminervacapri.com.* ⚓. *18 rooms.* A small hotel in the centre of Capri where you will feel pampered. Modern style in typical island architecture.

⌖✉✉ **Hotel Villa Sarah** – *Via Tiberio 3a. 081 83 77 817. www.villasarah.it.* ⚓. *19 rooms.* Spacious villa, bright rooms overlook sea or citrus orchard. Very charming.

Amalfi Coast

⌖✉ **B&B Villa Avenia** – *Via Torquato Tasso 83, Salerno. 349 19 61 657 (mobile). 4 rooms.* Magnificent villa overlooking the historic centre and the harbour. Wide panoramic gardens.

⌖✉ **La Fenice** – *Via G. Marconi 8. 1km/0.6mi E of Positano. 089 87 55 13. www.lafenicepositano.com.* ⚓. *12 rooms.* Two19C–20C villas, lush vegetation. Simple, pleasant rooms. Panoramic seawater pool.

⌖✉✉ **Antica Repubblica** ♨ – *Vico dei Pastai 2, Amalfi. 089 87 36 310. www.anticarepubblica.it. 7 rooms.* Former palace has vaulted ceilings. Cosy, well kept, modern comforts. Beautiful roof terrace.

⌖✉✉ **La Maliosa d'Arienzo** – *Via Arienzo 74. 089 81 18 73. www. lamaliosa.it. 12 rooms.* Beautiful B&B outside Positano. Olives, lemon and orange blossoms. Comfortable.

⌖✉✉ **Villa San Michele** – *Via Carusiello 7, Ravello. Castiglione di Ravello, 5km/3mi S of Ravello. 089 87 22 37. www.hotel-villa sanmichele.it.12 rooms.* Atop the cliff-face, fine views over the Gulf and Capo d'Orso. Delightful setting, luscious garden, steps down to the beach. Tiled floors, sunny rooms.

SARDINIA

Emerald Coast

⌖ **Centro Vacanze Isuledda** – *Loc. La Conia, Cannigione, 6.5km/4mi NE of Arzachena. 0365 52 06 82. www.campingisuledda.com.* Great position above Maddalena Archipelago. Tents, bungalows, rooms, mobile homes and *tukul*. Supermarkets, shops, services.

⌖✉ **Hotel Selis** – *Loc. Santa Teresina, Arzachena, Strada provinciale (in the direction of*

Porto Cervo). 0789 98 630. www. selishotel.com. 18 rooms. Splendid stone building off the beaten track. Restaurant with tipycal dishes.

⌐⊜⊞ **Hotel Citti** – *Viale Costa Smeralda 197, Arzachena. 0789 82 662. www.hotelcitti.com.* ⌇ *51 rooms. Closed 22 Dec–9 Jan.* Excellent value, Costa Smeralda. On busy street. Spacious, comfortable rooms. Lovely sun lounge, pool.

⌐⊜⊞ **Hotel Da Cecco** – *Via Po 3, Santa Teresa di Gallura, 17km/10.6mi W of Palau on the S 133b. 0789 75 42 20. www.hotel dacecco.com. 30 rooms. Closed 20 Nov–25 Apr .* Magnificent view over the Straits of Bonifacio. Small, modern hotel. Sardinian hospitality.

⌐⊜⊞ **Hotel Villa Gemella** – *Loc. Baia Sardinia, Arzachena. 0789 99 303. www.hotelvillagemella.com.* ⌇*. 135 rooms.* Lovely flower-filled garden, swimming pool, near Bay of Sardinia. Light, tasteful rooms, some with terrace.

⌐⊜⊞ **Residence Hotel Riva Azzurra** – *Via Lampedusa, Loc. Banchina, Cannigione, 6.5km/4mi NE of Arzachena. 0789 89 20 05/6. www.residencerivaazzurra.com. 29 apts for 4 people.* Comfortable, two-roomed apts, lovely garden, near the beach. Friendly.

SICILY

Palermo
⌐ **Albergo Cavour** – *Via A. Manzoni 11 (5th floor with lift). 091 61 62 759. www.albergocavour.com. 9 rooms.* Renovated hotel on the fifth floor of an old palazzo near the railway station. Light, airy rooms with high ceilings. Functional.

⌐ **B&B La Fuitina** – *Via Garrafello 6. (4th floor without lift) 347 15 41 696 (mobile). bb-la-fuitina.hotel-palermo-it.com. 3 rooms (shared bathroom).* Near Vucciria market. Cosy, generous breakfast. Warm welcome. View of Palermo rooftops.

⌐⊜ **Hotel Moderno** – *Via Roma 276. 091 58 86 83. www.hotelmodern opa.com. 38 rooms.* Friendly, family-run, helpful staff. Simple, functional.

⌐⊜ **Hotel Alessandra** – *Via Divisi 99 (2nd floor). 091 616 5180. www.hotelalessandrapalermo.it. 20 rooms.* Near Palazzo Comitini. Simple, in the heart of the city. Bright, fresh rooms. Very friendly.

⌐⊜ **Al Giardino dell'Alloro** – *Vicolo San Carlo 8. 091 61 76 904. www.giardinodellalloro.it. 5 rooms.* In Kalsa, comfortable, mix of contemporary and traditional. Copious breakfast. Friendly.

⌐⊜⊞ **B&B 22** – *Corner between Via Pantelleria 22 and Largo Cav. di Malta. 091 32 62 14. www.bb22.it. 7 rooms and 1 apart (BB22 Palace 8 rooms).* In a little street in the historic centre. Charming, impeccably renovated. Bright rooms mix modern design.

⌐⊜⊞ **Ambasciatori** – *Via Roma 111 (5th floor with lift). 091 61 66 881. www.ambasciatorihotel palermo.net. 24 rooms.* Spacious rooms, good facilities. Breakfast on roof terrace and restaurant.

⌐⊜⊞ **Gallery House** – *Via M. Stabile 136. 091 61 24 758. www. hotelgalleryhouse.com. 13 rooms.* Very cosy hotel. Pleasant, rooms a bit luxurious. Attentive staff.

⌐⊜⊞ **Massimo Plaza Hotel** 🏛 – *Via Maqueda 437. 091 32 56 57. www.massimoplaza hotel.com. 15 rooms and 5 aparts.* Opposite Teatro Massimo. Excellent service comfortable rooms, parquet floors, modern furnishings.

⊜⊜⊜ **Hotel Posta** ⚤ – *Via A. Gagini 77. 091 58 73 38. www. hotelpostapalermo.it. 30 rooms and 5 aparts.* Behind busy Via Roma. Family-run, popular with actors in nearby Teather Massimo.

Erice
⊜⊜⊜ **Azienda Agrituristica Tenuta Pizzolungo** – *Contrada San Cusumano. 0923 56 37 10. www. pizzolungo.it. 2 rooms and 9 aparts.* Rustic, romantic 19C farmhouse; luxuriant garden near sea. Apts with kitchen.

⊜⊜⊜ **Hotel Baglio Santacroce** – *Contrada Ragosia (2km/1.2mi E of Valderice on the SS 187). 0923 89 11 11. www.bagliosantacroce.it. ⌇. 67 rooms.* Delightul 17C farmhouse, bucolic setting, magnificent views Golfo di Cornino. Small rooms, wood-beamed ceilings.

Siracusa
⊜⊜ **B&B Dolce Casa** ⚤ – *Via Lido Sacramento 4, loc. Isola (S 115 towards Noto, left to loc. Isola). 0931 72 11 35. www. bbdolcecasa.it. 8 rooms and 1 apart.* Between Siracusa and the sea, friendly. Light, spacious rooms. Beautiful garden.

⊜⊜⊜ **Agriturismo La Perciata** – *Via Spinagallo 77, 14km/8.7mi SW of Siracusa on P 14 (from Maremonti, to Canicattini, to Floridia). 0931 71 73 66. www. perciata.it. ⌇. 9 rooms, 4 aparts. Restaurant ⊜⊜.* Mediterranean villa. Tennis, horse riding, massage.

⊜⊜⊜⊜ **Albergo Domus Mariae** – *Via Vittorio Veneto 76, Siracusa. 0931 24 854. www.domusmariae benessere.com. 21 rooms.* Elegant rooms, terrace ocean views. Run by Ursuline nuns. Spa with pool.

Taormina
⊜⊜ **B&B Villa Regina** – *Via San Giorgio 12, Castelmola, 5km/3mi from Taormina. 0942 28 228. www.villareginataormina.com. 12 rooms.* Simple guesthouse has a cool, shady garden, delightful view of Taormina and the coast.

⊜⊜⊜ **Hotel Villa Sonia** – *Via Porta Mola 9, Castelmola, 5km/3mi from Taormina. 0942 28 082. www.hotelvillasonia.com. Closed Nov–Feb. 44 rooms.* Attractive villa tastefully decorated with period items and Sicilian handicrafts.

Eolian Islands
⊜⊜⊜ **Hotel La Canna** – *Contrada Rosa, Filicudi. 090 98 89 956. www.lacannahotel.it. ⌇. 14 rooms and 9 aparts. Closed 15 Oct–22 Apr.* Excellent location overlooking Filicudi port and sea. Two rooms have small terraces, a romantic hideaway. Pool, sun terrace and restaurant.

⊜⊜⊜ **Hotel Poseidon** ⚤ – *Via Ausonia 7, Lipari. 090 98 12 876. www.hotelposeidonlipari.com. 18 rooms and 2 villas.* Central. Mediterranean style. Spotless, modern, practical rooms. Polite service. Pleasant sun terrace.

⊜⊜⊜⊜ **Hotel Ericusa** – *Via Regina Elena, Alicudi. 090 98 89 902. www.alicudihotel.it. 20 rooms.* Small, simple, on the beach. Sun, sea and solitude. Restaurant serves fresh fish, simple salads.

⊜⊜⊜⊜ **Locanda del Barbablù** – *Via Vittorio Emanuele 17/19, Stromboli. 090 98 61 18. www. barbablu.it. 5 rooms. Closed Nov– Mar.* Pleasant, fusion of modern, Arte Povera and period styles.

HOTELS

ITALY

INDEX

INDEX

INDEX

INDEX

INDEX

Map Index